Richard Henry Stoddard

Personal Recollections of Lamb, Hazlitt, and Others

Richard Henry Stoddard

Personal Recollections of Lamb, Hazlitt, and Others

ISBN/EAN: 9783337218935

Printed in Europe, USA, Canada, Australia, Japan

Cover: Foto ©Thomas Meinert / pixelio.de

More available books at **www.hansebooks.com**

PERSONAL RECOLLECTIONS

OF

LAMB, HAZLITT, AND OTHERS.

BRIC-A-BRAC SERIES.

Each 1 vol. sq. 12mo. Per vol. $1.50.

Sent, post-paid, on receipt of price by the Publishers.

Scratched on Copper from Life in 1825 by his friend Brook Pulham.

Charles Lamb

Bric-a-Brac Series

PERSONAL RECOLLECTIONS

OF

LAMB, HAZLITT, AND OTHERS

EDITED BY

RICHARD HENRY STODDARD

NEW YORK

SCRIBNER, ARMSTRONG, AND COMPANY

1875

PR
453
57

\

RIVERSIDE, CAMBRIDGE:
STEREOTYPED AND PRINTED BY
H. O. HOUGHTON AND COMPANY.

CONTENTS.

PREFACE.

MONG the motives which impel to the writing of books, there may be singled out from the number, the belief that the writer has something to say which the world will be willing to hear, the intention of making money, and the desire for fame. The consciousness of a literary mission is an agreeable one, for however delusive it may be, it raises its possessor for the time being above his fellows, and places him in his own estimation among the benefactors of his race. Not less agreeable is the hope of deriving profit from one's pleasure, for though it is seldom fulfilled, it is never perhaps entirely abandoned; most men, I fancy, — most authors, I am sure, — would rather become rich by Literature than by Trade. We respect the mercantile mind, as we should, but something tells us that it is inferior to pure Intellect. We reverence genius more than gunny-bags, and would rather witch the world with noble horsemanship on the back of Pegasus than be carried more comfortably to oblivion in a palace-car. But fame —

> Fame is the spur that the clear spirit doth raise,
> (That last infirmity of noble minds,)
> To scorn delights and live laborious days."

The desire for fame is one of the highest by which man

is actuated.   I can conceive of nothing grander than the
love of fame by which so many are governed, and nothing sadder than the disappointment to which they are
doomed.   It is confined to no station, and no sex.   The
smallest have felt it equally with the greatest, and the
greatest have not felt it all.   That Shakespeare was without it appears as certain as that it was, after duty, the
chief incentive to the literary life of Milton.   The rickety
little papist Pope construing his Tully at Binfield ; the stu-
dious scholar Gray annotating his books in the cloisters
of Cambridge ; the marvelous boy, Chatterton, poring
over old parchments in the muniment room at St. Mary
Redclyffe's ; the stalwart Scottish peasant at Mossgiel,

> " Behind his plough along the mountain side ; "

the irascible young lord, carrying war into the enemy's
camp over his claret ; who does not recall them, and
their struggles and triumphs ?   But the Kirke Whites, the
Bloomfields, the Dermodys, the Clares, and the crowd of
nameless singers, whose pursuit of fame was as eager as
that of their masters, — whoever thinks of them, and of
their aspirations and failures ?   They followed a Will-o'-
the-wisp, which so far from guiding them to

> " The steep where Fame's proud temple shines afar,"

went out in darkness, and left them to die in poverty
and neglect.   Clearly, it is as true of Literature, as of
a weightier matter, that many are called, but few chosen.
   The life of an author is about the last life which any
sensible man would choose, and the life of Charles Lamb
is certainly the first from which he would turn with aversion.   It was not Life in the full sense, but endurance
of existence, — a period of denial and disappointment.
There was no enjoyment in it ; nothing in which a vigor-

ous nature could sun itself; only the twilight of creature comforts. His happiest days were perhaps those which he spent in Christ's Hospital, where he became acquainted with Samuel Taylor Coleridge, a blue coat boy like himself, and where he picked up his "small Latin and less Greek," being, in the language of the school, in Greek, but not a Deputy Grecian. He left Christ's Hospital in his fifteenth year, and entered the South Sea House, under his elder brother John, a cold-hearted, selfish man, who cared nothing for his family. His parents were poor, his father, John Lamb, being the clerk of Mr. Salt, one of the benchers of the Inner Temple. A duller home than that of the Lambs cannot well be imagined, for as the years went on the father fell into dotage, the mother became bedridden, and the daughter Mary shattered her health by needle-work all day, and incessant watches throughout the night. Hours of happiness were occasionally vouchsafed to the young clerk, the best of which were spent in the society of Coleridge at the Salutation and Cat, a little public-house in the neighborhood of Smithfield, where the whilom charity boys used to sup, and smoke and talk, long after they heard the chimes of midnight, beguiling the cares of life with poetry. For Charles was a poet, a sonneteer in a small way, who was, or thought he was, in love with a fair-haired maid, whom he christened Anna, and whom his biographers conjecture to have been one Miss Alice Winterton, or Winn, they are not certain which. In the autumn of 1796, his twenty-second year, his life was darkened by a tragedy, the shadow of which surrounded all his after days. His sister, who had been deranged, became insane, and seizing a case knife one day, while the family was preparing for dinner, she plunged it into the heart of her mother.

It was a dreadful picture which met the eyes of the landlord, who came hurrying into the room ; the mother life-
less in her chair, the daughter standing wildly over her
with the fatal knife, and the old man, her father, weeping
by her side, bleeding at the forehead, from the effects of
a blow from one of the forks which she had been hurling
madly about. Charles snatched the knife from his poor
demented sister, who was carried to a mad-house, where
she remained until she had recovered her reason, and
where, a few months later, he followed her.

Lamb's father soon died, and an old aunt who had
lived with them, and he and Mary were alone. His
brother was still living, but he might as well have been
dead, for all the help he afforded them in their trouble.
They lived for each other, or rather Charles lived for
Mary, who henceforth was the sole object of his anxiety.
What had been might have been forgotten (she at least
ceased to grieve over it) but for the cloud which brooded
above them, and was ready at any moment to burst upon
their devoted heads. There was no security in the household, for Mary was out of her head again and again ; the
only consolation they had was that she knew when it was
going to happen, and could be prepared for it. When
the hour approached they used to go to the Asylum at
Foxton together, weeping bitterly along the way. The
burden would have crushed him, one would think, but
strength was given him, and he rose and bore it manfully.
There was something heroic in the determination with
which he gave his life to his sister, and it is to be hoped
that it sustained him, for there was little else to sustain
him. He made no great professions of religion — his
friends were a little doubtful about his orthodoxy ; but if
Christianity consists in a life-long performance of duty,

he was certainly a Christian. He solaced himself with old books — Burton, and Fuller, and Walton, and her Grace, the eccentric Duchess of Newcastle, and indulged in the dream of one day making a name as a poet. His friend Coleridge patronized and altered his verse, and published a sample of it in a collection of his own poems, together with a sample of the verse of their common friend, Charles Lloyd. A year later the two friends sallied from behind the shield of the greater Ajax, and challenged fame on their own account. It was accorded to neither. Lamb now changed his "'prentice han'," and brought out the little prose story of " Rosamond Gray," which was too artless for the time, if not for any time.

The life of Lamb during the next twenty years was uneventful. It may be traced in outline in his letters to his correspondents, who were the most prominent members of the Lake school of poets, Coleridge, Southey, and Wordsworth, and others of less note, Manning, Montague, etc., and in the little volumes upon which he employed his leisure hours. The influence of the old books which he read so ardently is evident in his writings, and nowhere so much as in " John Woodvil," which is the most faithful reproduction of the Elizabethan Drama, so called, that we possess ; a reproduction as perfect in its way as the strange dramas of Beddoes, and the dramatic fragments of *Barry Cornwall.* " John Woodvil " might have been written by a post-Shakespearean dramatist, and had it been published as by one, I question whether any critic known to us could have successfully disputed its authenticity. " Hang the age," Lamb wrote after one of his failures, " I will write for antiquity." " John Woodvil " was written for antiquity, and only failed to reach its address because it was written two

centuries too late.   It is affecting, in a primitive fashion,
but as artless as the babbling of a child.   That Lamb
should ever have supposed that it could be acted successfully is a striking evidence of his inability to understand modern literature, dramatic or otherwise.   He was
born out of his time, and had to pay a penalty for the
tardiness of nature.   " John Woodvil " failed to make
a mark, even among Lamb's friends, upon whom its most
poetical passages were lost.   He had no motive to write,
except the necessity of diverting his mind, and the possibility of adding to his income, but he wrote, nevertheless,
his sister assisting him, or he assisting her, it is not easy
to say which.   They produced together, " Tales from
Shakespeare " (1807), and " Mrs. Leicester's School "
(1809).   Between these he had published " The Ad-
ventures of Ulysses" (1808), of which he was the sole
author, and, in conjunction with his sister, two little volumes of " Original Poetry for Children " (1809), which
is only known to us through extracts in a later publication, the whole original edition having disappeared, apparently beyond recovery.   More important than either
of these works was his " Specimens of English Dramatic
Poets " (1808), a collection of extracts, which was the
fruit of his devotion to old English literature, and which
ought to have placed him at the head of the critics of his
time.   It must have been a revelation to its readers, who
for the most part were unacquainted with the early poets
whom it laid under contribution, and whom it introduced
to their notice.   His critical comments, brief as they are,
have never been excelled, and never approached, except
perhaps by Coleridge, whose knowledge of the old dramatists was not so extensive as Lamb's, and whose appreciation is chiefly confined to their master, Shakespeare.

The "Specimens" is a book which scholars love ; one of
the "books which are books," and which will never be
out of date.

Lamb had no inducements to continue to write. He
had made no money, or at least but yeoman's wages, and
fame was as far from sounding his praises as when he sat
and talked o' nights with Coleridge, in the little smoky
room at the Salutation and Cat. Did he care for fame?
I am inclined to think not. It was not that which he
sought, but recreation and forgetfulness, — compensation
for his daily drudgery at the India House, and distrac-
tion from the anxieties which filled his household. The
authors in whom he most delighted were not the most
famous ones, — his prime favorites were not famous at
all. If they had missed fame, who was *he* that he should
achieve it? He was obscure, no doubt, but he was in
good company — there could be no better, — and he was
content. What did his masters think of fame? What
did well-languaged Daniel, for example, think of it?

> " Alas, poor Fame ! in what a narrow room,
>   As an encaged parrot, as thou pent
> Here amongst us ? when even as good be dumb
>   As speak, and to be heard with no attent :
> How can you promise of the time to come,
>   When as the present is so negligent ? "

Or Lord Brooke, in whom, as he well says, the understanding must have held a mystical predominance ?

> " Who worship fame commit idolatry ;
>   Make men their god, fortune and time their worth ;
> Form, but reform not, mere hypocrisy :
>   By shadows, only shadows bringing forth :
> Which must, as blossoms, fade e'er true fruit springs,
> Like voice and echo joined, yet diverse things."

Or Middleton, for whom he had a generous sympathy, as

is shown by his comparison of his witches with the weird
sisters in Macbeth : —

> " The fame that a man wins himself is best :
> That he may call his own : honors put to him,
> Make him no more a man than his clothes do,
> And are as soon ta'en off : for in the warmth,
> The heat comes from the body, not the weeds :
> So man's true fame must strike from his own deeds."

In a graver and sadder mood he may have exclaimed,
with Davenant : —

> " For fame (whose custom is to have a care
> Only of those who her familiars are)
> Does with a proud neglect o'er strangers fly,
> As if unworthy of her voice or eye :
> *She seldom is acquainted with the young,*
> *And weary is of those who live too long.*"

The books of Lamb, though they did not make him
known to the world, made him known to his friends, the
circle of which was gradually enlarging. He lost none
of the old ones, and the new which gathered around him,
when he had once taken them into his confidence, clung
to him to the last. They were mostly men of letters, like
himself, and were not popular favorites. He was the
centre of a little set, who believed in themselves, and
in each other, and who looked askance at their more fortunate and famous brothers. What Holland House was
to the latter, they imagined they found in the chambers
of Lamb, whose Wednesday suppers surpassed, they
were sure, the rarest breakfasts of Rogers. They visited him and Mary, played whist, talked books, punned,
ate cold meat, drank porter, and made merry generally.
One of the earliest of the new brood was Hazlitt, who
made Lamb's acquaintance in 1805, and who paid him
the dubious honor of painting his portrait. Another was

Leigh Hunt, a slashing theatrical critic, who was soon
to be incarcerated for calling the Prince Regent a fat
Adonis of fifty. Coleridge sometimes came, and Wordsworth, when he was in town, but the great names whom
the world delighted to honor held aloof. They would
not have been at home with Lamb, and Lamb would not
have been at home with them, so there was no loss on
either side. They had their enjoyments, which if brilliant were frivolous, as the reader may satisfy himself
by running over the pages of Moore's Diary; and Lamb
had his enjoyments, the choicest of which came to him
in midnight hours as he pored over his beloved folios.
He read and read, and when he was thirsty sipped his
tumbler of brandy and water. He had a decanter of
brandy on his table, and, the story goes, that it ebbed
before he went to bed. He had given up smoking years
before, but not for good, for, in spite of his " Farewell
to Tobacco," he resumed the habit in moderation, treating the resolution that had enabled him to overcome it.

Of Lamb's personal appearance we have the following
description from the pen of *Barry Cornwall*, whose
memory appears to date from the first year of his acquaintance, 1817. " Persons who had been in the habit
of traversing Covent Garden at that time, might, by ex-
tending their walk a few yards into Russell Street, have
noticed a small, square man, clothed in black, who went
every morning, and returned every afternoon as the
hands of the clock moved towards certain hours. You
could not mistake him. He was somewhat stiff in manner, and almost clerical in dress, which indicated much
wear. He had a long, melancholy face, with keen, penetrating eyes, and he walked with a short, resolute step city-
wards. He looked no one in the face for more than a

moment, yet contrived to see everything as he went on.
No one who ever studied the human features could pass
him by without recollecting his countenance ; it was full
of sensibility, and it came upon you like a new thought,
which you could not help dwelling upon afterwards ; it
gave rise to meditation, and did you good. This small
half-clerical man was Charles Lamb." Hazlitt pronounced Lamb's head to be " worthy of Aristotle," and
Hunt called him " a compound of the Jew, the gentleman, and the angel."

The establishment of the " London Magazine," in
1820, was an epoch in the life of Lamb. It numbered
among its contributors most of the rising writers of the
time, Hazlitt, De Quincey, Carlyle, Allan Cunningham,
Keats, Hood, Darley, Landor, Julius Hare, and, greatest of all, Lamb. He adopted a signature, which has
become immortal, — that of *Elia*, a former clerk in the
India House, and wrote upon whatever came uppermost
in his mind, with a humor and a pathos which have never
been excelled. There was a flavor of antiquity in his style,
as if he had caught the spirit of the old writers whom he
loved, and had made it his own. It was quaint, dramatic,
felicitous. There was no trace of imitation in it ; it suggested no model ; it was original and individual. The
Essays of Elia are unlike any that preceded them, and any
that have succeeded them ; they are unique. Lamb had
found his true vocation ; the world which had turned a
deaf ear so long, listened to him now, or rather to his shadow
Elia, not divining at first that it was his veritable self.

The life of a man of letters is seldom, or never, depict-
ured accurately by his biographers. They write when it
is finished, gathering information concerning it and him
from his acquaintances, and tracing, as well as they can,

the history of his mind in his books. It is an interesting task which they undertake, but is a task, nevertheless, and one which generally baffles them before they are done with it. They cannot put themselves in the place of the men and women whom they are dissecting, for what after all is biography but dissection, the *post-mortem* examination of hearts that have ceased to beat, and brains that have ceased to think? The publication of the Essays of Elia strikes us as an important event in the life of Lamb, but if the truth were fully known, we should find, I think, that it was really very little to him. It did not enrich him, and it did not surround him with crowds of new admirers. The world knew him not, and when he came in contact with its favorites they considered him a queer customer. Moore characterizes him in his Diary as a clever fellow, but full of villainous and abortive puns, which he miscarried of every moment, and flippantly refers to his sister as the poor woman who went mad with him in the diligence on the way to Paris. He mentions Lamb's receiving £170 (that, if I remember rightly, is the figure) for his two years' contributions to the "London Magazine," of which he was then the hero, and wonders, as he well might, at the smallness of the sum. There was nothing in common between the fashionable and petted author of "Lalla Rookh" and the old-fashioned, black gaitered little man who was masquerading as *Elia*, and it would have been strange if they had understood each other. It was otherwise with Rogers, whom Lamb knew later, and whose brother's death he celebrated in one of his best sonnets.

The last days of Lamb were passed in comparative ease. He left the India House in 1825, after thirty-three years' faithful service at his desk, and found that he had

made a mistake in so doing. His time hung heavily
on his hands ; he knew not what to do, and in consequence increased his libations of porter. Mary perpetually charged him to refrain, but the public-houses that lay
in wait along the roads that he was accustomed to travel,
were too tempting to be avoided. He moved from place
to place, restless everywhere, and finally settled at Edmon-
ton, where he died in his sixtieth year. His last days
were clouded by insanity, as were also those of his sister,
who was out of her mind when he passed away. She
survived him over twelve years, falling asleep at last at
the age of eighty-two.

Such was the life of Charles Lamb, which was not
known in its entirety until after the death of his sister.
It was a tragedy, but it was manfully borne. To sacrifice himself, as he did, to the care of this poor demented
creature, was an act of life-long heroism, which has endeared his memory to the world. He is beloved, as few
writers have been, and his reputation is steadily increasing. A literature has sprung up from his ashes. We
can trace his career from youth to age ; can read his
poems, his essays, and his letters ; can see the houses
in which he lived, and be present in imagination at his
midnight studies. If his gentle spirit knows this, we
may be sure that it compensates it for all the ills it suffered in the flesh.

The friendship of Lamb and Hazlitt, if we may dig-
nify their intimacy by that name, was intellectual rather
than personal. They differed in many things, notably
in politics, which Lamb detested, but at heart each re-
spected the sterling qualities of the other. " I should
belie my own conscience," Lamb wrote in 1823, " if I
said less than that I think W. H. to be, in his natural and

healthy state, one of the finest and rarest spirits breathing.
So far from being ashamed of that intimacy which was
betwixt us, it is my boast that I was able for so many
years to have preserved it entire, and I think I shall go
to my grave without finding, or expecting to find, such
another companion." When the intimacy of Lamb and
Hazlitt began we are not told, but probably in 1803.
There was a woman in it; a Miss Sarah Stoddart, the
daughter of Lieutenant John Stoddart, R. N., whose
acquaintance the Lambs had made, and who was one
of Miss Lamb's correspondents. Her share of the correspondence has survived, and, bating its tediousness, it
is curious reading. It turns upon love and marriage, in
which Miss Stoddart was naturally interested. She was
twenty-eight, and she wanted a husband. A lady in this
predicament generally makes a confidant of one of her
own sex. She discloses her little secrets of feeling, and
discourses about her lover, or lovers. She is sure she
needs sympathy, and thinks she needs advice ! Miss
Stoddart bared her tender bosom to Miss Lamb, who
medicated its wounds with the traditionary simples of
old maids. She is of two minds, is Miss Stoddart, for
while she is engaged to one lover, a Mr. Turner, who was
her brother's choice, she is writing to a certain W. H.,
who is her own. A Mr. White makes matrimonial over-
tures, which amount to nothing, and is followed by a Mr.
Dowling. At last she is engaged to Hazlitt.

Whether authors are more eccentric than other men,
may admit of discussion ; but that in their relations with
women they are singular admits of none. The history
of their loves may be entertaining, but it is not the history which most of us would prefer to have written about
ourselves. If there is a moral attached to it, it is that

genius is a doubtful, if not dangerous possession, — a
possession which insures neither its own happiness, nor
the happiness of others.   It is a law to itself ; let us be
thankful that it is not a law to us.   We may not be very
wise, but we are wiser than many men of genius.   We
make fewer and lesser mistakes, and when we make mistakes we abide by them.   More gifted souls perpetually
repent, but never amend.   Such an one was Hazlitt,
whose married life was comically unfortunate.   He married Miss Stoddart in 1808 ; lived with her ten or twelve
years, and then, by her consent, was divorced from her.
Before the divorce was obtained he fell in love with a
tailor's daughter, whom he would have married.   It was
a temporary flame, which burned intensely while it lasted,
more intensely than the Hymeneal torch that lighted him
to the couch of his Sarah (the tailor's daughter, by the
way, was a Sarah, too, Miss Sarah Walker), and which
was soon to be rekindled, for a similar blessed purpose.
Disappointment in a wife, and rejected by a maid, he
espoused a widow named Bridgewater, with whom he
made a tour on the Continent, and who left him in
about a year, giving no other reason than the womanly
one that they had parted forever !

   I do not propose to write even a sketch of Hazlitt's
life, for apart from its matrimonial infelicities, it was
uneventful.   What interest it had was literary, for except when he labored under the delusion that he was a
painter, a delusion which Thackeray shared when young,
he was a man of letters, and nothing else.   His inclination was towards metaphysics, his forte was criticism.
He was an admirable critic, though rather intolerant to
the moderns, and the most brilliant and eloquent essayist
that ever committed his thoughts to paper.   A vein of

autobiography runs through his writings, which is not the least of their charms. We share his tastes, his sympathies, his prejudices even, and are inspired by a warm personal feeling. We do not love him, as we do Lamb, but we respect him as the profounder thinker. His life was a warfare, and his death, which occurred in his fifty-third year, was a release. His last words were, " Well, I 've had a happy life."

The life of Lamb has been written by Talfourd and Procter, who were acquainted with him in his later years, and the life of Hazlitt has been written by his grandson, Mr. W. Carew Hazlitt; who was not acquainted with him at all. The biographies of Talfourd and Procter are what might be expected, — elegant, but superficial studies of a singular nature. They were gentlemen, and Lamb — I say it in no invidious spirit — was not. He was a man of genius, — a whimsical creature, with a mad sister, and lots of queer people about him. His biographers surveyed him from without, not from within, and of course missed much that was characteristic of him. They painted him as they would have had him, not as he was, and the most that can be said of their sketches is that they bear some resemblance to the original. He is more truly portrayed, I think, by others, and by none more truly than by Mr. P. G. Patmore, in " My Friends and Acquaintance," a collection of personal reminiscences of deceased celebrities of the nineteenth century (3 vols. London, 1854). Mr. Patmore was not a man of note, though acquainted with notabilities ; his chief distinction, and it is not a remarkable one, being that he was the father of Coventry Patmore, the poet. He wrote a romance entitled, " Chatsworth," which was attributed to Mr. R. P. Ward, a dull novelist of fifty years ago, "Marriage in May Fair," and I know not what besides. We are not interested in him on his own account, but on account of the people whom he knew, Lamb, Hazlitt, and others who figure here. I have not gone beyond his reminiscences, except in the case of Hazlitt, certain episodes of whose erratic life, his divorce, his affair with Sarah Walker, etc., are amusing enough to be remembered. For these I am indebted to the two volumes of " Memoirs," published by his grandson in 1867, — a bumptious book-maker, profusely addicted to scissors and paste. He has edited Constable, Lovelace, and other old English worthies, who never did him any harm, and, besides taking the life of his grandfather, has disturbed the ashes of Charles and Mary Lamb.

" Insatiate archer, could not one suffice ? "

Enough, however, of Mr. Hazlitt and Mr. Patmore, who shall now introduce the reader to their betters.

R. H. STODDARD.

Dear Sir

It is not unknown to you, that about sixteen years ago I published "Specimens of English Dramatic Poets, who lived about the time of Shakespeare". For the scarcer plays I had recourse to the Collection bequeathed to the British Museum by Mr. Garrick — But my time was but short, and my subsequent leisure has discovered in it a treasure rich and inexhaustible, beyond what I then imagined — For it is to be found almost every production in the shape of a play, that had appeared in print, from the times of the old Mysteries and Moralities to the days of Greene and D'Urfey. Imagine the luxury to one like me, who, above every other form of Poetry have ever preferred the Dramatic, of sitting in the princely apartments, (so such they are,) of poor condemned Montague House, which I predict will not speedily be followed by a handsomer, and culling at will the flower of some thousand Dramas. It is like having the range of a Nobleman's Library, with the Librarian to your friend. Nothing can exceed the courteousness and

attention of the Gentleman who has the
chief direction of the Reading Rooms here;
and you have scarce to ask for a volume
before it is laid before you. — If the occasional
extracts which I have been tempted to
bring away may find an appropriate
place in your Table Book, some of them
are weekly at your service; to those
who remember the "Specimens", they must be
considered as mere after gleanings,
supplementary to that work, only comprising
a longer period. — You must be content with
sometimes a scene, sometimes a song;
a speech, or a passage, or a poetical
image, as they happen to strike me. — I
read without order of time; I am a
poor hand at dates; and for any
biography of the dramatists, I must
refer to writers who are more skilful
in such matters. — My business is
with their poetry only.

Your serv't—writer

C. Lamb

January 27
1827

CHARLES LAMB.

CHARLES LAMB.

PATMORE'S FIRST ACQUAINTANCE WITH LAMB.

Y first introduction to Charles Lamb took place accidentally, at the lodgings of William Hazlitt, in Down
Street, Piccadilly, in 1824, and under circumstances
which have impressed it with peculiar vividness on
my memory. Mr. Colburn had published anonymously, only
two or three days before, a *jeu-d'esprit* of mine,[1] which aimed
at being, to the prose literature of the day, something like what
the " Rejected Addresses " was to the poetry, — with this
marked difference, however, that my imitations were in a great
measure *bonâ fide* ones, seeking to reproduce or represent,
rather than to ridicule, the respective qualities and styles of the
writers imitated ; merely (for the sake of " effect ") pushing
their peculiarities to the verge of what the truth permitted.

As I was very young in author-craft at that time, and pro-
portionately nervous as to the personal consequences that might
attend a literary adventure of this peculiar character, I had
called on Hazlitt on the day in question, in the hope of learning
from him anything that might have transpired on the subject
in his circle, he himself, and several of his personal friends,
being among the imitated. We met from opposite directions
at his door, and he had (what was the rarest thing in the world
with him) a book in his hand, the uncut leaves of which he had
been impatiently tearing open with his finger as he came along,

[1] *Rejected Articles.*

and before we had reached the top of the stairs I found, to my no small alarm, it was the book which occupied all my thoughts. This was an ominous commencement of my investigation ; for the book contained a portrait of Hazlitt himself, drawn with a most unsparing hand, because professing to be *his own*, and to have been " Rejected," for obvious reasons, from his own " Spirit of the Age," then recently published. Hazlitt's looks, however, which were an infallible criterion of the temper of his mind at the moment of consulting them, were quite sufficient to satisfy me that he was not displeased with what he had been reading. But before anything could be said on the matter beyond his asking me if I had seen the book, the door opened, and two persons entered, whom, though I had never before seen either of them, I at once *felt* to be Charles Lamb and his sister.

The plot now thickened ; for scarcely had I been introduced to the new-comers, when Hazlitt pointed to the book, which he had laid on the table on their entrance, and said to Miss Lamb, " There 's something there about Charles and you. Have you seen it ? "

Miss Lamb immediately took up the book, and began to read to herself (evidently with no very good will) the opening paper which was an imitation of an Essay by Elia.

Here was an accumulation of embarrassments, which no consideration could have induced me to encounter willingly, but which, being inevitable, I contrived to endure with great apparent composure ; though the awkwardness of my position was not a little enhanced by Miss Lamb presently turning to her brother, and expressing feelings about what she had read, which indicated that her first impression was anything but a favorable or agreeable one. Lamb himself seemed to take no interest whatever in the matter.

They stayed but a very short time, spoke only on the ordinary literary topics of the day, and on taking leave, Lamb pressed me to visit him at Islington, where he then resided.

During this brief interview with the Lambs, nothing in the smallest degree characteristic occurred ; and if I had not seen

Charles Lamb again, I might have set him down as an ordinary
person, whose literary eccentricities and oddities had been
gratuitously transferred by report to his personal character and
way of life.

I visited Lamb shortly afterwards at his house in Colnbrook
Row, and an intimacy ensued which lasted till his death, if,
indeed, one is entitled to describe as intimacy an intercourse
which, as in the case of all the rest of Lamb's friends, consisted of pleasant visits on the one part, and a gratified and
grateful reception of them on the other, which seemed intended
to intimate that there was nothing he did not owe you, and was
not willing to pay, in return for the dispensation you granted
him from the ceremony of visiting you in return : for the Lambs
rarely left home, and when they did, were never themselves
till they got back again.

The foregoing remarks point at what I afterwards learned
to consider as the leading and distinctive feature of Lamb's intellectual character, and also that of his sister — at least at
and after the time at which I first became acquainted with
them. All their personal thoughts, feelings, and associations
were so entirely centred in those of each other, that it was
only by an almost painful effort they were allowed to wander
elsewhere, even at the brief intervals claimed by that social intercourse which they nevertheless could not persuade themselves wholly to shun. They had been for so many years accustomed to look to each other alone for sympathy and support, that they could scarcely believe these to exist for them
apart from themselves ; and the perpetual consciousness of
this mutual failing, in a social point of view, and the perpetual
sense of its results upon their intellectual characters respectively, gave to both of them an absent and embarrassed air —
always excepting when they sought and found temporary shelter from it in that profuse and somewhat indiscriminate hospitality, which, at this period, marked their simple home at
Islington.

It is true they were, perhaps, never so happy as when surrounded by those friends and acquaintances who sought them

at their own house. But this was at best a happiness little
suited to the intellectual habits and temperament of either,
and one, therefore, for which they paid much more than it was
worth to them — *so* much more that they, not long after the
period to which I am now alluding, sought refuge from the
evil in a remedy that was worse than the disease. Always in
extremes, and being now able, by his retirement from the India House, to fix their whereabout wherever they pleased, they
fled from the too exciting scenes of the great metropolis to the
(for them) anything but "populous solitude" of that country
life for which they were equally unfitted and unprepared.

What I have further to say of Charles Lamb, I shall leave
nearly in the words in which it was recorded shortly after his
death in 1834, while the impression of his remarkable intellectual qualities, and their results upon his personal character,
were fresh in my recollection, and therefore likely to be less
unworthy the reader's attention than anything I could now
substitute in their place.

What immediately follows, however, was written during
Lamb's life-time ; and as it will serve as a sort of *personal* introduction of him to the reader, I shall give it precedence of
those recollections which were not written till after his death.
The following descriptive passages are part of what was intended to form a group of Sketches from Real Life, the imaginary scene of which was the Athenæum Club House.

Observe that diminutive figure, all in black (the head and
face only half visible from beneath the penthouse of an ill-fit-
ting hat), that has just entered the splendid and luxurious
apartment in which we are taking our sketches, and is looking
about with an air of odd perplexity, half timid, half bold, as
if —

"Wondering how the devil it got there."

And well it may, for its owner is as little dependent on modern luxury for *his* comforts, as if he had just been disinterred
by the genius of Bulwer from the oblivion of Pompeii.

Doubtless in passing down Waterloo Place, from his friend

Moxon's, with the intention of *losing* his way home to Islington through St. James's Park, the statue of the Goddess of
Wisdom over our portico attracted his eye, and his thoughts
naturally jumped to the conclusion that the temple over which
her effigy presides can be devoted to no less dignified purposes
than she was wont to patronize in those times of which this
"ignorant present " is apt to make such little use. And that
such a temple should be other than open to all comers, our exquisite " modern antique " could not for an instant doubt. In
therefore he walks, unmolested by the liveried menials of the
vestibule; for " there 's a divinity doth hedge " a man of genius, that makes his person in some sort sacred, even to the
wearer of a laced coat, be he lackey or lord. During the gaping wonder of the waiters at his advent, he has mounted the
staircase, — glancing with a look of momentary surprise at the
undraped figure of the Goddess of Love and Beauty, which
strikes him as a novel but by no means inappropriate introduction into a temple of wisdom ; and entering the first door that
seems likely to lead towards the penetralia of the place, behold
him among us ! . . . . It is odd how appearances sometimes belie themselves. If all here present were compelled to
guess the worldly calling of the object of our attention, nine
out of ten would pronounce for his being a half-starved country curate, who has wandered up to the metropolis on a week's
leave of absence, to make his fortune, and immortalize his
name, by a volume of MS. sermons. And the rusty suit of
black, the knee breeches met by high gaiters of the same, and
the contemplative gravity of the face and air, aid the delusion
— a delusion which those who know him cannot think of without a smile, and which he himself would hail the announce-
ment of with a shout of laughter, of a kind seldom heard
within these refined and fastidious walls, — laughter, however,
in which there would be no touch of derision at the association
that called it forth.

But see — he has removed his hat ; and all vestige of the
vestry has disappeared ; for the operation has revealed a countenance, the traits and characteristics of which never yet ap-

pertained to the follower of *any* exclusive profession or calling
— not even the sacred one which has for its object to lift men
from the commerce of earth to that of immortality.

If read aright, there is not a finer countenance extant than
that of Charles Lamb, nor one that more exquisitely and eloquently shadows forth the soul and spirit that give it life and
speech. It is a face that would have taxed the genius of
Titian himself to set it forth truly — so varied and almost contradictory in appearance are the evidences and intimations it
includes. There are lines of the loftiest thought and the
purest wisdom, intersected by others traced by the hand of
Folly herself while sporting there in her cap and bells. There
is the deepest and the gentlest love for mankind, inextricably
mingled with marks of the most bitter and biting contempt
for men and their ways and works. There is the far-darting
glance of high and searching intellect quelled, and as it were
hoodwinked, by an ever-present sense of the petty and peddling limits of even its widest and wildest range. There is
the profound melancholy of the poetic temperament, brooding
fondly over the imagination of what it feels to be unattainable,
— mixed into a "chance medley" of all sorts of quips, quib-
bles, and quiddities of the brain. There is the gravity of the
sage contending with the gayety of the humorist; the pride
and solemnity of the philosophic observer of human nature,
melting into the innocent playfulness of the child, and the mad
fun of the school-boy. In short, to sum up the case as para-
doxically as we have been tempted, from the peculiar nature
of the theme, to commence and carry it on, Charles Lamb's
face, like his other attributes, amounts to a "contradiction in
terms," — with this special qualification in every particular of
the case, that the contradiction is invariably in favor of right,
of truth, and of good, wherever these are brought into momentary contention with their opposites.

So much for a sketch that, in its accessories at least, is in
some sort a "fancy" one. The details of the description
which follows refer to a period immediately preceding his
death.

I do not know whether Lamb had any oriental blood in his veins, but certainly the most marked complexional characteristic of his head was a *Jewish* look, which pervaded every portion of it, even to the sallow and uniform complexion, and the black and crisp hair standing off loosely from the head, as if every single hair were independent of the rest. The nose, too, was large and slightly hooked, and the chin rounded and elevated to correspond. There was altogether a *Rabbinical* look about Lamb's head which was at once striking and impressive.

Thus much of form chiefly. In point of intellectual character and expression, a finer face was never seen, nor one more fully, however vaguely, corresponding with the mind whose features it interpreted. There was the gravity usually engendered by a life passed in book-learning, without the slightest tinge of that assumption and affectation which almost always attend the gravity *so* engendered ; the intensity and elevation of general expression that mark high genius, without any of its pretension and its oddity ; the sadness waiting on fruitless thoughts and baffled aspirations, but no evidences of that spirit of scorning and contempt which these are apt to engender. Above all, there was a pervading sweetness and gentleness which went straight to the heart of every one who looked on it ; and not the less so, perhaps, that it bore about it an air, a something, seeming to tell that it was not *put on* — for nothing would be more unjust than to tax Lamb with assuming anything, even a virtue, which he did not possess — but preserved and persevered in, spite of opposing and contradictory feelings within, that struggled in vain for mastery. It was a thing to remind you of that painful smile which bodily disease and agony will sometimes put on, to conceal their sufferings from the observation of those they love.

I feel it a very difficult and delicate task to speak of this peculiar feature of Lamb's physiognomy ; and the more so that, from never having seen it noted and observed by others of his friends, I am by no means sure of meeting with an accordance in the opinions, or rather the feelings, of those who

knew him as well, or even better than I did. But I am sure
that the peculiarity I speak of was there, and therefore venture to allude to it for a moment longer, with a view to its
apparent explanation. The truth then is, that Lamb was what
is by no means so uncommon or so contradictory a character
as the unobservant may deem it: he was a gentle, amiable, and
tender-hearted misanthrope. He hated and despised men
with his mind and judgment, in proportion as (and precisely
because) he loved and yearned towards them in his heart ;
and individually, he loved those best whom everybody else
hated, and for the very reasons for which others hated them.
He generally through life had two or three especial pets, who
were always the most disagreeable people in the world — *to*
the world. To be taken into Lamb's favor and protection you
had only to get discarded, defamed, and shunned by everybody else ; and if you deserved this treatment, so much the
better ! If I may venture so to express myself, there was in
Lamb's eyes a sort of sacredness in sin, on account of its sure
ill consequences to the sinner ; and he seemed to open his
arms and his heart to the rejected and reviled of mankind in
a spirit kindred at least with that of the Deity.

Returning to my description of Lamb's personal appearance, — his head might have belonged to a full-sized person,
but it was set upon a figure so *petite* that it took an appearance of inappropriate largeness by comparison. This was the
only striking peculiarity in the *ensemble* of his figure ; in
other respects it was pleasing and well-formed, but so slight
and delicate as to bear the appearance of extreme spareness,
as if of a man air-fed, instead of one rejoicing in a proverbial
predilection for "roast pig." The only defect of his figure
was that the legs were too slight even for the slight body.

Lamb had laid aside his snuff-colored suit long before I
knew him, and was never seen in anything but a suit of black,
with knee-breeches and gaiters, and black worsted or silk
stockings. Probably he was induced to admit this innovation
by a sort of compromise with his affection for the color of
other years ; for though his dress was, by courtesy, "black,"

he always contrived that it should exist in a condition of rusty brown. The only way in which I can account for Lamb's having been faithless to his former color, after having stood by it through a daily ordeal, for twenty years, at the Long Room of the India House, is, that he was placarded out of it by his dear friend Wordsworth's description of the personal appearance of his *ideal* of a poet, which can scarcely have been drawn from any but Lamb himself — so exact is the likeness in several of its leading features.[1] Now, Lamb did not like to be taken for a poet, nor, indeed, for anything else in particular; so latterly he made a point of dressing so as to be taken, by ninety-nine people out of every hundred who looked upon him, for a Methodist preacher — which was just the very last he was like, or would like to be taken for! This was one of his little willful contradictions.

AT HOME, ABROAD, AND AMONG HIS BOOKS.

I am bound to say that my acquaintance with Charles Lamb, during his residence at Islington, offered little to confirm the associations which Hazlitt has connected with those palmy days when his residence was the resort of all those who "called Admiral Burney friend." When I knew him, his house had, for various reasons wholly unconnected with any change in the Lambs themselves, degenerated, for the most part, into the trysting-place of a little anomalous *coterie* of strenuous idlers and "Curious Impertinents," who, without the smallest power of appreciating the qualities of mind and character which nominally brought them together, came there

---

[1] See "A Poet's Epitaph," in the *Lyrical Ballads.*

"But who is he *with modest looks,*
And clad in homely russet brown,
Who murmurs near the running brooks
A music sweeter than their own?

"He is retired as noon-tide dew,
Or fountain in a noon-day grove;
And you must love him ere to you
He will seem worthy of your love."

to pass the time under a species of excitement a little different from their ordinary modes of a social intercourse — alternating "an evening at the Lambs'" with a half-price to the
play, or a visit to the wild beasts at Exeter 'Change. Certain
it is, that not one out of twenty ever came there with the re-
motest thought of enjoying the society of Lamb and his sister,
and quite as little for that of the distinguished men who still
occasionally sought the residence of Lamb with that view.
Still more certain is it that Lamb himself did not shine in this
sort of "mixed company"—this strange *olla-podrida* of intellect, oddity, and commonplace. It might be an "Entertaining
Miscellany" to him, but it was one in which he rarely or never
published any of those exquisite Eliaisms of which his mind
and heart were made up. He was everything that was kind
and cordial in his welcome to all comers, and his sister used
to bustle and potter about like a gentle housewife, to make
everybody comfortable ; but you might almost as well have
been in the apartments of any other clerk of the India House,
for anything you heard that was deserving of note or recollection.

The fact is, that in ordinary society, if Lamb was not an
ordinary man, he was only an odd and strange one — display-
ing no superior knowledge or wit or wisdom or eloquence, but
only that invariable accompaniment of genius, a moral incapacity to subside into the conventional cant or the flat commonplace of every-day life. He would do anything to gratify
his guests but that. He would joke, or mystify, or pun, or
play the buffoon ; but he could not bring himself to prose, or
preach, or play the philosopher. He could not be *himself*
(for others, I mean) except when something out of himself
made him so ; but he could not be anything at variance with
himself to please a king.

The consequence was, that to those who did not know him,
or, knowing, did not or could not appreciate him, Lamb often
passed for something between an imbecile, a brute, and a
buffoon ; and the first impression he made on ordinary people
was always unfavorable — sometimes to a violent and repul-

sive degree. Hazlitt has somewhere said of him in substance (with about an equal portion of truth and exaggeration, but with an exact *feeling* of the truth in the very exaggeration) that Lamb was always on a par with his company, however high or however low it might be. But, somehow or other, silly or ridiculous people have an instinct that makes them feel it as a sort of personal offense if you treat them as if you fancied yourself no better than they. They know it to be a hoax upon them, manage it how you may, and they resent it accordingly.

Now Lamb was very apt to play fast and loose with his literary reputation in this way, and would certainly rather have passed with nine tenths of the world for a fool than for a philosopher, a wit, or a man of letters. And I cannot help thinking it was his deep sympathy with mankind, and especially with the poor, whether in spirit or in purse, that was the cause of this. He did not like to be thought different from his fellow-men, and he knew that, in the vocabulary of the ordinary world, "a man of genius" seldom means anything better, and often something worse, than an object of mingled fear, pity, and contempt.

The truth is, that the Elia of private life could be known and appreciated only by his friends and intimates, and even by them only at home. He shone, and was answerable to his literary and social reputation, only in a *tête-à-tête*, or in those unpremeditated colloquies over his own table, or by his own fireside, in which his sister and one or two more friends took part, and in which every inanimate object about him was as familiar as the "household words" in which he uttered his deep and subtle thoughts, his quaint and strange fancies, and his sweet and humane philosophy. Under these circumstances, he was perfectly and emphatically a *natural* person, and there was not a vestige of that startling oddity and extravagance which subjected him to the charge of affecting to be "singular" and "original" in his notions, feelings, and opinions.

In any other species of "company" than that to which I

have just referred, however cultivated or intellectual it might
be, Lamb was unquestionably liable to the charge of seeming
to court attention by the strangeness and novelty of his opinions, rather than by their justness and truth — he was *liable*
and open to this charge, but as certainly he did not *deserve*
it ; for affectation supposes a something assumed, put on,
pretended — and of this, Lamb was physically as well as morally incapable.   His strangeness and oddity under the one
set of circumstances, was as natural to him as his naturalness
and simplicity under the other.   In the former case, he was
not at ease — not a free agent — not his own man ; but

> " Cabined, cribbed, confined
> Bound in by saucy doubts and fears "

that were cast about him by his " reputation " — which tram-
meled and hampered him by claims that he had neither the
strength cordially to repudiate, nor the weakness cordially to
embrace ; and in struggling between the two inclinations, he
was able to exhibit nothing but the salient and superficial
points of his mind and character, as moulded and modified by
a state of society so utterly at variance with all his own deliberate views and feelings, as to what it might be, or at least
might have been, that he shrank from the contemplation of it
with an almost convulsive movement of pain and disgust, or
sought refuge from it in the solitary places of his own thoughts
and fancies.   When forced into contact with " the world's
true worldlings," being anything but one of themselves, he
knew that he could not show like them, and yet feared to pain
or affront their feelings by seeming too widely different ; and
between the two it was impossible to guess beforehand what
he would do or be under any given circumstances ; he himself
being the last person capable of predicating on the point.
The consequence was, that when the exigency arrived, he was
anything or nothing, as the turn of the case or the temper of
the moment might impel him ; he was equally likely to outrage or to delight the persons in whose company he might
fall, or else to be regarded by them as a mere piece of human

still-life, claiming no more notice or remembrance than an old-fashioned portrait, or a piece of odd-looking old china.

What an exquisite contrast to all this did Lamb's intercourse with his friends present! Then, and then only, was he himself; for assuredly he was not so when in the sole company of his own thoughts, unless when they were communing with those of his dearest friends of all — his old books — his "midnight darlings," as he endearingly calls them somewhere, in a tone and spirit which prove that he loved them better than any of his friends of the living world, and cared not if the latter knew it.

Yet I'm afraid it does not follow that Lamb was happier among his books than with his friends; he was only more *himself.* In fact, there was a constitutional sadness about Lamb's mind, which nothing could overcome but an actual personal interchange of thought and sentiment with those, whoever they might be, whose tone and cast of intellect were n some sort correspondent with his own. And though in his intercourse with his beloved old books, he found infinitely more of this correspondence than the minds of his most choice living friends could furnish; yet in the former there was wanting that *reciprocal* action which constitutes the soul of human intercourse. Lamb could listen with delight to the talk of his books, but they could not listen to him in return; and his spirit was so essentially and emphatically a *human* one, that it was only in the performance and interchange of human offices and instincts it could exist in its happiest form and aspect. Unlike his friends, Coleridge and Wordsworth, Lamb was not a man whose mind was sufficient to itself, and could dwell forever, if need were, in the world of its own thoughts, or that which the thoughts of others had created for it. He delighted to *visit* those worlds, and found there, it may be, his purest and loftiest pleasures. But the *home* of his spirit was the face of the common earth, and in the absence of human faces and sympathies, it longed and yearned for them with a hunger that nothing else could satisfy.

16 *CHARLES LAMB.*

LAMB'S LETTERS.

Just before the Lambs quitted the metropolis for the voluntary banishment of Enfield Chace, they came to spend a day
with me at Fulham, and brought with them a companion, who,
"dumb animal" though it was, had for some time past been
in the habit of giving play to one of Charles Lamb's most
amiable characteristics, that of sacrificing his own feelings
and inclinations to those of others. This was a large and
very handsome dog, of a rather curious and singularly saga-
cious breed, which had belonged to Thomas Hood, and at the
time I speak of, and to oblige both dog and master, had been
transferred to the Lambs, who made a great pet of him, to
the entire disturbance and discomfiture, as it appeared, of all
Lamb's habits of life, but especially of that most favorite and
salutary of all, his long and heretofore solitary suburban
walks : for Dash (that was the dog's name) would never allow
Lamb to quit the house without him, and, when out, would
never go anywhere but precisely where it pleased himself.
The consequence was, that Lamb made himself a perfect slave
to this dog, — who was always half a mile off from his companion, either before or behind, scouring the fields or roads in
all directions, up and down "all manner of streets," and keeping his attendant in a perfect fever of anxiety and irritation,
from his fear of losing him on the one hand, and his reluctance to put the needful restraint upon him on the other.
Dash perfectly well knew his host's amiable weakness in this
respect, and took a due dog-like advantage of it. In the Regent's Park in particular Dash had his quasi-master completely
at his mercy ; for the moment they got within the ring, he used
to squeeze himself through the railing, and disappear for half
an hour together in the then inclosed and thickly planted
greensward, knowing perfectly well that Lamb did not dare to
move from the spot where he (Dash) had disappeared till he
thought proper to show himself again. And they used to take
this walk oftener than any other, precisely because Dash liked
it and Lamb did not.

The performance of the Pig-driver that Leigh Hunt describes so capitally in the "Companion," must have been an easy and straightforward thing compared with this enterprise of the dear couple in conducting Dash from Islington to Fulham. It appeared, however, that they had not undertaken it this time purely for Dash's gratification ; but (as I had often admired the dog) to ask me if I would accept him, — "if only out of charity," said Miss Lamb, "for if we keep him much longer, he'll be the death of Charles."

I readily took charge of the unruly favorite, and soon found, as I suspected, that his wild and willful ways were a pure imposition upon the easy temper of Lamb ; for as soon as he found himself in the keeping of one who knew what dog-decorum was, he subsided into the best bred and best behaved of his species.

A few weeks after I had taken charge of Dash, I received the following letter from Lamb, who had now removed to Enfield Chace. Exquisitely characteristic of their writer as are the "Elia" Essays of Charles Lamb, I doubt if any one of them is superior in this respect to the letter I am about to cite : —

CHARLES LAMB TO P. G. PATMORE.

" Mrs. Leishman's, Chace, Enfield.

"DEAR PATMORE, — Excuse my anxiety — but how is Dash ? (I should have asked if Mrs. Patmore kept her rules and was improving — but Dash came uppermost. The order of our thoughts should be the order of our writing.) Goes he muzzled, or *aperto ore?* Are his intellects sound, or does he wander a little in *his* conversation ?[1] You cannot be too careful to watch the first symptoms of incoherence. The first illogical snarl he makes, to St. Luke's with him. All the dogs here are going mad, if you believe the overseers ; but I protest they seem to me very rational and collected. But nothing is so deceitful as mad people to those who are not used to them. Try him with hot water. If he wont lick it up, it is a sign he does not like it. Does his tail wag horizontally or perpendic-

[1] A sly hint, I suspect, to one who did — and does.

2

ularly? That has decided the fate of many dogs in Enfield.
Is his general deportment cheerful? I mean when he is
pleased — for otherwise there is no judging. You can't be
too careful. Has he bit any of the children yet? If he has,
have them shot, and keep *him* for curiosity, to see if it was the
hydrophobia. They say all our, army in India had it at one
time — but that was in *Hyder-*Ally's time. Do you get paunch
for him? Take care the sheep was sane. You might pull out
his teeth (if he would let you), and then you need not mind if
he were as mad as a bedlamite. It would be rather fun to see
his odd ways. It might amuse Mrs. Patmore and the children. They'd have more sense than he! He'd be like a
Fool kept in the family, to keep the household in good humor
with their own understanding. You might teach him the mad
dance set to the mad howl. *Madge Owl-et* would be nothing
to him. 'My, how he capers!' (One of the children speaks
this.) . . . .

(Here three lines are erased.)

" What I scratch out is a German quotation from Lessing
on the bite of rabid animals : but, I remember, you don't read
German. But Mrs. Patmore may, so I wish I had let it stand.
The meaning in English is, ' Avoid to approach an animal
suspected of madness, as you would avoid a fire or a preci-
pice : ' which I think is a sensible observation. The Ger-
mans are certainly profounder than we.

" If the slightest suspicion arises in your breast, that all is
not right with him (Dash), muzzle him, and lead him in a
string (common packthread will do ; he don't care for twist) to
Hood's, his quondam master, and he'll take him in at any
time. You may mention your suspicion or not, as you like, or
as you think it may wound or not Mr. H.'s feelings. Hood, I
know, will wink at a few follies in Dash, in consideration of
his former sense. Besides, Hood is deaf, and if you hinted
anything, ten to one he would not hear you. Besides, you will
have discharged your conscience, and laid the child at the
right door, as they say.

" We are dawdling our time away very idly and pleasantly, at

a Mrs. Leishman's, Chace, Enfield, where, if you come a-hunt-
ing, we can give you cold meat and a tankard. Her husband
is a tailor; but that, you know, does not make her one. I
knew a jailer (which rhymes), but his wife was a fine lady.
  " Let us hear from you respecting Mrs. Patmore's regimen.
I send my love in a —— to Dash.   C. LAMB."

  On the *outside* of the letter (a letter sent by the public post)
is written : " Seriously, I wish you would call on Hood when
you are that way. He's a capital fellow. I sent him a couple
of poems : one ordered by his wife, and written to order ;
and 't is a week since, and I 've not heard from him. I fear
something is the matter.
  " Omitted within :
  " Our kindest remembrance to Mrs. P."
  Is the reader acquainted with anything in its way more exquisite than this letter, in the whole circle of our epistolary
literature — anything more buoyant with wit, drollery, and
humor, and, at the same time more pregnant with that *spirit
of self-contradiction* which was so singularly characteristic
of Lamb in almost all he said and did ? His broadest jokes
have a sentiment in them, and his most subtle and refined
sentiment always takes the form of a joke. Whole pages
or chapters of critical comment on his intellectual character would not speak its chief features more clearly and
emphatically than the three first lines of this letter, especially
when coupled with the three last — " Excuse my anxiety — but
how is Dash ? I should have asked if Mrs. Patmore kept
her rules, and was improving ; but Dash came uppermost."
" Let us hear from you respecting Mrs. P.'s regimen. I send
my love in a —— to Dash." Lively and sincere as was the
interest that he felt for the lady referred to (whose health was
at that time in a very delicate state), he never would have
written the letter at all, but for his still livelier interest about
Dash. And he could not, and would not conceal the truth —
though he did not object to disguise it in the form of a seeming joke.

As Dash was one of the very few objects of Lamb's " Hero-
worship," the reader may like to learn a little more about him
from my reply to the foregoing letter : —

P. G. PATMORE TO CHARLES LAMB.

" DEAR LAMB, — Dash is very mad indeed. As I knew you
would be shocked to hear it, I did not volunteer to trouble
your peaceful retreat by the sad information, thinking it could
do no good, either to you, to Dash, to us, or to the innocent
creature that he has already bitten, or to those he may (please
God) bite hereafter. But when you ask it of me as a friend,
I cannot withhold the truth from you. The poor little patient
has resolutely refused to touch *water* (either hot or cold) ever
since, and if we attempt to force it down her throat, she
scratches, grins, fights, makes faces, and utters strange noises,
showing every recognized symptom of being very mad indeed.
. . . . As for your panacea (of shooting the bitten one),
we utterly set our faces against it, not thinking death ' a happy
release' under any given circumstances, and being specially
averse to it under circumstances given by our own neglect.

" By the bye, it has just occurred to me, that the fact of the
poor little sufferer making a noise more like a cat's than a
dog's, may possibly indicate that she is not quite so mad as
we at first feared. Still there is no saying but the symptom
may be one of aggravation. Indeed I should n't wonder if the
' faculty' preferred the *bark*, as that (under the queer name of
quinine) has been getting very fashionable among them of late.

" I wish you could have seen the poor little patient before
we got rid of her — how she scoured round the kitchen among
the pots and pans, scampered about the garden, and clambered
up to the tops of the highest trees. (No symptoms of *high*-
drophobia, you will say, in that.) . . . .

" By the bye again, I have entirely forgotten to tell you, that
the injured innocent is not one of *our* children, but of the
cat's; and this reminds me to tell you that, putting cats out of
the question (to which, like some of his so-called ' betters,'
Dash has evidently a ' natural antipathy '), he comports him-

self in all other respects as a sane and well-bred dog should
do. In fact, his distemper, I am happy to tell you, is clearly
not insanity, but only a temporary hallucination or monomania
in regard (want of regard, you will say) to one particular species of his fellow-creatures — *videlicet*, cats. (For the delicate
distinctions in these cases, see Haslam *passim ;* or pass him,
if you prefer it.) . . . .

" With respect to the second subject of your kind inquiries
— the lady, and the success of her prescribed regimen — I
will not say that she absolutely *barks* at the sight of water
when proffered to her, but she shakes her head, and sighs
piteously, which are bad symptoms. In sober seriousness,
her watery regimen does not yet show any signs of doing her
good, and we have now finally determined on going to France
for the summer, and shall leave North End, with that purpose,
in about three weeks.

" I was going up to Colnbrook Cottage on the very Monday
that you left ; but (for a wonder) I took the precaution of calling on your ancient friend at the factory in my way, and
learned that you had left. . . . . I hope you will not feel
yourselves justified in remaining long at Enfield, for if you
do, I shall certainly devise some means of getting down to
see you, in which case I shall inevitably stay very late at night,
and in all human probability shall be stopped and robbed in
coming back ; so that your sister, if not you, will see the propriety of your returning to town as soon as may be.

" Talking of being stopped on the King's Highway, reminds
me of Dash's last exploit. He was out at near dusk, down
the lane, a few nights ago, with his mistress (who is as fond of
him as his master — please to be careful how you construe
this last equivocally expressed phrase, and don't make the
'master' an accusative case), when Dash attacked a carpenter,
armed with a large saw — not Dash, but the carpenter — and
a 'wise saw' it turned out, for its teeth protected him from
Dash's, and a battle royal ensued, worthy the Surrey Theatre.
Mrs. Patmore says that it was really frightful to see the saw,
and the way in which it and Dash gnashed their teeth at each
other. . . . .   Ever yours, P. G. P."

The Lambs' Domestic Arrangements.

Another characteristic instance of Lamb's sacrifice of his own most cherished habits and feelings to those of other people was in the case of a favorite servant, " Beckey," to whose will and pleasure both Charles Lamb and his sister were as much at the mercy as they were to those of Dash. This Beckey was an excellent person in her way, and not the worse that she had not the happiness of comprehending the difference between· genius and common sense — between "an author" and an ordinary man. Accordingly, having a real regard for her master and mistress, and a strong impression of what was or was not "good for them," she used not seldom to take the liberty of telling them "a bit of her mind," when they did anything that she considered to be " odd " or out of the way. And as (to do them justice) their whole life and behavior were as little directed by the rules of commonplace as could well be, Beckey had plenty of occasions for the exercise of her self-imposed task, of instructing her master and mistress in the ways of the world. Beckey, too, piqued herself on her previous experience in observing and treating the vagaries of extraordinary people ; for she had lived some years with Hazlitt before she went to the Lambs.

In performing the duties of housekeeping the Lambs were something like an excellent friend of mine, who, when a tradesman brings him home a pair of particularly easy boots, or any other object perfectionated in a way that peculiarly takes his fancy, inquires the price, and if it happens to be at all within decent tradesmanlike limits, says, " No — I cannot give you that price — it is too little — you cannot afford it, I 'm sure — I shall ‚give you so and so " — naming a third or fourth more than the price demanded. . If the Lambs' baker, for example, had charged them (as it is said bakers have been known to do) a dozen loaves in their weekly bill, when they must have known that they had not eaten two thirds of that number, the last thing they would have thought of was complaining of the overcharge. If they had not consumed the proper quantity to remunerate him for the trouble of serving them, it was not the baker's fault, and the least they could do was to pay for it !

Now this kind of logic was utterly lost upon Beckey, and she would not hear of it. Her master and mistress, she fully admitted, had a right to be as extravagant as they pleased ; but they had no right to confound the distinctions between honesty and roguery, and it was what she would not permit.

There are few of us who would not duly prize a domestic who had honesty and wit enough to protect us from the consequences of our own carelessness or indifference ; but where is the one who, like Lamb, without caring one farthing for the advantages he might derive from Beckey's unimpeachable honesty, and her genius for going the best way to market, could not merely overlook, but be highly gratified and amused by, the ineffable airs of superiority, amounting to nothing less than a sort of personal patronage, which she assumed on the strength of these ? The truth is, that Beckey used to take unwarrantable liberties with her quasi-master and mistress — liberties that amounted to what are usually deemed, in such cases, gross and unpardonable impertinences. Yet I do not believe any of their friends ever heard a complaint or a harsh word uttered of her, much less *to* her ; and I believe there was no inconvenience or privation they would not have submitted to, rather than exchange her blunt honesty for the servile civility, whether accompanied by honesty or not, of anybody else. And I believe, when Beckey at last left them, to be married, it was this circumstance, much more than anything else, which caused them to give up housekeeping, never afterwards to resume it.

Another notable instance may here be cited of Lamb's habitual disposition to bend and veil his own feelings, inclinations, and personal comforts to those of other people. When they left off housekeeping, and went to reside at Enfield, they boarded for some time in the house of a reputable old couple, to whom they paid, for the plainest possible accommodation, a price almost sufficient to keep all the household

twice over, but where, nevertheless, they were expected to
pay for every extra cup of tea, or any other refreshment, they
might offer to any occasional visitor. Lamb soon found out
the mistake he had made in connecting himself with these
people, and did not fail to philosophize (to his friends) on their
blind stupidity, in thus risking what was almost their sole
means of support, in order to screw an extra shilling out of
his easy temper. But he endured it patiently, nevertheless.
One circumstance I remember his telling me with great glee,
which was evidently unmixed with any anger or annoyance
at the cupidity of these people, but only at its blindness.
Wordsworth and another friend had just been down to see
them, and had taken tea ; and in the next week's bill *one* of
the extra "teas" was charged an extra sixpence, and on
Lamb's inquiring what this meant, the reply was, that "the
elderly gentleman," meaning Wordsworth, " had taken such a
quantity of sugar in his tea."

Yet this sort of thing Lamb bore patiently, month after
month, for years, under the feeling, or rather on the express
plea of — What was to become of the poor people if he left
them ?

The Protectionists never pleaded harder for their "vested
rights " than did Lamb for the claims of these people to
continue to live upon him, and affront him every now and
then into the bargain, because they had been permitted to
begin to do so.

LAMB'S SYMPATHIES AND SELF-SACRIFICES.

I 'm afraid it must not be concluded that Lamb gained in
personal comfort and happiness by the change of life consequent on his removal from London. It is true he got rid of
all those visitors who sought him only for his oddity or his
reputation, and retained those only between whom and himself there could be any real interchange of intellect and affection. But it may be doubted whether the former were not
more necessary to him than the latter ; for it was with the
poor and lowly (whether in spirit or in purse) that Lamb chiefly

sympathized, and with them he could hold communion only in the busy scenes of metropolitan life ; and that communion, either in imagination or in fact, was necessary to the due exercise and healthy tone of his mind. The higher class of communion he could at all times find, when he needed it, in books ; but that living sympathy which alone came home to his bosom, he could compass nowhere but in the living world of towns and cities.

In fact, Lamb's retirement, first from the pleasant monotony of a public office, and afterwards from the busy idleness of his beloved London, was the crowning one of those self-sacrifices which he was ever ready to make at the shrine of human affection ; sacrifices not the less noble and beautiful that they were submitted to with an ill grace ; for what sacrifices are those which it costs us nothing to make ? It was for the greater security of his sister's health that Lamb retired from London ; and, in doing so, he as much offered himself a sacrifice for *her* well-being as the martyrs and heroes of other times did for their religion or their country.

And why should the truth be concealed on this point ? "The country" was to Lamb precisely what London is to thoroughly country people born and bred, — who, however they may long to see it for the first time, and are lost in a week's empty admiration at its "sights" and wonders, — would literally die of home-sickness if compelled to remain long in it. I remember, when wandering once with Lamb among the pleasant scenery about Enfield shortly after his retirement there, I was congratulating him on the change between these walks and his accustomed ones about Islington, Dalston, and the like. But I soon found that I was treading on tender ground, and he declared afterwards, with a vehemence of expression extremely unusual with him, and almost with tears in his eyes, that the most squalid garret in the most confined and noisome purlieu of London would be a paradise to him, compared with the fairest dwelling placed in the loveliest scenery of "the country." "I *hate* the country !" he exclaimed, in a tone and with an emphasis which showed not

only that the feeling came from the bottom of his soul, but
that it was working ungentle and sinister results there, that he
was himself almost alarmed at. The fact is that, away from
London, Lamb's spirits seemed to shrink and retire inwards,
and his body to fade and wither like a plant in an uncongenial
soil. The whole of what he felt to be the truly vital years of
his existence had been passed in London; almost every pleasant association connected with the growth, development, and
exercise of his intellectual being belonged to some metropolitan locality ; every agreeable recollection of his social intercourse with his most valued friends arose out of some London
scene or incident. He was born in London ; the whole even
of his school-life was passed in London ; [1] he earned his living in London, — performing there for thirty years that to
him pleasantly monotonous drudgery which gave him his ultimate independence ; [2] in London he won that fame which,
however little store he might seem to set by it, was not without a high and cherished value in his eyes. In short, London
was the centre to which every movement of Lamb's mind
gravitated — the pole to which the needle of his affections and
sympathies vibrated — the home to which his heart was tied
by innumerable strings of flesh and blood, that could not be
broken without lacerating the being of which they formed a
part. In Lamb's eye and estimation the close passages and
grim quadrangles of the Temple (one of his early dwelling-
places) were far more pleasant and healthful than the most
fair and flowery spots of

" Auburn, loveliest village of the plain."

To him, the tide of human life that flowed through Fleet
Street and Ludgate Hill, was worth all the Wyes and Yarrows
in the universe ; there were, to his thinking, no " Green
Lanes " to compare with Fetter Lane or St. Bride's ; no garden like Covent Garden ; and the singing of all the feathered

[1] At Christ's Hospital, where he was contemporary with Coleridge, and where
their life-long friendship commenced.
[2] He was a clerk in the India House for that period, but before I knew him had
retired on half-pay.

tribes of the air "grated harsh discord" in his ear, attuned as it was only to the drone or squall of the London ballad-singer, the grinding of the hand-organ, and the nondescript "London cries," set to their cart-wheel accompaniments.

And yet, when Lamb lived in the country he used to spend the whole of the fore part of his days, winter and summer alike, in long walks and wanderings — not in search of any specific scenes or objects of interest or curiosity, but merely for the sake of walking — its movement and action being congenial to the somewhat torpid and sluggish character of his temperament; for, when sitting still alone, his thoughts were apt to brood and hover, in an uneasy slumberousness, over dangerous and intractable questions, on which his strong common sense told him there was no satisfaction to be gained, but from which his searching spirit could not detach itself.

There was another inducement to these long walks. In whatever direction they lay, Lamb always saw at the end of them the pleasant vision of a foaming pot of ale or porter, which was always liked the better for being quaffed

"In the worst inn's worst room."

The reader, who has accompanied me thus far in my personal recollections of Charles Lamb, will not object to my dwelling for a few moments on a habit of his latter years, which is one of those on which a man's *friends* are apt, without sufficient reason, to interdict themselves from speaking; thus abandoning the topic to the tender mercies of his enemies.

The truth is, that as "to the pure, all is pure," so to the wise and good, all is wise and good. Now, there never was a wiser and better man than Charles Lamb, and the habit to which I am about to refer more definitely than in the above passage, was one of the wisest to which he addicted himself; and if it now and then lapsed into folly, what is the merely human wisdom which does not sometimes do the like?

When Lamb was about to accompany a parting guest half a mile, or half a dozen miles on his way to town (which was his almost constant practice), you could always see that his sister

had rather he stayed at home ; and her last salutation was apt
to be, " Now, Charles, you 're not going to take any ale ? "
" No, no," was his more than half-impatient reply. Now, this
simple question, and its simple reply, form the text on which I
ask leave to preach my little homily on the imputed sin of an
extra glass of gin and water.

The truth, then, is, that Lamb's excellent sister, in her over-
anxious and affectionate care in regard to what she looked at
too exclusively as a question of *bodily* health, endeavored latterly to restrict her brother too much in the use — for to the
abuse he was never addicted — of those artificial stimuli which
were to a certain extent indispensable to the healthy tone of
his mental condition. To keep him from the chance of being
ill, she often kept him from the certainty of being well and
happy — not to mention the keeping others from partaking in
the inestimable results óf that health and happiness. I have
listened delightedly to the intellectual Table Talk of a large
proportion of the most distinguished conversers of the day, and
have ever found it, as a rule, to be infinitely more deeply im-
bued with wisdom, and the virtues which spring from wisdom,
and infinitely more capable of impressing and generating these,
than the *written* words of the same teachers. But I have no
recollection of any such colloquies that have left such delightful and instructive impressions on my mind as those which
have taken place between the first and the last glass of.gin and
water, after a rump-steak or a pork-chop supper in the simple
little domicile of Charles Lamb and his sister at Enfield Chace.
And it must not be overlooked that the aforenamed gin and
water played no insignificant part in those repasts. True, it
created nothing. But it was the talisman that not only unlocked
the poor casket in which the rich thoughts of Charles Lamb
were shut up, but set in motion that machinery in the absence
of which they would have lain like gems in the mountain, or
gold in the mine.

No really good converser, who duly appreciates the use and
virtue of that noble faculty, ever talks for the pleasure of talking, or in the absence of some external stimulus to the act.

He talks wisely and eloquently only because he thinks and feels wisely and eloquently, and he is always fonder of listening than of talking. He talks chiefly that he may listen, not listens merely that he may talk.

Now Charles Lamb, who, when present was always the centre from which flowed and to which tended the stream of the talk, was literally tongue-tied till some slight artificial stimulus let loose the sluggish member; and his profound and subtle spirit itself seemed to wear chains till the same external agency set it at liberty. Indeed, compared with what it really contained, his mind remained a sealed book to the last, as regards the world in general. I mean that his writings, rich and beautiful as they are, were but mere spillings, or forced overflowings, from the hidden fountains of his mind and heart. It was a task of almost insuperable difficulty and trouble to him to write; for he had no desire for literary fame, no affected anxiety to make his fellow-creatures wiser or better than he found them, and no fancied mission to do so; nor had he any pecuniary necessities pressing him on to the labor. So that I do not believe he would ever have written at all but for that salutary " pressure from *within*," which answered to the divine afflatus of the oracles of old, and *would* have vent in speech or written words. His thoughts were like the inspirations of the true poet, which must be expressed by visible symbols or audible sounds, or they drive their recipient mad. What was " the Reading Public " to Charles Lamb ? He did not care a pinch out of his dear sister's snuff-box whether they were supplied to repletion with " food convenient for them," or left to starve themselves into mental health for the want of it. He knew that, in any case, what he had to offer would be " *caviare* " to them.

But it was a very different case with regard to the little world of friends and intimates that his social and intellectual qualities had gathered about him. When with them, it was always as pleasant and easy for him to talk as it was to listen; but never more so; for the truth is, he did not care much even about *them*, so far as related to any pressing desire or necessity for their admiration or appreciation of his mental parts or acquirements : so that latterly nothing enabled or rather induced him to talk at all but that artificial stimulus which for a time restored to him his youth, and chased away that spirit of indifference which had pervaded the whole of his moral being during the last ten years of his life.

In the country, too, this mental apathy and indifference gathered double weight and strength by the absence of any of those more legitimate means of resisting them, which were always at hand in London : for Lamb was not, as I have hinted, among those fortunate persons who

> " Find tongues in trees, books in the running brooks,
> Sermons in stones, and good in everything : "

on the contrary, he saw about him on every side an infinite deal of bad, and no means of turning it to good; while the good that there really is, he saw perpetually overlooked, or turned to bad, by those who should apply and administer it.

The reader must not for a moment suppose, from anything I have now said, that Charles Lamb was in the habit of indulging in that "inordinate cup " which is so justly said to be "unblest, and its ingredient a devil." My very object and excuse in alluding to the subject has been to show that precisely the reverse was the case — that the cup in which *he* indulged was a blessing one, no less to himself than to others, and that for both parties "its ingredient " was an angel.

ELIANA.

Hazlitt has somewhere said of Charles Lamb speculatively, that he was a man who would laugh at a funeral and cry at a wedding. How far the first branch of the proposition was true may be seen by the following exquisite effusion : —

CHARLES LAMB TO P. G. PATMORE.

" DEAR P., — I am so poorly ! I have been to a funeral, where I made a pun, to the consternation of the rest of the mourners. And we had wine. I can't describe to you the howl which the widow set up at proper intervals. Dash could, for it was not unlike what he makes.

" The letter I sent you was one directed to the care of E. White, India House, for Mrs. Hazlitt. *Which* Mrs. Hazlitt I don!t yet know, but A. has taken it to France on speculation. Really it is embarrassing. There is Mrs. present H., Mrs. late H., and Mrs. John H., and to which of the three Mrs. Wigginses it appertains I don't know. I·wanted to open it, but it's transportation.

" I am sorry you are plagued about your book. I would strongly recommend you to take for one story Massinger s 'Old Law.' It is exquisite. I can think of no other.

" Dash is frightful this morning. He whines and stands up on his hind legs. He misses Beckey, who is gone to town. I took him to Barnet the other day, and he could n't eat his victuals after it. ˙ Pray God his intellects be not slipping.

" Mary is gone out for some soles. I suppose it's no use to ask you to come and partake of 'em ; else there's a steam-vessel.

" I am doing a tragi-comedy in two acts, and have got on tolerably ; but it will be refused, or worse. I never had luck with anything my name was put to.   .

" Oh, I am so, poorly ! I *waked* it at my cousin's the book-binder's who is now with God ; or if he is not, it's no fault of mine.

" We hope the frank wines do not disagree with Mrs. Pat-more. By the way, I like her.

" Did you ever taste frogs ? Get them, if you can. They are like little Lilliput rabbits, only a thought nicer.

" Christ, how sick I am ! — not of the world, but of the widow's shrub. She's sworn under £6,000, but I think she perjured herself. She howls in E *la*, and I comfort her in B flat. You understand music ?

" If you have n't got Massinger, you have nothing to do but go to the first *bibliothèque* you can light upon at Boulogne, and ask for it (Gifford's edition), and if they have n't got it, you can have "Athalie," par Monsieur Racine, and make the best of it. But that 'Old Law ' 's delicious.

" ' No shrimps ! ' (That 's in answer to Mary's question about how the soles are to be done.)

" I am uncertain where this *wandering* letter may reach you. What you mean by Poste Restante, God knows. Do you mean I must pay the postage ? So I do to Dover.

" We had a merry passage with the widow at the Commons. She was howling — part howling and part giving directions to the proctor — when crash ! down went my sister through a crazy chair, and made the clerks grin, and I grinned, and the widow tittered — *and then I knew that she was not inconsolable.* Mary was more frightened than hurt.

" She 'd make a good match for anybody (by she, I mean the widow).

> ' If he bring but a *relict* away
> He is happy, nor heard to complain.'
> SHENSTONE.

" Procter has got a wen growing out at the nape of his neck, which his wife wants him to have cut off ; but I think it rather an agreeable excrescence — like his poetry — redundant. Hone has hanged himself for debt. Godwin was taken up for picking pockets. Beckey takes to bad courses. Her father was blown up in a steam machine. The coroner found it Insanity. I should not like him to sit on my letter.[1]

" Do you observe my direction ? Is it Gallic ? — Classical ?[2]

" Do try and get some frogs. You must ask for '*grenouilles*' (green-eels). They don't understand ' frogs,' though it 's a common phrase with us.

" If you go through Bulloign (Boulogne) inquire if old Godfrey is living, and how he got home from the Crusades. He must be a very old man now.

---

[1] The reader need scarcely be told that all the above items of home news are pure fiction.

[2] By this it should seem that the direction was written before the letter, for the passage is not interlined.

" If there is anything new in politics or literature in France, keep it till I see you again, for I 'm in no hurry. Chatty-Briant (Châteaubriand) is well, I hope.

" I think I have no more news ; only give both our loves ('all three,' says Dash) to Mrs. Patmore, and bid her get quite well, as I am at present, bating qualms, and the grief incident to losing a valuable relation.   C. L."

" LONDRES, *July* 19, 1827."

If I give this incomparable letter in all its disjointed integrity, with its enormous jokes in the shape of pretended domestic news, about Procter, Hone, Godwin, Beckey, etc. ; its inimitable *tableau vivant* of the " merry passage with the widow at the Commons ; " its "and then I knew that she was not inconsolable," which cannot be paralleled out of Shakespeare ; its startling dramatic interpolations, " No shrimps ! " and " All three, says Dash ; " its sick qualms, curable only by puns ; its deliberate incoherencies ; its hypothetical invitation to dinner, (I was at Paris at the time) ; if I venture to give all these in their naked innocence, it is because I do not dare to tamper, even to the amount of a single word, with an epistolary gem that is worth the best volume of Horace Walpole's, and half the " Elegant Extracts " from Pope and Atterbury to boot.

INTELLECTUAL CHARACTER.

From much that I have said of Charles Lamb it will have been gathered that he was little qualified, either by temperament or habits, to live in what is called " the world." It may seem paradoxical to say so, but he was quite as little qualified to live out of it. In some sort wedded both to solitude and to society, so far from being able to make himself " happy with either," each was equally incapable of filling and satisfying his affections. The truth is that, deep and yet gentle as those affections were, his daily life gave token that in their early development they had received a sinister bias which never afterwards quitted them — perchance a blow which struck them from the just centre on which they seemed to have been origi-

3

nally destined to revolve, in a circle of the most perfect beauty
and harmony.

Those of Lamb's friends who felt a real and deep interest in
his intellectual character, and its results on his personal happiness, must, I think, have seen this influence at work in almost every movement of his mind and heart, as these developed themselves in his ordinary life and conversation ; for in
his published writings the evidences I allude to do not appear,
at least in any distinct and tangible form.   There, in short,
and there only, was Charles Lamb his own man — his early,
natural, original self ; as indeed is almost always the case with
those men who possess that peculiar idiosyncrasy which is
indicated by the term *genius*.

It would be a task as difficult as delicate, to adduce detailed
evidence of the peculiar condition of mind and heart, in
Charles Lamb, to which I have just alluded ; but I think that
some, at least, of his intimates, will call to mind such evidence,
especially in connection with the last few years of his life.   I
appeal to those intimates whether they ever saw Lamb wholly
at his ease for half an hour together — wholly free from that
restlessness which is incompatible with mental tranquillity ;
whether they ever saw him wrapt in that deep and calm *repose*, in the absence of which there can be no actual, soul-felt
satisfaction.

If, indeed, they have seen him alone in his book-room — he
unknowing of their presence — hanging in rapt sympathy over
the tattered pages of one of his beloved old folios, perchance,
quietly disentangling some ineffable mystery in " Heywood's
Hierarchy of Angels," or listening with his mind's ear to the
solemn music breathing from the funereal organ of Sir
Thomas Browne's Urn-burial — they may have seen him in a
condition of mind analogous to that self-centred repose which
is the soul of human happiness, but is not identical with it.

It is not the less true that Lamb was, for the moment, delighted at the advent of an unlooked-for friend, even though
he was thereby interrupted in the midst of one of these beatific communings.   But they must have read his character

ill, or with little interest, who did not perceive that, after the pleasant excitement of the moment was over, he became restless, uneasy, and " busied about many things " — about anything, rather than the settling down quietly into a condition of mind or temper, even analogous to that from which the new arrival had irretrievably roused him, for that day at least. Feeling the unseasonable disturbance *as* such, yet not for a moment admitting it to be such, even to himself, he became *over*-anxious to show you how welcome you were, — doing half a dozen things in a breath, to prove the feeling, — every one of which, if read aright, proved something very like the reverse. If it happened to be about dinner-time, he would go into the kitchen to see if it was ready, or put on his hat and go out to order an additional supply of porter, or open a bottle of wine and pour some out, — taking a glass himself to set you the example, as he innocently imagined, — but, in reality, to fortify himself for the task of hospitality that you had imposed upon him ; anything, in fact, but sit quietly down by the fire, and enjoy your company, or let you enjoy his. And if you happened to arrive when dinner or tea was over, he was perfectly fidgety, and almost cross, till you were fairly seated at the meal which he and his excellent sister insisted on providing for you, whether you would or not.

It is true that, by the time all these preliminaries were over, he had recovered his ease, and was really glad to see you ; and if you had come to stay the night, when the shutters were shut, and the candles came, and you were comfortably seated round the fire, he was evidently pleased and bettered by the occasion thus afforded for a dish of cosey table-talk. But not the less true is it that every knock at the door sent a pang to his heart ; and this without any distinction of persons : whoever it might be, he equally welcomed and wished them away ; and all for the same reason — namely, that they called him from the company of his own thoughts, or those still better communings with the thoughts of his dead friends, with whom he could hold an intercourse unclogged by any actual bodily presence.

In these respects, Lamb resembled the lover in Martial's epigram: he could neither live *with* his friends, nor without them. If they stayed away from him long, he was hurt and angry; and when they went to him, he was put out.

I believe those contradictory feelings of Lamb in regard to the visits of his friends, to have been in a great measure the secret of his daily and interminable rambles, which he pursued without aim or object, and certainly without any care about the scenes of external nature they might bring before him; for, as I have said, he was anything but fond of the country for itself, and took no sort of pleasure in any of the pursuits and amusements connected with it. Even a garden he was more than indifferent about. If compelled to walk in one, he could no more have confined himself to the regular *walks* than a bird could, and had it been his own, he would have trampled it all into one plot in a week. The garden attached to the cottage they first took at Enfield Chace was in the condition of a school play-ground — never having been touched by spade or hoe for the two years they occupied the place. In short, if such a truth may be told of one who was after all a true poet, Lamb was more than indifferent about flowers — he almost disliked them. In the world, as at present constituted, a man like Charles Lamb must hate *something;* and for him (Lamb) to hate a human being, or indeed any sentient being — even an adder or a toad — was impossible to his nature. Is it, then, speculating too curiously on his singularly-constituted mind and heart to suppose that he may have gone to the opposite extreme — for he lived in extremes — and hated that which seems made only to be loved, and which all the world fancy they love, or pretend to do, because they can find nothing in them to move their hate — flowers, fields, and the face of external nature?

Before quitting this perhaps too speculative portion of my recollections of Charles Lamb, I must remind his earlier and older friends that my knowledge of him extended only over the last nine or ten years of his life: and every lustre that he lived made him in many respects a new man.

ODD CORRESPONDENT OF LAMB.

Most literary men of extensive reputation have met with
odd and unexpected testimonies of the admiration they have
excited in quarters where they would have least looked for it,
and which has been set forth in a fashion drolly discordant
with their tastes and habits of feeling ; and Lamb was not
without these testimonies. One of them he related to me as
having mightily tickled his sense of the ludicrous. A young
gentleman in the country, of a "literary turn,"

> " A clerk foredoomed his father's soul to cross,
> Who penned a stanza when he should engross,"

solicited the favor of Lamb's correspondence and friendship :
and as an unequivocal testimonial of his claims to these, he
forwarded to the object of his admiration his miniature portrait ; the said effigy setting forth a form and feature such as
"youthful maidens fancy when they love."

It was excessively amusing to hear Lamb describe his droll
embarrassment, on the reception of this naive and original
mode of paying court to a man who almost piqued himself on
having no eye or taste for personal comeliness, even in
women, while anything like coxcombry in a man made him
sick ; and who yet had so exquisite a sense of what was due
to the feelings of others, that when a young lady who was
staying at his house, had been making some clothes for the
child of a poor gypsy woman in the neighborhood, whose
husband was afterwards convicted of sheep-stealing, would not
allow her (the young lady) to quit the village without going to
see and take leave of her unhappy *protégée*, — on the express
plea that otherwise the felon's wife might imagine that she
had heard of her husband's "misfortune," and was ashamed
to go near her. "I have a delicacy for a sheep-stealer,"
said he.

There are many who duly appreciate, and are ready enough
to extol, the beauty and the merits of this delicacy to the personal feelings of others, and a few who can sympathize with it

even in extreme cases like the one just cited ; but I never
knew any one who was capable of uniformly, and at all costs,
practising it, except Charles · Lamb and William Hazlitt, —
both of whom extended it to the lowest and vilest of man and
woman kind : would give the wall to a beggar if it became a
question which of the two should cede it, and if they had visited a convicted felon in his cell, would have been on tenter-
hooks all the time, lest anything might drop from them to indicate that they had less consideration for the object of their
visit than if he had been the most " respectable " of men.

The name of William Hazlitt reminds me that a writer [1] of
some pleasing "recollections " of Charles Lamb, in the number of the " New Monthly Magazine " immediately following
his death, speaking of Lamb's intimacy with Hazlitt, and of
the unshrinking manner in which he stood by him, " through
good report and through ill report," says, " He (Lamb) was,
we believe, the only one of Hazlitt's early associates who
stood beside his grave." He was not merely the only one of
Hazlitt's " early " associates, — he was the only one of all his
associates or friends, early or recent, excepting his own son,
and the writer of these pages. The fact offers a sorry evidence of the estimation in which purely intellectual endowments are held among us. And the case is not bettered by
the circumstance that, to this day, no one of the many who
knew him intimately through the whole of his literary life, has
taken the pains to rescue his name and character from the
load of undeserved obloquy that was cast upon them, during
his life-time, by those political enemies and opponents who
saw no other way of combating the "cannonade-reasoning "
and the terrible invective he was accustomed to bring to bear
against them.

But Hazlitt, to say nothing of his unpopular manners, and
his unlucky disposition to "call a knave a knave, and Chartres
Chartres," could not abstain from speaking the truth even of
his best friends, when they happened to treat him as he felt
that only an enemy should be treated ; and the man who does

[1] Mr. Forster, I believe.

this must reckon upon outliving every friend he has in the world, die when he may.

ANECDOTES.

As it is not the aim of this work to exalt or aggrandize the intellectual pretensions of the persons to whom it relates, but only to give true sketches of them as they appeared from the point of view from which the writer looked at them, I shall resort very sparingly to those daily records which I occasionally made, of my personal intercourse with them at set literary or other meetings, where they were more or less *on show*, and consequently never perfectly themselves — any more than a sitter for his portrait is until the artist has talked and enticed him into forgetfulness of the occasion of his visit. What I profess to know and to depict of the persons I treat of was gathered chiefly in that familiar *tête-à-tête* intercourse in which alone men show themselves for what they really are. The startling strangeness of Lamb's utterances at those social meetings in which he joined, either at his own house or elsewhere, though strikingly characteristic of the turn of thought and tone of feeling which prompted them, were anything but indicative of his personal and intellectual character, except as these were momentarily colored and modified by the circumstances acting upon them. Still, as these colorings and modifications are part and parcel of the picture he has left on my recollection, the reader may like, and, indeed, may be considered as entitled in Lamb's case, to see a few of those traits and touches which the self-painter was accustomed to throw in when the beloved solitude of his studio was disturbed by the presence of comparative strangers. And to this end I shall copy *verbatim* from a diary which, when made at all, was invariably made on the night of the day to which it refers.

"*December* 5, 1826. — Spent the evening at Lamb's. When I went in, they (Charles and his sister) were alone, playing at cards together.

"I took up a book on the table — ' Almack's ' — and Lamb said, ' Aye ; that must be *all max* to the lovers of scandal.'

" Speaking of Northcote, he related a story of him, illustrating his love for doing and saying little malicious things. It
was at a party at Sir Joshua Reynolds's, where Boswell was
present, and they were talking of Malone, and somebody said
that Malone seemed to live in Shakespeare, and not to have a
feeling or thought connected with anything else ; upon which
Northcote said, ' Then he must have been the meanest of
mankind. The man who sets up any other man as a sort of
God, and worships him to the exclusion of all other things and
thoughts, must be *the meanest of men;* and everybody,' said
Northcote (who was himself the original relator of the story),
' everybody turned and looked at Boswell.'

" We spoke of L. E. L., and Lamb said, ' If she belonged
to me, I would lock her up and feed her on bread and water
till she left off writing poetry. A female poet, or female author of any kind, ranks below an actress, I think.'

" —— was mentioned, and Lamb said he seemed to him to
be a sort of L. E. L. in pantaloons.

" Bernard Barton was mentioned, and Lamb said that he
did not write nonsense, at any rate — which all the rest of
them did (meaning the Magazine poets of the day). He was
dull enough ; but not nonsensical. ' He writes English, too,'
said Lamb, ' which they do not.'

" H. C. R. came in about half-past eight, and put a stop to
all further conversation — keeping all the talk to himself.

" Speaking of some German story, in which a man is made
to meet *himself* — he himself having changed forms with some
one else — the talk turned on what we should think of ourselves, if we could see ourselves without knowing that it *was*
ourselves. R. said that he had all his life felt a sort of horror
come over him every time he caught a sight of his own face in
the glass ; and that he was almost afraid to shave himself for
the same reason. He said that he often wondered how anybody could sustain an intimacy with, much less feel a friendship for, a man with such a face. Lamb said ' I hope you have
mercy on the barbers, and always shave yourself.'

" Speaking of names, Lamb said, ' John of Gaunt, time-

honored Lancaster,' was the grandest name in the world.
On this R. spoke of a Spanish pamphlet he had lately met
with, describing the Reformation, in which all the English
names were changed to Spanish ones, and the fine effect it
had. It began by relating that a great prince named Don
Henriquez (Henry VIII.) was married to a beautiful princess
called La Donna Catalina (Queen Catherine) — that he was
under the influence of a wily priest named Il Cardinal Bolseo
(Wolsey), who advised him to divorce his chaste wife La
Donna Catalina, and unite himself to a foul though beautiful
witch named La Donna Anna Volena (Anna Boleyn). Jane
Seymour was called La Donna Joanna Sumaro, and her house
(at Greenwich) the castle of Grenuccio.

"*Friday, July* 13. — Spent the evening at Leigh Hunt's,
with the Lambs, Atherstone, Mrs. Shelley, and the Gliddons.
Lamb talked admirably about Dryden and some of the older
poets, in particular of Davenant's "Gondibert." Of this Hunt
wanted to show that it consisted almost entirely of monosylla-
bles, which gave a most heavy and monotonous effect to the
versification ; and he read some passages to that effect. Lamb
would not admit this, and he read an admirable passage in
reply, about a Museum of Natural Curiosities in which Man,
the pretended Lord of all the other creatures, hung by the
wall, dry, like all the rest, and even Woman, the Lord of
Man, hung there too — 'and *she* dried by him.' The effect
of the passage was prodigious. . . . .

"He (Lamb) spoke of Dryden as a prodigious person, so far
as his wonderful power of versification went, but not a first-
rate poet, or even capable of appreciating such — giving instances from his prefaces in proof of this. He spoke of Dryden's prefaces as the finest pieces of *criticism*, nevertheless,
that had ever been written, and the better for being contradictory to each other, because not founded on any pretended
rules.

"Hunt was asking how it was necessary to manage in order
to get Coleridge to come and dine. Lamb replied that he
believed he (Coleridge) was under a kind of watch and ward

— alluding to the watchful care taken of him by the Gilmans, with whom he was then residing. 'Ah," said H., '*vain* is the watch (Mrs. G.), and *bootless* is the ward' (Mr. G.), who always wore shoes.

"Lamb repeated one of his own enormous puns. He had met Procter, and speaking of his little girl (then an infant), Procter said they had called her Adelaide. 'Ah,' said Lamb, 'a very good name for her — *Addle-head.*' "

The two following anecdotes are so characteristic that, although they reached me at second-hand, and may possibly, therefore, have been printed before, I will not omit them. They were told me by James Smith (of the " Rejected Addresses "), at a dinner at the late Charles Matthews's : —

Lamb and Coleridge were talking together on the incidents of Coleridge's early life, when he was beginning his career in the Church, and Coleridge was describing some of the facts in his *usual* tone, when he paused, and said : " Pray, Mr. Lamb, did you ever hear me preach ? " " Damme," said Lamb, " I never heard you do anything else."

The other anecdote was of a lady — a sort of social Mrs. Fry — who had been for some time *lecturing* Lamb on his irregularities.   At last, she said : " But, really, Mr. Lamb, I 'm afraid all that I 'm saying has very little effect on you. I 'm afraid from your manner of attending to it, that it will not do you much good." " No, ma'am," said Lamb, " I don't think it will.   But as all that you have been saying has gone in at *this* ear (the one next her) and out at the other, I dare say it will do this gentleman a great deal of good," turning to a stranger who stood on the other side of him.

LAMB, HAZLITT, AND SOUTHEY.

In ·glancing through the foregoing " Recollections " of Charles Lamb, it seems probable that they may be deemed liable to the objection of not being sufficiently specific — of not dealing enough with facts — of expressing rather what the writer *thought* and *felt* of Lamb than what he *knew*.   Should this complaint be made, it will doubtless be a valid one for

those who make it ; but it is one against which I cannot defend myself, because it points at the precise object, not only
of *these* Recollections, but of all the others of which the work
consists. In fact, I did not go to Charles Lamb's house with
a note-book in my pocket, ready to slip aside at every opportunity, and record his "good things" for the benefit of the
absent, or the amusement of those who, had they been present, would have disputed his wit because it was not dressed
in the received mode, and yawned over (if they had not felt
scandalized at) his wisdom, because it was dictated by the
heart rather than the head. Moreover, Lamb was anything
but what is understood by "a wit" and a *diseur de mots*, in
the ordinary and "company" sense of the phrase, — as the
respectable Lord Mayor who invited him to the city feast of
Lord Mayor's Day in that capacity would have found to his
cost, had Lamb, in that spirit of contradiction which sometimes beset him, accepted the invitation. Though for the
mere sitters-by it would have been capital fun to see him
mystifying my Lord Mayor, scandalizing my Lady Mayoress,
confounding the sheriffs, and putting the whole Court of Al-
dermen and their wives into a fever of mingled wonder and
indignation, at the unseemly revival of an exploded barba-
rism ; for they would doubtless have mistaken our incomparable Elia for the Lord Mayor's Fool.[1] The Boswells of the
literary world are excellent and admirable persons in their
way — that is, when they have Doctor Johnson to deal with.
But Lamb was, of all men that ever lived, the least of a Doctor Johnson ; and Heaven preserve us from a Boswell in his
case ! — for he would infallibly dissipate the charm and the
fragrance that at present encircle the personal memory of
Lamb in the minds of his friends, and which, if not so disturbed, may descend with him to that posterity which his
name and writings will surely reach.

[1] I am supposing that Lamb did *not* accept this tribute offered to his literary
fame ; but he may have done so for anything I know to the contrary. What I am
sure of is, that if he had gone, he would have taken care to remunerate his inviter
as well as himself in a manner and to an effect something like that which I have
supposed in the text. The story of the invitation I find in Hazlitt's notice of him
in *The Spirit of the Age.*

As my opening recollections of Charles Lamb have necessarily connected themselves with the name of William Hazlitt,
I shall, perhaps, not be improperly departing from the spirit
of my theme if I allow my closing remarks to again couple
them together. And I do so the rather that my impulse to
the act involves in its explanation certain characteristic features in the minds of both these remarkable men.

The truth is, that though Lamb and Hazlitt were strangely
different from each other in many features of their minds, they
were singularly alike in many others — more so, perhaps, than
any other two men of their day. There was a general sympathy between them, which served to melt away, and as it were
fuse together, and bring into something like a friendly unison
and correspondence, those differences themselves, — till they
almost took the character of meeting-points, which brought
the two extremes together, when perhaps nothing else could.

In confirmation of this seemingly fanciful theory, I would
refer to two facts only, as almost demonstrative of it : I allude
first to that magnanimous letter of Charles Lamb's to Southey,
on the latter paying him some public compliment which could
only be accepted, as it was only offered, at the 'cost of some
imputation on Hazlitt's character and pursuits. Lamb, on that
occasion, flung back to Southey, with a beautiful indignation
almost bordering on contempt, and in a tone of but half-sup-
pressed bitterness which I do not believe he ever exhibited on
any other occasion, a testimony to his talents and character
which he could not have merited, had the qualifying insinua-
tion, or regret, or whatever it might be called that accompanied it, *also* been deserved. If I remember the circumstances
rightly (for I have no means at hand of referring to the record
of them on either side), the gist of Southey's double offense was
a mingled remonstrance and lamentation at the melancholy
fact, that *such a man as Lamb* should consort with *such a man
as Hazlitt !* As if any two men that ever lived were more exquisitely constituted and qualified to appreciate and admire the
large balance of good over evil that existed in each, and to explain, account for, and excuse the ill, than those two men !

Lamb never did a more noble or beautiful or characteristic thing than the writing of that memorable letter ; and Hazlitt never experienced a higher purer intellectual pleasure than in reading it ; and though at the period of its publication Hazlitt had for a long time absented himself from Lamb's house and society, on account of some strange and gratuitous crotchet of his brain, respecting some imagined offense on the part of Lamb or of himself (for in these cases it was impossible to tell which) — the letter instantly brought them together again ; and there was no division of their friendship till Hazlitt's death, fifteen years afterwards.

The other proof I would offer of the natural sympathy between Lamb and Hazlitt, of which I have spoken, is to be found in the fact, that of all the associates of Hazlitt's early days — indeed of his whole literary and social life — the only one, except his son and myself, who followed him to his grave was Charles Lamb.

But, perhaps, those readers who are unacquainted with the literary table-talk of the last twenty years, or have become acquainted with it through a discoloring and distorting medium, may imagine that there was some good and sufficient reason for the double-edged insult of Southey, and the seeming desertion of Hazlitt by his early friends and associates.

If any reader of this page has imbibed such a notion, I call upon him, in the name of our common nature, and of that sense of justice which is its fairest and noblest feature, to disabuse himself of the unworthy and utterly unfounded impression. And that he is bound in truth and honesty to do so, I appeal to every individual who really knew Hazlitt during the last fifteen years of his life. That Hazlitt had great and crying faults, nobody intimately acquainted with him will deny. But they were faults which hurt himself alone, and were, moreover, inextricably linked with the finer qualities of his nature. The only one of those faults which brought upon him the obloquy to which the peace and comfort of his life were sacrificed, was the result of a virtue which nine tenths of the world (his maligners included) have the wit to divest

themselves of — what he thought and felt about other people,
whether friends or foes, *that* he spoke or wrote, — careless of
the consequences to himself, and sparing himself as little as
he spared any one else. Moreover, if a man smote him on
one cheek, he did not meekly turn the other, and crave for it
the same process ; nor could he ever persuade himself to
carry away the affront quietly, merely because it might consist
with his worldly interest to do so. If he was hated and feared
more than any other living man, it was because he saw more
deeply than any other man into the legitimate objects of
hatred, and was, by habit as well as temper, not amenable to
those convenient restraints and mental reservations which custom has imposed, in order to guard against the social consequences of such untoward discoveries. Iago says it was the
virtue of the Venetian dames of his day, "not to leave un-
done, but to keep unknown." It was Hazlitt's virtue — or
vice, if you please — not merely "to spy into abuses" (for
that we can all of us do), but to feel a sort of moral necessity
for dragging them into the light, when he had found them.
He could neither conceal nor palliate a single fault or weakness of his own. Was it likely, then, that he would be at the
trouble of throwing a veil over those of other people — especially when the only passion of his soul was a love of
Truth !

Charles Lamb knew and appreciated these qualities of
Hazlitt's mind more truly and entirely than any one else, because he found the types of them in his own ; the only but
signal difference being, that he (Lamb), while he saw the
truth with an intellectual vision as clear as that of Hazlitt, was,
by the gentleness and moral sweetness of his nature, not
merely deterred from exposing it to those who might have
overlooked it, but was impelled to transform or translate it
into symbols of its most striking opposite. Like the "sweet
Ophelia," he "turned to favor and to prettiness" all the moral
evil and deformity that presented itself to his observation.
He could not, or would not see ugliness anywhere, — except as
a sort of beauty-spot upon the face of beauty ; but beauty he

could see everywhere, and nowhere shining so brightly as when in connection with what others called ugliness.

There is something inexpressibly shocking in first hearing of a dear friend's death through the medium of a public newspaper, at a time, perhaps, when you believe him to be in perfect health, and are on the point of paying him a too long delayed visit. Such was my case in respect to Charles Lamb. Still more painful was the case of a lady, formerly a distinguished ornament of the English stage, to whom Lamb was attached by the double tie of admiration and friendship.[1] Several days after Lamb's death, she was conversing of him with a mutual friend, who, taking for granted her knowledge of Lamb's death, abruptly referred to some circumstance connected with the event, which for the first time made her acquainted with it.

[1] Miss Kelly.

WILLIAM HAZLITT.

.

4

yours,

W. Hazlitt

WILLIAM HAZLITT.

PATMORE'S FIRST INTRODUCTION TO HAZLITT.

Y acquaintance with William Hazlitt commenced before his name emerged from the "illustrious obscurity" of that private and local fame which had gathered round it, in the small *coterie* to which he had till then addicted himself, and just as it was rising into that "bad eminence" to which the abuse and scandal of his political and personal enemies (not unaided by his *friends*) soon after lifted it. My first interview with him took place in the committee-room of a literary institution, of which I was at that time one of the managers, and had been deputed by my colleagues to arrange with Hazlitt respecting the details of a course of lectures, which it was proposed he should deliver in the theatre of the institution; an office to which he had been recommended by an influential member of the institution, the late Mr. Alsager, of the "Times" newspaper.

Having been previously cautioned not to be surprised or repelled by any "strangeness" that I might observe in Hazlitt's manner and personal appearance, I was shown into the room where he was by the librarian, who merely named each to the other, and then left us together.

On entering, I saw a pale anatomy of a man, sitting uneasily, half on half off a chair, with his legs tucked awkwardly underneath the rail, his hands folded listlessly on his knees, his head drooping on one side, and one of his elbows leaning (not resting) on the edge of the table by which he sat, as if in fear of its having no right to be there. His hat had taken an odd position on the floor beside him, as if that, too, felt itself as much out of its element as the owner.

He half rose at my entrance, and, without speaking a word, or looking at me, except with a momentary and furtive glance, he sat down again, in a more uneasy position than before, and seemed to wait the result of what I might have to say to him, with the same sort of desperate indifference with which a culprit may be supposed to wait the sentence of his judge, after conviction. He was to learn from me whether his proffered services, as a lecturer, were accepted or rejected : and, to a man of his habits and temperament, and under his circumstances, either alternative took the shape of an intolerable penalty — like those to Romeo, of "Death" or "Banishment." If the lectures he proposed to deliver were rejected, he probably did not know where to meet the claims of to-morrow. On the other hand, if they were accepted, his condition was still more trying : for I learned from him that not a line of the lectures were written, nor even their materials prepared ; they had been merely *thought of.* It was a case, too, in which punctuality was indispensable ; yet such were his uncertain and desultory habits, that the fulfillment of an engagement to be at a given place and time, on a given day, for ten successive weeks, then and there to address a miscellaneous audience for "an hour by Shrewsbury clock," was what few who knew him could have believed to be among possible contingencies.

The picture which Hazlitt presented when I first saw him in the little dark, dungeon-like committee-room referred to, was not unlike that of Sir Joshua's "Ugolino." There he sat, his anxious and highly-intellectual face looking upon vacancy ; pale and silent as a ghost ; emaciated as an anatomy ; loose, unstrung, inanimate, as a being whose life is leaving it, from sheer emptiness and inanition. And this "poor creature" (as he used sometimes to call himself) — apparently with scarcely energy enough to grapple with an infant or face a shadow — was the launcher forth of winged words that could shake the hearts of princes and potentates, and make them tremble in

their seats of power; this effigy of silence was the utterer of
floods of indignant eloquence, that could rouse the soul of apathy itself, and stir the blood like the sound of a trumpet; this
"dish of skimmed milk" was the writer of the celebrated re-
plies to "Vetus," in the "Times" newspaper; the invectives
of the "Catalogue Raisonné;" and the essays on "The Spirit
of Monarchy," and "The Regal Character." Nay, more — he
was the only man of letters in England who had dared openly
to stand by the French Revolution, through good and through
evil report; and who had the magnanimity never to turn his
back on its "child and champion."

Though nothing worth particular record occurred in this my
first interview with William Hazlitt, I have been tempted to
dwell on it thus long, because it has left a more vivid and
picturesque impression on my mind than any subsequent one,
except the last, which took place when he was on his death-
bed.

It was not till two or three years after the period above referred to, that a strict intimacy commenced between Hazlitt
and myself, and that I had the full and fair means of appreciating his remarkable, and in all respects self-consistent
character. I shall, therefore, not dwell upon the intercourse
which ensued upon our first acquaintance, except to contrast
the impression I gained of him before I really knew him, with
that which was the due and just result of an intimate and
unrestricted insight into his mental and moral constitution
— a contrast which may, in some degree, account for the
strangely contradictory feelings and impressions which prevailed in the world respecting him, according to the amount
of actual knowledge or ignorance possessed, concerning his
character and the springs of it. I remember the time — and
I remember it without shame, because the impressions under
which I then felt and spoke of Hazlitt were the *natural* ones
— that is to say, the only ones naturally resulting from the
circumstances under which I had formed my judgment — I
remember the time when no words could express the horror I
felt at the (supposed) personal character of William Hazlitt,

or were deemed too strong to openly set forth those feelings.
But my first impressions were derived, not from my own observations, but from the report of those who ought to have
known better, and who certainly would have known better,
had not their personal feelings been enlisted into the cabal
against him, either by their having been the subject of one
of those insane assaults that he was every now and then
making on his best friends, under a false (or true) impression
of their occasional treatment of him, or (still worse) in consequence of some " good-natured " acquaintance repeating some
of those unpalatable truths which Hazlitt was in the habit of
telling of *all* his friends in their absence. For he professed
to lay no restraint upon his tongue in this particular : he considered the foibles of our friends to be as fair game as those
of our enemies, always provided they were pursued and hunted
down without the cognizance of the owner. He recognized
no Game Laws in this particular. The axiom which bids
us " never speak ill of a man behind his back " (as if one
might do it with propriety before his face !), was not one of
those ranked by Hazlitt among " the wisdom of nations."
On the contrary, he spoke what he thought of people, everywhere but in their hearing ; trusting (rather too implicitly, I
am afraid) to that tacit compact which recognizes the sacredness of social intercourse. And he cared not what you said
of him in return, nor if he heard your injurious estimate of
him repeated by half the town ; or if he sought to make reprisals, it was on the hawker, not the originator, of the
affront. But a *personal* slight or incivility he held to be the
most unpardonable of offenses, and to be punished and
avenged as such. You might think and call him a rascal or a
reprobate as much as you pleased ; you might " prove " him
to be a bad writer and a worse man, with perfect impunity ;
but if you looked askance upon him in company, or "cut "
him in the street, or even gave him reason to fancy that you
had done so, there was (as we shall see hereafter) no limit to
the revenge he would take on you, and no rest for him till he
had taken it.

But I will not go farther wide of my intended mark, which is that of painting William Hazlitt as I knew him ; not describing or estimating his general character, but leaving the reader to form an estimate for himself, from the personal traits that I may be able to furnish, in addition to those which may be gathered from his writings.

Our first interview, as above alluded to, lasted but a few minutes, and was concluded by an arrangement for the early delivery of a course of lectures — those on the Comic Writers ; and I saw nothing more of William Hazlitt till a day or two before the delivery of the first lecture, when I addressed a note to him, stating my intention of giving a critical notice of the lectures in " Blackwood's Magazine," and asking him for such facilities as he might choose to afford me, with a view to offering specimens of the matter. His reply was a request to see me at his residence in York Street, Westminster.

HAZLITT'S RESIDENCE.

It is, perhaps, worth remark, that my early intercourse with William Hazlitt has left on my memory a singularly vivid impression of the *local* circumstances and objects connected with it. I remember every room in which I have seen him, as clearly as if I were now sitting in it, and the exact situation and attitudes in which I was accustomed to see him sit or stand when conversing with him. I make the observation, because it would not be applicable to my intercourse with any other of the distinguished men of the day. The reason probably is, that our susceptibility to external impressions at any given time, and our consequent power of retaining them, is proportioned to the *interest* we feel in the immediate source of those impressions. I have not slightly or unduly appreciated and enjoyed the intercourse that has fallen to my lot with a large proportion of the remarkable men of our day, in every department of human acquirement; but I have never been induced to feel that any one of them claimed or justified that profound intellectual study which I was always (in spite of myself) called upon to apply in the case of William Hazlitt;

or it may be that he alone was always *susceptible* of that study, by reason of the beautifully simple and natural cast of his character; in which spring and evidence of true greatness of capacity I do not believe him to have been surpassed by any man that ever lived. If "to know a man truly were to know *himself*," then was William Hazlitt's character, though the least common in the world, so legibly written in his daily conduct and converse, that for those who saw much of him to mistake it was next to impossible. Yet no character was ever so mistaken and misrepresented.

Leaving the *onus* of this charge to be divided between the willful blindness of his friends and the willful falsehood of his enemies, I will say, that I believe the certainty of not coming away empty-handed was the secret of the strong and unwearied interest that I always felt in his society, even at the very time when I felt an inexpressible horror and dread of his supposed personal character, — as was the case at the time I am now speaking of. From all that I had heard, both from his enemies (and even from his so-called friends) and the little I had hitherto seen for myself, I looked upon him, personally, as little better than an incarnate fiend: and those who recollect the *looks* that occasionally came over him (as if, against his will, to warn by-standers of their danger), will scarcely deem this an exaggerated description of the feeling. Yet my desire to see and know him was not the less strong and urgent; and hence, as I conceive, the peculiar vividness with which I retain my impressions of the local circumstances under which we met.

I went to him in York Street, in consequence of the note referred to above; and, though I have never since (until this moment) attempted to recall the scene, it lives before me now as if it were of yesterday. On knocking at the door, it was, after a long interval, opened by a sufficiently "neat-handed" domestic. The outer door led immediately from the street (down a step) into an empty apartment, indicating an uninhabited house, and I supposed I had mistaken the number; but, on asking for the object of my search, I was shown to a door which opened (a step from the ground) on to a ladder-like staircase, bare like the rest, which led to a dark, bare landing-place, and thence to a large square wainscotted apartment. The great curtainless windows of this room looked upon some dingy trees; the whole of the wall, over and about the chimney-piece, was entirely covered, up to the ceiling, by names written in pencil, of all sizes and characters, and in all directions — commemorative of visits of curiosity to "the house of Pindarus."[1] There was, near to the empty fire-place, a table with breakfast things upon it (though it was two o'clock in the afternoon); three chairs and a sofa were standing *about* the room, and one unbound book lay on the mantel-piece. At the table sat Hazlitt, and on the sofa a lady, whom I found to be his wife.

My reception was not very inviting; and it struck me at once (what had not occurred to me before) that in asking facilities for criticising William Hazlitt in "Blackwood's Magazine," I had taken a step open to the suspicion of either mischief or mystification, or both. However, I soon satisfied him that my object and design were anything but unfriendly. To be what he called "puffed" in so unlooked-for a quarter was evidently deemed a godsend; it put him in excellent humor accordingly; and the "Lake Poets" being mentioned, and finding me something of a novice in such matters (and moreover an excellent listener), he talked for a couple of hours, without intermission, on those "personal themes," which he evidently "loved best," and with which, in this instance, he mixed up that spice of malice which was never, or rarely, absent from his discourse about his quondam friends, Wordsworth, Coleridge, and Southey, and which so strangely interferred with his general estimate of their pretensions — or rather (for such I believe to have been the case) with that perfect *good faith* with which he was accustomed to give his estimates to the world : for I believe the above-named were the only instances in which he did not say of celebrated men all

[1] The house had been the residence of Milton, and now belonged to Jeremy Bentham, over whose garden it looked.

the *good* that he thought, as well as the bad. But to put the
seal of his critical fiat to the fame of men whom he believed to
have treated him personally as Wordsworth, Coleridge, and
Southey were supposed by him to have done, was scarcely in
human nature.

The above was my first initiation into themes of this nature ;
and I must confess that the way in which Hazlitt stripped off
the attributes of divinity with which I had hitherto invested
those idols of my boyish worship, was not so unpalatable to
my taste as I should myself have expected it to be. The
truth is, we are not sorry to learn that any of our fellow-beings
are less immaculate or superlative in *personal character* than
our imaginations, excited by their written works, had led us to
suppose them : nor do I know that it in the least degree
interferes with the effect which their works are calculated to
produce upon us afterwards, or to impair those we already
possess. On the contrary, it perhaps aggrandizes our impressions of them, from the seeming inadequacy of the source
whence they flow, and soothes our personal feelings into the
belief that we ourselves are not so immeasurably inferior to
these "gods of the earth " as we had been accustomed to
deem ourselves. We do not think the less of Shakespeare
for being told that he was a link-boy or a deer-stealer ; and
we *do* think very considerably less of Goethe from knowing
that he was, for his worldly wisdom, deemed fit to be the privy
councilor, and for his unimpeachable morals and manners the
personal friend and associate, of an absolute prince. The only
difference is, that after the new light has come to us, the pro-
duct is thenceforth one thing, and the producer another ;
whereas they were before inextricably linked and blended together ; and our impressions of the latter, as derived from the
former, besides being altogether gratuitous, were infinitely
more likely to be the false interpretation than the true one.
To which it may be added, that what the human soul instinct-
ively yearns for and reaches after, as the hart pants for the
water-brooks, is not this or that vague generality, or empty
and unmeaning abstraction, but THE TRUTH. Whatever it may

be, or wheresoever it may lead, truth is the goal to which the
undiverted tendency of the human mind points all its affections ; and it is never satisfied or at rest till this is reached.
The natural and healthful condition of any given mind may, in
a great degree, be estimated by the strength or weakness with
which it retains and is acted upon by this bias ; and the lingering love which is perpetually pointing to it, after it has been
destroyed by the conventional ordinances of the world, is a
proof and a measure of its original amount. We love all
other things for something else not inherent in themselves ;
but we love the truth for itself alone. In this sense it is that
" Beauty is Truth, Truth Beauty." We desire, first and fore-
most, to know *what* a thing is : it is time enough afterwards
to inquire the why and wherefore — the how and when.
These are very well as matters of amusement and curiosity ;
but the truth is the only *pabulum* of our mental and moral existence — the only real necessity — the only veritable " staff
of life." We can live by it in health and vigor, deprived of
all other things ; and *with* all others, *that* wanting, we pine
and pule and fret away our fruitless days, in an empty and uneasy search after that which is not to be found. Nor when
the truth is once attained on any given point of inquiry, is the
searcher at a moment's loss in the recognition of it, nor does
he seek to proceed another step in his pursuit. They say
" marriages are made in heaven," and that when the objects
destined for each other meet, the recognition is instant and
mutual. At least it is so with Truth and the Human Soul ; and
it is a marriage which, when once consummated, cannot know
division or divorce. We may pass from the cradle to the
grave without meeting with this bride of our souls ; or we may
meet with a thousand " false Florizels," and mistake each of
them for the true one ; but we cannot meet with the true one
and mistake or reject *her*. It is not in the nature of things.

The reader will I hope excuse this digression, in favor of
the occasion which suggested itself ; for if ever there was a
human mind devoted and self-sacrificed to the love of truth,
it was that of William Hazlitt ; and he pursued the search of

it with a fearless pertinacity only equaled by the sagacity
which pointed out and applied the means and materials of the
discovery. This love of truth was the leading feature of his
mind, and it was the key to all its weaknesses, errors, and inconsistencies, as well as to all its extraordinary powers and
the successful application of them. He used to boast of
being "a good hater." If the boast and the habit were un-
charitable ones, they were the offspring of that love of truth
which was the passion of his soul, and that power of eliciting
it which was the great characteristic of his intellect. If,
while conscious of his own errors and failings, he felt and expressed too bitter a scorn for those of others, it was because
others instead of owning and despising their frailties as he
did, insist on monstering them into virtues and subjects of personal vanity, and the world abets and encourages them in the
mischievous self-deception. If, instead of being content to use
his great powers in calmly exposing the false pretensions of
the world to that contempt which they merit, he was too apt to
seize upon them with a savage fury, and tear them to pieces, as
the wild beast tears and rends the cloak that is flung upon it
to blind its eyes from the attacks of its enemies, it was because
his self-control was less than his detestation of the debasing
consequences that spring from the admission of those pretensions ; it was because it drove him mad to see whole nations,
generation after generation, dragged like slaves and idiots at
the chariot-wheels of a few empty and vulgar idols — bound
there by lilliputian threads that a breath might have broken.

This first lengthened interview of mine with Hazlitt ended
by his promising to let me have the MS. of his lectures, to do
what I pleased with, and we parted on a better footing than
we had met ; though evidently with as little prospect as before
of our ever becoming intimate associates : for the way in
which he handled his quondam friends, as above described,
did anything but decrease the dread I had been taught to entertain of his personal character.

IN THE STREETS.

As it is of my *intimacy* alone with Hazlitt that I propose to treat in any detail, I shall pass hastily over that mere desultory acquaintance which ensued on his delivery of the lectures above alluded to. Two or three trifling but characteristic circumstances growing out of that acquaintance are, however, worth referring to.

I well remember, after the successful delivery of his first lecture on the Comic Writers, my walking home with Hazlitt from the institution to his house in Westminster. Let those who knew the personal bearing and habits of William Hazlitt, conceive of a man almost a stranger to him — who had only exchanged words with him in a sort of *official* capacity — let the intimates of Hazlitt conceive of such a person volunteering to walk home with him, for the purpose of having a little pleasant conversation by the way ! Nay, in my innocence, I actually *offered him my arm*, WHICH HE TOOK ! and so we walked, arm in arm, through the whole of Fleet Street, the Strand, Parliament Street, etc.

The "general reader " will wonder what there was extraordinary in this ; but the initiated will not believe it. They can fancy him sitting sulkily in the stocks, or walking doggedly round in the pillory ; for a superior physical force might have placed him there, and being there, he was too much of a logician to quarrel with necessity. But to walk straight home at ten o'clock at night, "in a respectable and gentlemanlike manner !" It cannot have been ! Arm in arm, too, and with a very young gentleman in a point device costume ! I think I hear Charles Lamb exclaim, " Why, the angel Gabriel could not have persuaded Hazlitt to walk arm in arm with him for half the length of Southampton Buildings." Perhaps not — but with a *writer in " Blackwood's Magazine "* it was different ; one, too, who had tacitly engaged to give a favorable account of him in that terror and bugbear of his *coterie.* The chance was not to be thrown away ; for Hazlitt, with all his boasted non-conformity, piqued himself on his prudence and

world-wisdom, when he thought the occasion of sufficient
moment to his personal comfort to call for these. In fact,
this trait formed the only serious stain in his personal character, or rather it sprang out of that quality which was so.

Let me here, once for all, get over this only painful and
repugnant portion of the task I have undertaken ; for that once
off my conscience, I shall go forward much more to my own
satisfaction, and therefore to the reader's. In resolving to tell
what I know, or have been led to feel, of William Hazlitt, I
have determined to "nothing extenuate." I at once, then,
confess that the plague-spot of his personal character was an
ingrained selfishness, which more or less influenced and modified all the other points of his nature.

This is a hard stone to fling at a man of whom one is proud
to be deemed the friend in spite of it. But now that it cannot
hurt him, the truth may be told : nay, I verily believe that, had
it been told in his life-time, in the spirit in which it is told now, .
he would have had the magnanimity not merely to admit the
charge, but to forgive the maker of it. And if this noble frank-'
ness is not enough to wash out the "damned spot," it may at
least serve — as, in fact, it did serve in practice — to prevent
the spread of the poison to the vital parts of his character.

Let me still further guard against being mistaken by Hazlitt's friends and misinterpreted by his enemies. The defect
which I have noticed in his character was little in amount. I
never knew him do a base or mean action ; and I have known
him do many that might fairly claim to be deemed magnanimous, in the ordinary acceptation of the term. It would be
the basest of libels upon Hazlitt to describe him as a mean-
souled man. But the tendency, the taint was there ; though it
seldom showed itself in overt acts, and never without a sort of
half-struggle to overcome it ; or in default of that, a half-os-
. tentatious exposure of the weakness, as one of which he was
not merely conscious, but took to himself more shame for it
than his worst enemies would have cast upon him.

I shall leave it to those enemies to collect proofs and illustrations of this "original sin" of Hazlitt's temperament. I

have done my self-prescribed duty in declaring the existence
of the evil, and shall now quit the painful and ungrateful
theme, after having ventured on one more remark in connection with it. I have said that the above-named trait in Hazlitt's character was, like Othello's declension into the vale of
years, "not much." I will add, that like that, it was (prac-
tically) fatal to his peace of mind; for he could not choose but
be deeply conscious of it, and this gave him an ever-present
sense of his own comparative unworthiness, and made him
listen more eagerly to the suggestions of that self-raised
demon, who, Iago-like, was ever at his elbow, urging him on
to insane jealousies and suspicions of the good faith of those
on whom his heart and spirit yearned to rest and repose.
Hazlitt had strong and burning affections, which could never
find a fit object whereon to lean for support ; so that, like the
projections of a disease-worn frame, at whatever points they
touched external objects, they corroded, and cankered, and
turned to poisonous sores. Had Hazlitt believed that any one
human being (especially one of the other sex), whatever his or
her station or character, could have loved him with an undivided and unfailing love, he would have been a happy and a
happy-making man. But the unfounded belief which beset
him, that he was despised and contemned wherever he turned
for sympathy, and the still stronger belief *that he in some sort
deserved to be so*, made and kept him the most miserable of
human beings.

To return to our "progress" from Blackfriars to Westminster, after Hazlitt's first lecture on the Comic Writers. I
remember he declined my offered arm at first — which I interpreted as an evidence of his excessive modesty ! I pressed
it, however, and he then took it — but as if it had been a bar
of hot iron — holding it *gingerly*, with the tips of his fingers,
much after the fashion in which he used to shake hands with
those friends who were inadvertent or absent enough to proffer
that ceremony.

Nevertheless, we talked bravely by the way (though every
third sentence on his part was concluded by a " Sir ") till we

got to that broad part of Parliament Street opposite to the Admiralty and the Horse Guards. Here, however, we met with a rather unseemly interruption, in the form of sundry petitioners ; and I shall never forget the air of infantine simplicity with which Hazlitt received and answered them. That I should see anything exceptionable in the acquaintance seemed not to enter his thoughts ; but his surprise and horror were extreme at the *breach of etiquette* committed by his unhappy *protégées*, in thus addressing him in the presence of a third person ! And this feeling was evidently not on his own account, but on mine. His forbearance and charity for the " unfortunate " persons in question were without limits ; and he did not care if all the world knew it, and witnessed the results that ensued whenever his pocket was on a par with his humanity in this particular. But it by no means followed that others might have reached the same philosophic pitch of benevolence : and, with the fewest "prejudices " of any man I ever knew, Hazlitt was the last to shock those of other people. His consternation on the above occasion was extreme accordingly, and his uneasiness and confusion were in proportion ; for he found himself between the horns of a dilemma. He must either run the risk of horrifying *me* by entertaining these not very creditable applicants, or he must outrage *them* by a harsh and unlooked for repulse. I will not say whether his humanity was stronger than his sense of the *bienséances ;* or whether he might not consider the incident as a fairly-earned penalty for the breach of them which *I* had committed, in forcing my company where the desire of companionship was evidently not mutual ; not to mention that it might prove a convenient guard against a repetition of the intrusion. Certain it is, that the claimants in question were repulsed with the gentlest hand in the world.

I shall make no apology for relating this incident ; for those who feel a sufficient interest in the character of the late William Hazlitt to have accompanied me thus far in my recollections of him, are not likely to be troubled with that false delicacy which could alone have induced or demanded the suppression of it.

I shall conclude the record of my first acquaintance with Hazlitt, by referring to another incident, still more character-istic than the above, of the mind and character I would help to delineate. I had, as the reader has seen, been the occasion of securing to Hazlitt what he considered and called "the best job" he ever had as a professed author ; for, besides the sum he was to receive for the delivery of the course of lect-ures, he had sold the copyright of them for a handsome price. I had, moreover, not merely kept his lectures from being abused in " Blackwood's," but had praised them there to the full amount of his expectations.[1] And, to crown the climax of (so-called) obligation, I had, if I remember rightly, at his earnest request, procured the consent of the committee of managers to pay him *in advance* the whole or part of the price of his services ; a benefit, in his estimation, "worth the other two." Such was the relative state of things between us, when, in an unfortunate article which I wrote in " Blackwood's," I happened to use some phrase or illustration which he (Hazlitt) had used on the same subject just before, in the "London Magazine," and without referring to him as the origin of the joke, or witticism, or whatever it was : for it is not worth the trouble of turning to the passage for verification.

Let the reader judge of my mingled horror and astonish-ment at finding, in the next number of the "London Maga-zine," a ferocious personal attack on myself, almost by name, in which my innocent and unconscious adoption of a worth-less phrase or word of his was characterized as an atrocious appropriation of his property, and the doer of it written down, in so many words, a "petty-larceny rascal," and threatened with redoubled vengeance in future if he did not leave off his pickpocket proceedings !

[1] In order to show that Hazlitt was not unreasonable or exigent in his require-ments in cases of this nature, I subjoin the note he wrote me on the occasion of my sending him in MS. the article in question : —

"DEAR SIR, — I am very well satisfied with the article, and obliged to you for it. I am afraid the censure is truer than the praise. It will be of great service if they insert it entire, which, however, I hope. . Your obliged,

"W. HAZLITT."

Being totally unconscious of any *other* cause of offense
against Hazlitt than the above, I confess that the savage manner in which he made his reprisals both shocked and disgusted
me ; and so matters rested between us for a considerable
length of time, and of course without any thought on my part
of the acquaintance being renewed ; all the ill that I had
heard of Hazlitt being thus confirmed to me by this (as I *then*
considered it) atrocious, because wholly unprovoked act.

It is astonishing how quickly a *personal* proof of this kind
brings conviction to one's mind on a doubtful point, when
nothing else can. I had heard repeated instances of Hazlitt
committing unprovoked outrages of this description on his
best friends ; but knowing and feeling them to be against nature, I would not allow myself to believe them. But the moment he committed one of a similar kind *against myself,* I not
merely believed it, but believed all the rest in virtue of it ;
though it was even more inexplicable, on any received principle of human action, than all the rest, and more against all my
previous experience.

I hope the reader anticipates the true explanation in my
case, and, through it, in all the rest. The fact is, Hazlitt (as
I learned afterwards) believed that I had committed against
him what he justly deemed an unpardonable offense. I had,
he thought, *cut* him in the street ! And whenever anything of
this kind happened to him, there was no limit to the " wild
kind of justice " which he was disposed to wreak upon the
offending party. I do not believe that he could have slept in
peace till he had *righted* himself, in any case of this kind ; and
when the individual was not one against whom he could use
his pen, he made his tongue the medium of reprisal.

I do not know how it may have been with Hazlitt's friends
in cases similar to that which I have just referred to, or how
it might have been with myself had I at that time ranked
among them ; though I believe that, even in that case, my
angry feelings (if I had experienced any) would have arisen
solely from his supposing me capable of the unspeakable
meanness in question. But merely as an acquaintance, and

that acquaintance sought by myself, and almost forced upon him, I (on receiving the explanation of the act, and believing that he was satisfied as to the alleged cause for it) thought then, and think now, that he had not only a *right* to do what he did but that there was a kind of magnanimity in flinging aside all the supposed claims of obligation which I have alluded to in the outset of this little history (and which were no obliga- tions at all, but done purely to please and satisfy *myself*), and "doing himself a pleasure and a right," out of that pure and irrepressible sense and love of abstract justice which are among the noblest and rarest attributes of the human mind, and were especially conspicuous in his. The "taste" in which the thing was done is another matter, and one which, luckily, Hazlitt cared nothing about ; for had he been the man to do so, the world would have been without some of the noblest writings of their class which it can boast.

DINNER WITH HAZLITT AT JOHN SCOTT'S.

Shortly after the period of my receiving the above explana- tion of Hazlitt's supposed outrage upon me, I was sitting one morning with the late John Scott, at his lodgings in York Street, Covent Garden, when he told me that he was every moment expecting Hazlitt to call on him by appointment ; and knowing my *then* feelings about the attack in the magazine (for it was he who had furnished me with an explanation of it, and from Hazlitt's own lips), he proposed that I should meet him, but not then, for he felt that it would not be *safe* to introduce Hazlitt *unprepared* into the room with a man whom he (Hazlitt) felt that he had outraged. In fact, so intense was Hazlitt's sense of what was due to a man's immediate *personal feelings* when face to face with him, that he would never have forgiven Scott the *indiscretion* of bringing himself and me to- gether again, without the full consent of both parties. Briefly, it was settled that we should dine with Scott the same day, if Hazlitt did not object ; and accordingly we met as if nothing had happened : for Hazlitt's sensitiveness on matters of this nature precluded the slightest allusion to the indirect occasion

of our meeting, nor was it ever afterwards referred to in the
most remote manner ; and the rest of the day (and night) was
spent in talk such as I scarcely remember to have enjoyed
either before or since. I never knew Hazlitt so entertaining
and brilliant, yet so subtle, penetrating, and profound. He
seemed determined to make me amends for the undeserved
injury he had done me. It was also, I remember, the first
fair renewal of John Scott's intimacy with him, which had
been broken off for several years ; and they mutually made
it the occasion of such a vivid and various calling back of the
scenes, characters, and histories of the then, alas ! defunct
coterie who were accustomed to meet at Basil Montagu's,
Charles Lamb's, Leigh Hunt's, and all those who had once
"called Admiral Burney friend," that I became as familiar
with them all as if I had been one among them — a boon the
bestowal of which was like adding a score of years to one's
life, "without the illness should attend them." Scott, too,
who had recently returned from a lengthened residence in
Italy, had many excellent things to tell, which were new to
Hazlitt (who was as good a listener as he was a talker) ; in particular, several capital ones about Lord Byron, with whom he
had been recently spending a week at Venice.

Two of these anecdotes I particularly remember. Until
their meeting at Venice, there had been an estrangement
between Byron and Scott, in consequence of the part the
latter had taken in the "Champion," relative to the publication of the celebrated "Farewell ; " but they were now reconciled, and were on the water together in Byron's gondola,
under circumstances which led Scott to express a strong sense
of danger as to their position. "Oh ! " said Byron, in a tone
of perfect seriousness, "you need not be afraid of anything
happening to you while you are with me, *for we are friends
now.*" And Scott explained that Byron had the most intimate
persuasion, that any of his friends who had quarreled with
him were never safe from some strange accident, until they
had ".made it up."

The other anecdote related to one of those *bonnes fortunes*

on which Byron so much piqued himself. He told Scott,
that during the heyday of his popularity, he was on a visit
at a noble house in the country, where a large party of both
sexes was assembled ; and that among them was a lady of
rank, beauty, and immaculate reputation, with whom he fell
desperately in love, and determined to urge his passion, notwithstanding the presence of her husband, to whom she was
evidently attached. For several days his unwearied assidu-
ities produced no effect beyond that of an evident desire, on
the lady's part, to avoid them without infringing the usages
of society. Two or three times, during the siege and defense,
Byron had taken opportunities of offering the lady a *billet-
doux*, in which he had expressed his passion in terms not, as
he thought, to be resisted by mortal woman, at least in the
class of society in which this one moved ; but on every occasion she had contrived to avoid the proffered insult, without
being obliged to recognize it as such. At last, as Byron declared, he grew desperate, and determined to run all risks
rather than be foiled in his pursuit. Confident in what he believed to be his knowledge of the female heart, he contrived
to be conversing with the lady, in a billiard-room that was
situated apart from the rest of the house, at the precise moment when he knew that her husband would enter the room.
The husband entered : at *that* moment Byron pressed into
her hand his letter ; in the alarm and confusion of the moment *she took it* — concealed it hastily — he instantly left her
— and (so, at least, Byron declared) the daring *ruse* succeeded ! She " deliberated " for an instant whether or not
she should denounce to her husband the insulting outrage ;
and in that instant she was lost !

Such was Byron's account of one of the many love-pas-
sages of his strange life. Let those believe it who can.

From this night it was that my *intimacy* with Hazlitt commenced. Henceforward, with the exception of two or three
brief intervals, when either Hazlitt or I was abroad, we met
almost daily ; and although our intercourse was wholly free
from conventional restraint, neither of us ever disguising or

concealing an opinion or a sentiment in deference to those of the other, our intimacy was never broken, or even jarred or disturbed, from the above-named period to that of his death — an interval of more than twelve years ! This fact may well bear a note of admiration for those who knew the nature of Hazlitt's mind and temperament, and the doubts, suspicions, and misgivings to which they perpetually made him a prey, and the total incapacity that he labored under, of abstaining from *acting upon* those doubts and suspicions as if they were demonstrated truths.

On the other hand, it is proper for me to caution the reader against supposing that, at any period of our intercourse, anything like a *friendship* subsisted between Hazlitt and myself, in the "sentimental" sense of the phrase. It was a melancholy defect of his mind, that it was wholly incapable of either exciting or entertaining any such sentiment. I have (with deep reluctance) glanced at one of the *natural* reasons of this sad deficiency. Others of an adventitious character, but more than sufficient to account for it, will develop themselves hereafter. In the mean time, it is no less true than it may seem paradoxical, that, with the most *social* disposition of any man I ever met with, and an active and ever present sympathy with the claims, the wants, and the feelings of every human being he approached, Hazlitt was, even by nature, but by circumstance still more so, *a lone man*, living, moving, and having his being, for and to himself exclusively; as utterly cut off from fulfilling and exercising the ordinary pursuits and affections of his kind, and of his nature, as if he had been bound hand and foot in a dungeon, or banished to a desert. And so, indeed, he was — bound in the gloomiest of all dungeons — that built for us by our own unbridled passions — banished to that dreariest of all deserts, spread out for us by seared hopes and blighted affections.

We are told that on the summit of one of those columns which form the magnificent ruins of Hadrian's Temple, in the plain of Athens, there used to dwell a hermit, who never descended from his strangely-chosen abode ; owing his scanty food and support to the mingled admiration and curiosity of the peasants who inhabited the plain below. Something like this was the position of William Hazlitt, from the period at which I first became acquainted with him. Self-banished from the social world, no less by the violence of his own passions, than by those petty regards of custom and society which could not or would not tolerate the trifling aberrations from external form and usage engendered by a mind like this; at the same time, those early hopes, born of the French Revolution, which first awakened his soul from its ante-natal sleep, blighted in their very fruition, and the stream that fed them flung back upon its source, to stagnate there, and turn into a poisonous hatred of the supposed causes of their disappointment ; his spirit refused to look abroad or be comforted. Such being the melancholy condition of his intellectual being at the period I am speaking of, he became, as regarded himself personally, heedless of all things but the immediate gratification of his momentary wants or wishes ; careless of personal character, indifferent to literary fame, forgetful of the past, reckless of the future ; and yet so exquisitely alive to the claims and the virtues of all these, that the abandonment of his birthright in every one of them opened a separate canker in his heart, and made his life a living emblem of that early death which it foretokened.

Thus (like the hermit alluded to above) perpetually sur-rounded by objects of interest, beauty, and grandeur, and en-abled by the elevated position which his noble intellect gave him, to look abroad over them all with the ken of an almost superhuman intelligence, he yet dwelt amidst them all "a man forbid ; " self-exiled from that social intercourse which he was born to brighten and to love ; rejected and reviled by his own heart and affections ; dreaded, and therefore hated, by his foes ; feared, and therefore not loved, even by his (so-called) "friends : " with such a man, so constituted and so circum-stanced, there could exist no reciprocity of personal sentiment, no fair interchange of affection, and, therefore, no true friend-ship. So that (recurring to the immediate occasion of the foregoing remarks) I repeat, these Recollections must not be received as the blind tribute of an overweening affection, seeking to defend from obloquy a sort of other self; but, as a free-will offering, urged by a sense of justice towards a man whose errors and weakness have been "monstered" into the attributes of a demon; while his many rare and excellent qualities — his noble simplicity of heart and mind — his irrepressible love of truth and justice — and his almost sublime hatred of that oppression and wrong which a systematic violation of those had so long spread abroad over human hopes and institutions throughout the world: all these were overlooked or disregarded, or, when not so, were held up to the world as their direct opposites — as themes for obloquy, rather than claims to admiration.

PERSONAL BEARING AND ITS CAUSES.

Hazlitt is considered by some of his friends to have had many points of intellectual character and temperament in common with Rousseau. But I do not know how they would set about to make out the resemblance, except in one isolated feature — that of the morbid feeling which possessed Hazlitt as to the sinister effects of his personal appearance and manner, on ordinary observers. Rousseau fancied that his friends were always hatching plots and conspiracies against him; in like manner, Hazlitt fancied that everybody (*except* his friends) who looked upon him, perceived something about him that was strange and *outré*.

There was about as much and as little foundation for the feeling in the one case as the other: it was in fact the result of a consciousness in both that there *was* something within, which each would have desired to conceal. But there was this vital difference between the two, that in the case of Rousseau the weaknesses and errors of which he feared the discovery and promulgation, were such as all men consent to be ashamed of: whereas, in the case of Hazlitt, his extreme sensitiveness pointed at failings that could hurt nobody but himself. Moreover, what *he* chiefly feared from the eyes of the world was, that they should see in him, not himself, but that effigy of him which the inventions of his political and personal enemies had set up; he feared that vulgar eyes would discover in him, not the man he was, but the "pimpled Hazlitt" that his Tory critics had placarded him on every bare wall that knew no better throughout the empire.

There are few things that exercise a more marked and unequivocal influence over the lives and characters of men of great susceptibility of temperament, than any *personal* peculiarity, especially when it is one obvious to all the world : witness the case of Byron, to whose lameness might probably be traced every one of the leading events and features of his strange and melancholy career.. And the same might perhaps be said of Hazlitt, with this aggravating qualification — that in his case the peculiarity was wholly imaginary, except in so far as the imagination, while acting upon his mind, made that into a fact which had else been only a figment of his own brain. If Hazlitt had not in his moody moments fancied himself a mark for vulgar and ignorant wonder " to point the slow unmoving finger at," he might have been living among us now, one of the most delightful ornaments of social life, and the noblest examples of the advancing spirit of his day and country — the pride and pleasure of his friends, and himself the happy witness of the coming on of that glorious dawn of better things which his own writings have materially helped to bring about.

The result of this morbid imagination — this one idea which haunted him like a visible phantom — this falsehood, which knowing it to be such, he nevertheless palmed off upon himself as a palpable truth, till at last he believed it — the result of this was, that, with the most social disposition in the world, and with social qualities of unsurpassed amount and value, Hazlitt, during the latter years of his life, lived almost alone in the world, simply because he could not persuade himself to seek that social intercourse which he had lost the power of purchasing at the ordinary price, of complying with all the minutiæ in the received usages of modern life and manners. He felt, in this respect, like a man who is travelling in a strange or savage country, with his pockets full of gold, for which nobody will give him bread in exchange, because his coin has not the conventional stamp of the place, or because the people he has to deal with set no value on anything but those smooth shells and glittering beads with which he has neglected to provide himself.

There can be little doubt that Hazlitt's manner, superinduced upon him by his own morbid mistake as to his personal appearance, had more to do with his peculiar and painful destiny, as regards the private relations of life, than any one but himself would perhaps have been willing to admit. And therefore it is that it becomes a point worthy of especial notice in these Recollections. Indeed, there probably never occurred a more striking example of the vast influence of external trifles over the moral and intellectual condition of man ; nor can I conceive a finer theme for the pen of Hazlitt himself to have descanted upon and illustrated ; for he was even more intensely aware of the facts of the case, and of their causes and consequences, than if any one else had been the subject of them. And this knowledge was a perpetual aggravation of the evil, without, on the other hand, contributing in the smallest degree to its cure. It was one of those fatal cases in which the sufferer "weeps the more because he weeps in vain."

Nothing could be more curious, and at times affecting, than to observe (as those who thoroughly knew Hazlitt might often do) the working of these feelings, in his occasional intercourse with society. It might be supposed, perhaps, that the external deference and respect, not to mention the personal homage and admiration, of a man like Hazlitt, were reserved for the distinguished philosophers, men of science, poets, scholars, and statesmen of the day. Alas ! the Chancellor Oxensteirn himself had not a more contemptuous notion of the means and materials it takes to make "a great man," in the estimation of the world (whether of fact or of opinion) which great men are destined to govern. Accordingly, in the presence of these, even the most deservedly celebrated among them, Hazlitt felt himself perfectly at ease and on an equality. But bring him face to face with one of those sleek favorites of fortune who are supposed to find especial favor in fair eyes, or (above all) one of those happily constituted persons who combine the several attributes and peculiarities of manner, look, attire, etc., which go to form the "gentleman" of modern times, and he was like a man awe-struck, and confounded with a sense of his own comparative insignificance.

I remember once gaining his leave to introduce to him a person whose only error in these respects was, that he carried them all to the verge of coxcombry ; but who, *en revanche*, had the most earnest and sincere admiration for Hazlitt, and was, in all other respects, a cultivated and accomplished man. My friend had long solicited me to bring about this meeting ; and though, in the early part of my acquaintance with Hazlitt, I had avoided it, as a service of danger to all parties, I soon found that it might be effected, not only without any peril to my friend, but with real gratification to Hazlitt himself, who had the most unmingled admiration for the qualities in question, unimpaired by the slightest touch of envy towards the owner of them.

The meeting took place at Hazlitt's chambers ; and after a little of the same sort of blank embarrassment and school-boy shyness that one may fancy a country recluse might have exhibited on being called upon to sustain a personal interview with George the Fourth, I never knew Hazlitt spend a happier evening, or one more entirely free from those occasional fallings back into his other and less natural self, which were at once the sin and the curse of his social life. With the exception of this one occasion, I do not know that I have ever passed an evening with him, the intellectual enjoyment of which was not at intervals broken in upon by *looks* passing over his noble countenance, which, where they did not move the observer to terror or wonder, could not fail to excite the deepest pain and pity. But on the evening I am referring to, I particularly remarked that nothing of this kind occurred. .

The reason of this, on after reflection, became obvious to

me. Our talk was, almost without exception, on the ordinary
topics of the passing hour — the public and social events of
the day, the theatres, the actors and actresses, our mutual
friends (not forgetting their weaknesses), a little" scandal about
Queen Elizabeth " — in short, anything and everything but
books, book-making, book-learning, and those exclusively *literary* themes which Hazlitt liked less than any others that
could be started. The consequence was, that old associations
and painful recollections never once came back to him ; broken
friendships and buried affections found no unoccupied place
in his mind on which to cast their shadows ; present annoy-
ances were crowded out of doors ; future contingencies were
as if they could never happen ; and the too often moody,
gloomy, constrained, and taciturn recluse, was (to the no small
astonishment of my other friend) free and fresh-hearted as a
school-boy among his mates — gay and voluble as a bird in
spring — making the room echo with those shouts of laughter,
in the thorough heartiness of which no one surpassed him.

The strange and unhappy mistake of Hazlitt, respecting the
effect of his manner and bearing on casual observers, was
peculiarly active in regard to women ; nor could any evidences,
however strong and unequivocal (and the reader will see hereafter that such were far from wanting), remove or weaken this
feeling, which amounted to nothing short of monomania. In
proof of this I could, if the nature of the case permitted, al-
lege numerous instances in which the most indisputable marks
of female favor and distinction (whether accorded to his intellectual pretension or not, no matter), were looked upon and
resented by him as *personal affronts!* In his numerous "affairs of the heart " (for, like his favorite, John Buncle, he was
always in love with somebody or other), to the fair one's indifference he was indifferent, and continued to love on : if she
recognized his homage and was angry at it, he accepted the
token as a kind of involuntary compliment ; but if she smiled
on him, he was confounded and cured ! It was clear that
she meant, first to entangle, and then to laugh at and insult
him !

I may have some singular matter to unfold in connection with this part of my subject hereafter. In the mean time, the curious reader is growing anxious for the removal of the veil which hides this supposed Mokanna from view. What will he or she say, when, in dropping it, I exhibit a form of excellent symmetry, surmounted by one of the noblest heads and faces that ever symbolled forth a refined, lofty, capacious, and penetrating intellect.

The truth is, that for depth, force, and variety of intellectual expression, a finer head and face than Hazlitt's were never seen. I speak of them when his countenance was not dimmed and obscured by illness, or clouded and deformed by those fearful indications of internal passion which he never even attempted to conceal. The expression of Hazlitt's face, when anything was said in his presence that seriously offended him, or when any peculiarly painful recollection passed across his mind, was truly awful — more so than can be conceived as within the capacity of the human countenance ; except, perhaps, by those who have witnessed Edmund Kean's last scene of " Sir Giles Overreach " from the front of the pit. But when he was in good health, and in a tolerable humor with himself and the world, his face was more truly and entirely answerable to the intellect that spoke through it, than any other I ever saw, either in life or on canvas ; and its crowning portion, the brow and forehead, was, to my thinking, quite unequaled, for mingled capacity and beauty.

For those who desire a more particular description, I will add, that Hazlitt's features though not cast in any received classical mould, were regular in their formation, perfectly consonant with each other, and so finely "chiseled" (as the phrase is), that they produced a much more prominent and striking effect than their scale of size might have led one to expect. The forehead, as I have hinted, was magnificent ; the nose precisely that (combining strength with lightness and elegance) which physiognomists have assigned as evidence of a fine and highly cultivated taste ; though there was a peculiar character about the nostrils, like that observable in those of

a fiery and unruly horse.   The mouth, from its ever-changing
form and character, could scarcely be described, except as to
its astonishingly varied power of expresssion, which was equal
to, and greatly resembled, that of Edmund Kean.   His eyes,
I should say, were not good.   They were never brilliant, and
there was a furtive and at times a sinister look about them, as
they glanced suspiciously from under their overhanging brows,
that conveyed a very unpleasant impression to those who did
not know him.   And they were seldom directed frankly and
fairly towards you ; as if he were afraid that you might read
in them what was passing in his mind concerning you.   His
head was nobly formed and placed ; with (until the last few
years of his life) a profusion of coal-black hair, richly curled ;
and his person was of the middle height, rather slight, but well
formed and put together.

Yet all these advantages were worse than thrown away, by
the strange and ungainly manner that at times accompanied
them.   Hazlitt entered a room as if he had been brought back
to it in custody ; he shuffled sidelong to the nearest chair, sat
himself down upon one corner of it, dropped his hat and his
eyes upon the floor, and, after having exhausted his stock of
conventional small talk in the words, "It's a fine day"
(whether it was so or not), seemed to resign himself moodily
to his fate.   And if the talk did not take a turn that roused or
pleased him, thus he would sit, silent and half-absorbed, for
half an hour or half a minute, as the case might be, and then
get up suddenly, with a "Well, good morning," shuffle back to
the door, and blunder his way out, audibly muttering curses on
his folly, for willingly putting himself in the way of becoming
the laughing-stock of — the servants ! for it was of *that* class
and intellectual grade of persons that Hazlitt alone stood in
awe.   Of the few private houses to which his inclinations ever
led him, he perfectly well knew that, even if there had been
(which, as we have seen, there was not) anything unusual or
outré in his appearance, his intellectual pretensions would
alone have been thought of.   But there was no reaching the
drawing-room without running the gauntlet of the servants'

hall ; and this it was that crushed and confounded him. I am satisfied that Hazlitt never entered a room — scarcely even his own — that he was not writhing under the feelings engendered during his passage to it ; and that he never knocked at a door without fearing that it might be opened by a new servant, who would wonder what so " strange " a person could want with their master or mistress.

To those who are not accustomed to the mental vagaries of men of genius, this must seem like a species of insanity. But there would, I think, be no difficulty in accounting for it on perfectly rational principles ; at least, I am sure *he* would have found no difficulty in doing so, even in his own case, much less in that of another person. I shall not myself attempt this explanation ; but I will venture to hint at the grounds of it, because they belong to the subject of which I have undertaken to treat. Those grounds are to be sought, as I conceive, first, in that radical defect in Hazlitt's moral conformation, at which I have reluctantly glanced in the outset of these Recollections. Secondly, in that intensely vivid state of excitability in which his intellectual faculties, and especially his imagination, at all times existed, and that consequent intense perception of all things within and about him, which showed him, as with a microscopic eye, a thousand trifles that were invisible to ordinary observation. Thirdly, that oppressive and overweening self-consciousness which, as it were, projected the shadows and lights of his own mind upon all things on which he looked, and caused external objects to reflect back to him his own thoughts and sensations, as if they were bodily images ; thus creating an intellectual world which blended itself with the physical one, and prevented him from being wholly present in or occupied with either. Lastly, that despairing abandonment of all attempt at self-control, which (being fully and intensely conscious of it) made him stand in perpetual dread of himself, — uncertain that, from moment to moment, he might not be tempted to commit some incredible outrage against those rules and usages of civilized life, which, nevertheless, he was the last person in the world to hold in contempt.

The reader will, I hope, not suppose that I offer the above as anything more than the *materials* for an explanation of one of the most curious and interesting phenomena that ever arose out of the condition and operations of the human mind. The explanation itself might (as I have hinted) have formed an admirable theme for Hazlitt's own pen; but I scarcely think there is another left among us capable of handling it to any satisfactory result. For myself, I will not venture to pursue it further. But I will say, that, however the weakness in question used to pain and even shock me, I never felt the least surprise at it. On the contrary, it always struck me as a natural and intelligible commentary on the peculiar ,mental condition from which it sprang — a sort of physiognomical expression, as easy to be interpreted as those of the face itself : the only singularity of the case being, that whereas most other men are able to conceal all external evidences of what is passing or has passed in their minds except those which are written on their faces, Hazlitt was "all face."

HAZLITT'S HABITS.

Hazlitt's way of life was as little adapted to the ordinary course of things in a " regular " family, as can well be conceived. He always lived (during the period of my intimacy with him) in furnished lodgings, and those of a very secondary class ; the latter not from any lack of means, for he had only to take his pen in hand to, as it were, coin money ; still less was it from any parsimonious feeling, for he was profuse in his expenditure, so far as related to the personal comforts of himself and those dependent on him. But, on adopting this mode of life, he fancied that his peculiar habits would have subjected him to perpetual inconveniences and affronts, except from those to whom the moderate stipend he paid was a material object. But he was far from escaping them by this expedient, of descending in the scale of social order ; for the lower you descend in that scale, the less toleration there is for anything that does not precisely conform to the preconceived notions of the observer. In fact, this was one of the great mistakes that he made in "the act and practique part of life;" and it was the source of much bitterness and misery to him ; for, strange as it may seem in such a man, it was not from the flow and current of his own thoughts, feelings, and reflections, that his daily life took its tone and color, but from the petty events and outward accidents of the hour. And above all, it was on the personal civility and respect of those about him, that his very existence seemed to hang. Now, by keeping himself among a class of persons, to a certain degree removed from the mere vulgar, his name and pursuits would have secured him from personal disrespect, if they did not procure him the opposite ; whereas, in descending two or three steps lower in the scale, the effect of his intellectual pretensions was not merely nullified, but turned against him. In the former case, the gazers at the celebrated author did but "wonder with a foolish face of praise ; " but in the latter, they shrunk from him, as if he was a wizard, or stared at him as at a wild beast. And we are sadly too apt to become what people believe us, rather than what we seek and desire to be.

Hazlitt usually rose at from one to two o'clock in the day — scarcely ever before twelve ; and if he had no work in hand, he would sit over his breakfast (of excessively strong black tea, and a toasted French roll) till four or five in the afternoon — silent, motionless, and self-absorbed, as a Turk over his opium pouch ; for tea served him precisely in this capacity. It was the only stimulant he ever took, and at the same time the only luxury ; the delicate state of his digestive organs prevented him from tasting any fermented liquors, or touching any food but beef and mutton, or poultry and game, dressed with perfect plainness. He never touched any but *black* tea, and was very particular about the quality of that, always using the most expensive that could be got : and he used, when living alone, to consume nearly a pound in a week. A cup of Hazlitt's tea (if you happened to come in for the first brewage of it) was a peculiar thing ; I have never tasted anything like it. He always made it himself ; half filling the teapot with tea, pouring the boiling water on it, and then

6

almost immediately pouring it out ; using with it a great quantity of sugar and cream.

To judge from its occasional effect upon myself, I should
say that the quantity Hazlitt drank of this tea produced, ultimately, a most injurious effect upon him ; and in all probability hastened his death — which took place from disease of the
digestive organs. But its *immediate* effect was agreeable,
even to a degree of fascination ; and not feeling any subsequent reaction from it, he persevered in its use to the last,
notwithstanding two or three attacks, similar to that which
terminated his life.

To the very few who felt a real and deep interest in this extraordinary man, and to whom it was evident that his restless
and resistless passions, and his entire, and even willful, sub-
 · jection to them — added to other points, to be hereafter referred to, in his moral and physical constitution — made him
one of the most ˏwretched of human beings, it was no less
curious than pleasing to see him luxuriating over his beloved
tea, in a state of deep and still repose, that nothing could
disturb — not even the intrusion of a mere acquaintance or a
dun — events that, at other times, were but too apt to move
him from his propriety.

For the last four or five years of his life, Hazlitt never
touched any other liquid but tea. During the previous four or
five years, he used to drink large quantities of cold water.
I have frequently seen him take three or four quarts while
sitting after supper — which was his favorite meal. Wine,
and all fermented liquors, he had forsworn before I knew him ;
and he religiously kept to his resolution. *This*, he used to
say, was the reason why Blackwood's people called him
"*pimpled* Hazlitt " — thus holding him up to the world as a
dram-drinker ! [1]   Had they told nothing but the truth of him,

[1] Lord Byron took this imputation for granted, and discovered that the epithet
" pimpled " might also be applied to his writings! And so it might with about
equal fitness: for, as his face was as clear and pale as marble, so was his style the
most simple and transparent of the day. Sir Bulwer Lytton, in his admirable work
on " England and the English," has inadvertently adopted the invention as if it
were an unquestioned fact, merely disputing the utility of alleging it. " What pur-

they would not have made him out to the world as anything worse than he really was ; and he did not desire to pass for anything better. Whereas, by ascribing to him precisely *that* vice which was the farthest removed from his actual habits, they gained a great point against him. "Had I really been a gin-drinker and a sot," I have heard him say, "they would have sworn I was a milk-sop."

His breakfast and tea were frequently the only meals that Hazlitt took till late at night, when he usually ate a hearty supper of hot meat — either rump-steak, poultry, or game — a partridge or a pheasant. This he invariably took at a tavern — his other meals (except his dinner sometimes) being as invariably taken at home.

There were three or four houses only that he frequented ; for he never entered the doors of any one where his ways were not well known, or where there was any chance of his *bill* being asked for till he chose to offer payment of it. And when treated in a way that pleased him in this latter particular, he did not care what he paid. I have known him pay with cheerfulness accumulated sums of twenty or thirty pounds for suppers only or chiefly.

The houses Hazlitt frequented were the Southampton Coffee House, in Southampton Buildings, Chancery Lane ; Munday's, in Maiden Lane, Covent Garden, and (for a short period) the Spring Garden Coffee House. The first of these he has immortalized, in one of the most amusing of his Essays, "On Coffee-house Politicians." Here, for several years, he used to hold a sort of evening levee, where, after a certain hour at night (and till a very *un*certain hour in the morning) he was always to be found, and always more or less ready to take part in that sort of desultory "talk" (the only thing really deserving the name of "conversation") in which he excelled every man I have ever met with. But of this hereafter. Here,

pose," he asks, "salutary to literature, is served by hearing that Hazlitt had pimples on his face?" But he had no such thing! "Throw dirt enough, and some of it will stick." That was the axiom on which Hazlitt's enemies proceeded ; and there is no denying that, in his case, it succeeded to a miracle. Times are changed since, and the "dirt," when flung, sticks only to the fingers of the flinger.

however, in that little bare and comfortless coffee-room, have
I scores of times see the daylight peep through the crevices
of the window-shutters upon "Table Talk" that was worthy
an intellectual feast of the gods.

When Hazlitt dined at all — which was often not more than
two or three times a week — this meal seemed only a sort of
preliminary to his everlasting Tea, for which he returned
home as soon as he had dined, and usually sat over it for a
couple of hours. Afterwards he almost invariably passed two
or three hours at one or other of the large theatres, placing
himself as invariably in a back corner seat of the second tier
of boxes, and, if possible, shrouding himself from view, as if
he felt himself "a weed that had no business there," in such
a scene of light, gayety, and artificial seeming.

To the play itself, on these occasions, he paid scarcely any
attention, even when he went there in his critical capacity as
a writer for the public journals; for, notwithstanding the
masterly truth and force of most of his decisions on plays and
actors, I will venture to say, that in almost every case, except
those of his two favorites, Kean and Liston, they might be
described as the result of a few hasty glances and a few half-
heard phrases. From these he drew instant deductions that
it took others hours of observation to reach, and as many more
of labor to work out. In this respect his faculty was, I imagine, never before equaled or even approached; and his consciousness of, and confidence in it, led him into a few ridiculous blunders. Still, upon the whole, he was doubtless right
in trusting to these brief oracles and broken revelations,
rather than pursuing them to their ultimate sources — as
most others must do if they would hope to expound them
truly and intelligibly: for his was a mind that would either
take its own course or none; it was not to be "constrained
by mastery" of rule or discipline. It was a knowledge of
this truth, and his habit of acting on it, which constituted the
secret of his success as a writer.

HAZLITT AS A POLITICIAN.

Though no one could possess a more social turn of mind than Hazlitt did under ordinary circumstances, I never met with any other man who so little needed society. If ever there was a mind " sufficient to itself," it was that of Hazlitt ; and I believe that, bodily health and the appliances and means of personal comfort being supposed, he could have passed his life alone on a desert island, with perfect satisfaction, and even with high and constant intellectual enjoyment ; for with him thought and contemplation were ends in themselves, not merely means· to some end disjoined from them ; or, at all events, they were means to the attainment of that TRUTH which was, in itself, the great and all-sufficing end of his intellectual being.

What is understood by "society" in its ordinary sense, Hazlitt shunned altogether ; and, above all, that " literary " society in which his admirable powers of conversation qualified him to shine so conspicuously. He had enough of books and criticism and philosophy in the way of his profession ; it was the *business* of his life to " coin his brain for drachmas ; " the *pleasures* of it he wisely sought from other sources, and chiefly from calling back the feelings and recollections of the Past ; for it is, I think, remarkable that, though Hazlitt's views and sentiments respecting mankind were " as broad and general as the casing air," he never, or very rarely, employed his thoughts upon the Future.

The reason, I believe, was, that he could not do so without including *politics* in his speculations ; and this was an almost interdicted subject with him ; it was touching upon a string that " echoed to the seat where *hate* is throned." Politics offered the one point which acted on his temper like monomania. It was capable of changing him from a reasonable being into a wild beast. It stirred up the bitter and rancorous feelings that, to the very last, lay festering in his heart, and eating into its core like some " poisonous mineral " — deposited there by the events that had terminated the French Revolution ; and those feelings were still more firmly rooted by the subsequent downfall of his idol, Napoleon, and the restoration of the Bourbons. I have heard those who knew him in his early youth say, that it was the great events of the French Revolution, and the new era of thought and of things that they seemed to create throughout Europe, which first called forth Hazlitt's intellectual faculties from that dreamy torpor in which they might otherwise have lain for years longer, perhaps forever. His early metaphysical work, and many remarkable features of his after character, show us that those events found his heart filled with all tender and kindly affections towards his fellow-beings, and all high and happy hopes and aspirations as to their ultimate destiny. What those events, or rather their immediate sequents, *left* that heart, those only can know who had for years studied it as "a book where men might read strange matters." In brief, those events found his bosom the birth-place of universal Love ; they left it "the very heart and throne of tyrannous Hate."

I shall have more to say on this part of my subject hereafter. At present I glance at it accidentally, because it is the pivot on which moves the whole character of Hazlitt's actual life and destiny. Had his faculties and sensibilities opened and developed themselves at any other period, or under any other political aspect, than that of the first French Revolution, he might have been the very model of a wise and happy man. But as it was, his whole intellectual being — his temper, affections, passions, meditations, and pursuits — took a sinister turn from those events, which never afterwards left it, or at least which was never afterwards absent when its first exciting cause was recalled into action. On all matters but political ones Hazlitt's perceptions were almost superhumanly clear and acute, and his judgment was infallible. But about the political prospects, tendencies, and events of the day, he was like a child or a woman — either utterly indifferent to them, or, when not so, regarding them in a light directly opposed to the true one.

· I will give one or two remarkable instances of what I mean. The downfall of Napoleon, and the restoration of the Bourbons — which every man of ordinary political sagacity and foresight must have looked upon as the certain coming on of that natural supremacy of the MANY over the FEW, of which the first French Revolution did but furnish the rude foretaste and barbarous antitype — Hazlitt regarded as the final consummation of the triumph of "Legitimacy" and "Divine Right," and the utter extinction of human liberty from the earth. The writings and principles of Bentham and his friends and followers, which have already gone far towards creating a new era in human society, he looked upon and treated with utter and unmingled contempt. And as to the aristocracy of England, or of any other country, coming to feel and admit even the political expediency, much less the natural justice, of reform and social regeneration — he would as soon have looked for the Millennium.

The truth is, that many — perhaps it may be said most — of the commanding and first-rate intellects that have been among us, have not been so much in actual advance of their age as others of an inferior grade and a different temperament. It has seemed to be sufficient for them to *produce* the momentum, of which others could better feel, direct, and see the results. It was so with Bacon. We have no evidence that he anticipated the vast consequences to which his principles of philosophizing have led, and the still more vast ones to which they are now leading. Like Hazlitt in regard to morals, he was no "perfectibility" man, in respect of science and knowledge : and to anticipate *that* in the possible existence of which we have no faith, is a moral contradiction. Though Hazlitt would readily have admitted that the world has never been in the same moral or intellectual condition for any two centuries together, and that every nation has, from time to time, differed as much from itself as it has at all times differed from all others, yet he laughed at those who predicated for the future anything very different from that which has existed in the past. He sighed and wept over what he considered as the wreck of human liberty, its hopes, tendencies, and consequences, as he might be supposed to have done over a mortal bride and her offspring; seeming to forget that principles are imperishable, that truth and justice are unchangeable and immortal ; and, what is still more to the purpose, that the human mind has a natural and necessary sympathy with these, and a craving after them, which have the strength and the permanence of instincts, and therefore cannot be wholly eradicated or suppressed.

But Hazlitt's want of hope in the future condition of his fellow-beings was more a personal than an intellectual failing ; a thing arising more from his own individual circumstances and feelings than from the convictions or calculations of his understanding. He was a disappointed man ; and despondency was a disease, not a natural quality, of his mind. He had nothing in after life to look forward to for himself, and he had nothing to satisfy him in the present. The past was his only refuge ; and even there he found little that was personally gratifying to him — much that was deeply painful and disappointing, no less to his hopes than to his actual experience. And a man so placed is not likely to see too much good in prospect for his fellow-creatures ; for even the least desponding among us are but too apt to " lay the flattering unction to our souls " (for such it is) that misery is the destined lot of human nature. That we do so is at once the curse and the crime of that nature ; because (like jealousy) it makes the misery on which it feeds. Hope is more than a blessing — it is a duty and a virtue ; and in its absence we not only cannot accomplish the destiny that awaits us — we do not merit that destiny, and therefore shrink from admitting its existence, or even its possibility.

HAZLITT'S FRIENDS AND ACQUAINTANCE.

I can call to mind only one person for whom Hazlitt seemed habitually to entertain a sentiment of personal kindness and esteem, and one only (among his contemporaries) for whose intellectual powers he felt and uniformly expressed a general deference and respect. The first of these was Charles Lamb, the second was Coleridge.

Hazlitt went about (Diogenes-like) looking, by the light of

his acute and searching intellect, for a man made by Nature
in her happiest and simplest mould, and not afterwards marred
and curtailed of his fair proportions, on the Procrustes bed of
custom and society. He believed that there might be such a
man, because he felt that he himself retained much of the
character, though blended with more that deformed and de-
faced it. He sought such a man through the world — he
sought him in books — he sought him in the ideal places of
his own imagination ; but he found him in Charles Lamb
alone. He found there all his own exquisite sensibilities — all
his own simplicity and sincerity of heart — his uncompromising directness and singleness of spirit — his large and liberal
sympathies with his kind — together with all his own profound
sagacity of intellect and boundless range of thought. He also
found there *that* in the absence of which he would scarcely
have persuaded himself to believe that the other qualities
which he sought could exist : I mean, many of his own intellectual weaknesses and deficiencies ; much of that restless and
impatient yearning after good, which is the necessary consequence of perceiving without the power of compassing it ; not
a little of that willful mistaking of good for evil, and of evil
for good, which is the universal concomitant of such a condition of mind ; and not a few of those *crotchets* of the brain
and heart that were never yet absent from *such* a brain and
heart, when placed in the social circumstances which had
accompanied Lamb and Hazlitt through life. Hazlitt found
all these in Charles Lamb ; and he found them almost wholly
uncontaminated by that " baser matter " with which he felt
them to be so inextricably blended in his own nature, and
from which he had never found them dissevered in any
other.

Moreover, from Lamb, and from Lamb alone, among all his
friends and associates, Hazlitt had never received, or even
suspected, except on one occasion, any of those personal
slights and marks of disrespect which he did not feel or fear
the less because he was conscious of often deserving them —
using the phrase in its ordinary and social acceptation. From

Lamb alone, his errors, extravagances, and inconsistencies, met with that wise and just consideration which his fine sense of the weakness no less than the strength of our human nature dictated. There was no one who spoke more *freely* of Hazlitt, whether behind his back or before his face, than Lamb did ; but Lamb never spoke *disparagingly* of him. Lamb, in canvassing the faults of his character, never failed to bear in mind, and call to mind in others, the rare and admirable qualities by which they were accompanied, and with which, it may be, they were naturally and therefore inextricably linked.

No wonder, then, that Hazlitt felt towards Lamb a sentiment of personal kindness and esteem that was not extended, even in kind, to any other individual.[1]

There was but one house to which Hazlitt seemed to go, or to contemplate going (which with him answered almost the same purpose) with unalloyed pleasure ; and that was Charles Lamb's. Almost the only other houses to which he ever thought of going, after my acquaintance with him, were the late Mr. Basil Montagu's, in Bedford Square, the late Mr. Hume's, at Notting Hill, Mr. Northcote's, Mr. Leigh Hunt's, and my own. To the first of these he continued to go, partly on account of early associations, and in compliance with feelings which had been created by many acts of kindness. But he seemed to go in fear and trembling, and never without an even chance of coming away raging or sulking like a madman or a wild beast. There was a new footman, perhaps, who, not knowing him, would leave him "kicking his heels" in the hall, while he went to ascertain whether so."strange" looking a person could be admissible to the drawing-room ! And when anything of this sort happened, Hazlitt was upset for the

---

[1] I have sometimes felt that I might fairly extend this exception to myself. But I have as often been prevented from doing so by the consideration, that, in order to the existence of the sentiment in question, it was necessary, in this particular instance, that the party feeling it should entertain an admiration for the intellectual powers and pretensions of the object of it, little, if at all short of that which was due to his own. And in my case there was too little ground for this to induce me fairly to persuade myself that he felt more esteem for me than he did for the rest of his friends.

evening ; he was dumfounded, and would sit sulking and
scowling silently for a quarter of an hour or so, and then get
up and go away, to vent his rage in the open air ;' or if he
stayed, it was perhaps from sheer dread of having to repass
the ordeal of the ceremonious bell-ringing and the supercilious
lackey that preceded his exit.

In fact, Hazlitt never felt himself at ease for a moment,
where the outward observances proper to a certain class of
life were strictly maintained by those about him — much less
when they were expected from himself. Not that he overlooked or desired to depreciate their value and convenience ;
on the contrary, they were, perhaps, never more justly, and
therefore highly estimated by any one. But it did not follow
that he could himself conform to them ; and the impossibility
of his doing so was the very cause of the anger and uneasiness
he felt whenever he found himself in the way of failing in it.
The origin of this incapacity, and of its sad results as regarded
his personal comfort, would form a curious and interesting
subject of inquiry, in connection with Hazlitt's intellectual
character ; and, in fathoming it, the most recondite features
of that character would develop themselves. But I must not
venture to open the inquiry here. I must only observe that
none but the peculiar circumstances connected with his visits
to the house in question, could have induced Hazlitt to overcome the extreme repugnance he felt at placing himself within
the observation of *any* individuals, whether of the meanest or
the most exalted class, who were likely to look upon and treat
him according to his outward seeming. Nothing but the
pleasure he took in looking at the "coronet face " (as he has
called.it) of Mrs. M., and the Psyche-like form and features of
her daughter, and listening to the accomplished talk of the
one, and the quick wit and piquant satire of the other, could
have induced Hazlitt to undergo the ordeal of being formally
ushered into and out of a suite of spacious and well-appointed
drawing-rooms, by a liveried lackey who was all the while
(so at least Hazlitt persuaded himself)

" Wondering how the devil he got there."

There were other circumstances, too, which had, during the last three or four years of his life, prevented him from keeping up his former intercourse with the enlightened and accomplished family I have referred to above. He had, in his growing irritability, and the recklessness of consequences which attended it, and under the influence of those unworthy suspicions which always beset him when in that state of mind, committed some unpardonable outrages on one or more of the individual members of that family, in the form of offensive personal references to them in his writings ; at the same time adding to the outrage by everywhere pointing ít out to the attention of those who might otherwise have passed it over unnoticed ; for his misdeeds of this kind were of so vague, and often so utterly inapplicable a character, that nothing but his own voluntary confession of them could have fixed them upon him. And this self-accusation he never failed to furnish, and often (I am satisfied) from pure regret and remorse at the outrage and injustice he had committed. But the effect of it was ruinous to him nevertheless, and had latterly cut him off from almost all social intercourse, but that which was indispensable to the supply of his daily wants.

It is due to Hazlitt's memory, that I here mention his repeated expressions of a regret, almost amounting to a remorse, at one in particular of those insane outrages which he had, in a moment of ungovernable anger, been induced to commit, on the chief member of the family I have now referred to ; a man to whom he was indebted for many acts of substantial kindness and service, and (what Hazlitt was still more grateful for) that uniform evidence of personal esteem and consideration, which showed itself in outward civility and respect.

To Mr. Hume's, at Notting Hill, Hazlitt was now and then attracted by the cordial welcome he was sure to receive there, not merely from the "*one* fair daughter" of the worthy host, but from the half dozen, who were just sufficiently tinged with the literary hue to be aware of his pretensions. But an expedition of this kind was always a service of danger with

Hazlitt ; and he knew it to be so, and shrunk from it accordingly ; for such was his John Buncle-like susceptibility touching the merits and virtues of any unmarried lady between
the ages of fifteen and fifty, who might chance to smile upon
him, that even while despairing over the loss of one idol, he
was always prepared, at a moment's notice, to cast himself at
the feet of another.

To Mr. Northcote's, Hazlitt went frequently, and stayed
long ; at one time more frequently than to any other place.
But his visits to Northcote were in some sort professional :
and whatever he did with a view to business, or to any after
consideration whatsoever — anything which did not immediately
arise out of the impulse directing it — he did reluctantly and
with an ill grace. I have several times been present when
Hazlitt has been at Northcote's, and has taken part in those
admirable conversations with the venerable artist, in which
he (Hazlitt) professed that he used to take such delight. But
I never saw him for a moment at ease there, or anything like
himself — that self which he was when sitting in his favorite
corner at the Southampton, or by Lamb's or my fireside, or
(above all) his own. I do not mean to say, that in what he
has written on this subject, he has in the smallest degree exaggerated his impressions of the intellectual qualities of Northcote, or the charm of his conversation. But these were not the
things on which Hazlitt's personal ease and comfort depended
in his intercourse with others. There were points in Northcote's character for which Hazlitt felt the greatest dislike. But
what was of much more consequence to the mutual comfort of
their intercourse, he knew perfectly well that Northcote often
dreaded and therefore hated him ; and, when this feeling was
acting, only tolerated his presence, and talked to him the more
entertainingly, on that very account. I speak of the period
subsequent to Hazlitt's occasional publication, in the "New
Monthly Magazine," of portions of his Conversations with
Northcote, under the title of "Boswell Redivivus."

Hazlitt's mode of turning Northcote's conversation to a
business account, while the "Boswell Redivivus" was ap-

pearing in the " New Monthly Magazine," was sufficiently
curious and characteristic.   He used it more as a stimulus to
his own powers than in any other character, at least as related
to opinions and sentiments ; for, in reporting the curious facts
and personal anecdotes related to him by Northcote, he was
(as I have said elsewhere) correct, even to a literal setting
down of N.'s very words.   When the time was at hand for
preparing a number of the papers, he used to ask me, " Have
you seen Northcote lately ?   Is he in talking cue ? for I must
go in a day or two, and get an article out of him."   And, if
you happened to meet him anywhere on the evening of the
day on which he had paid one of these visits of business, he
was sure to be unusually entertaining.   He would relate every
word that had passed on any noticeable topic ; and almost any
topic, however dry or commonplace or exhausted, was sure to
furnish forth something novel and curious when he and Northcote got together.

     The simple truth on this matter is, that it was the astonish-
ing acuteness and sagacity of Hazlitt's remarks that called
into active being, if they did not actually create, much of
what was noticeable in Northcote's conversation.   Almost
everything that he said in the way of critical opinion, on any
topic that might be in question, was at least *suggested* by
something which Hazlitt would either drop in furtively as the
point arose, with a humble and deprecatory " But don't you
think, sir " — or it was supperadded to some inconsequent or
questionable observation of Northcote's with an assenting
" Yes, sir ; and perhaps " — adding the true statement of the
case, whatever it might be.   And with these intellectual
promptings, the truth and acuteness of which Northcote perceived and caught up immediately, he would go on talking " like
a book " (as Hazlitt used to describe it), for half an hour together ; and Hazlitt would sit listening in silent admiration, like
a loving pupil, to the precepts of his revered master — he the
pupil, being all the while capable of teaching or confounding
the master, on almost every point of inquiry that could by
possibility come into discussion between them.

The overstrained admiration which Hazlitt felt and expressed for the conversational powers of Northcote, has always seemed to me one of the most curious points in the
personal history of distinguished men ; and I could never satisfactorily account for it, until now that I have set myself to
recollect in detail the peculiar circumstances under which the
conversations between these two remarkable men took place.
But now I seem to see the explanation of it very clearly.
Northcote, by having preserved his intellectual faculties in all
their freshness up to the very great age at which Hazlitt first
became acquainted with him, and those faculties having always included an unusual justness of tact in observing the
ordinary circumstances to which the daily occurrences of life
directed them, had acquired a vast superiority over Hazlitt in
his actual personal knowledge of society, and its visible and
superficial results on individual men. He had also an inexhaustible fund of curious facts stored in his memory, in relation to a great number of persons about whom Hazlitt felt a
degree of interest and curiosity which he was wholly incapable
of entertaining towards *living* persons, however distinguished.
About Dr. Johnson, Sir Joshua, Burke, Goldsmith, and the
whole of that *coterie* of distinguished men of the last age,
Northcote had things to tell that would have furnished forth
half a dozen " Boswells Redivivus," in a much more apt sense
of the phrase than that in which Hazlitt used it ; and he told
them with a degree of tact, spirit, and dramatic effect that
has never been surpassed, if equaled, in any published detail
of these true gems of literary and personal history.

It was this which first attracted Hazlitt's attention towards
Northcote, and excited that interest in everything he said,
which Hazlitt never felt towards any other individual. He
looked upon Northcote as a connecting link — the only existing one that he knew of — between the last age and the present, and attached to him a portion of that (so to speak) tradi-
tional respect and deference which he could never persuade
himself to feel for any contemporary, however distinguished,
or withhold from any to whom posterity had agreed to award
them.

Another house to which Hazlitt sometimes went, but with a degree of reluctance for which it would be difficult to account, considering the partiality and personal interest which attracted him there, was that of Mr. Leigh Hunt. And these opposing influences (whatever they were) were so nearly balanced that I have often known him " of twenty minds," as the phrase is, whether he would go or not, for hours together, and not able to settle the question at last, until it was settled by the acquiescence or refusal of somebody else to go with him. Indeed this *vis inertiæ* was so strong in Hazlitt that, frequently, nothing but the actual and near prospect of absolute destitution could induce him to set about writing — except in the case of his having some subject in his head on which he desired to write, for the mere pleasure of expressing his sentiments and opinions on it : for in all other cases, the excitement derived from the mere distinction and profit of his writings was fully counterbalanced by the habitually contemplative turn of his mind, as opposed to its *active* qualities, and by his utter indifference to popular opinion or applause, except in so far as he felt these to be important to his immediate success as a writer by profession. No wonder, then, that the quality of mind I am alluding to should overcome the impulses of a mere passing inclination or a pleasant association.

There was no man of whose social qualities Hazlitt thought so highly as he did of Leigh Hunt's ; and no one with whom he had connected more pleasant associations, arising out of the earlier and happier part of his intellectual life. In fact, there was no man to whom Hazlitt felt himself more *attracted*, actively speaking, than towards Leigh Hunt — no one in whose society he enjoyed more of the double pleasure arising from receiving and communicating intellectual excitement. Yet the impulse to seek that pleasure where alone it was to be found, in the instance in question, was never strong enough to overcome the negative disposition to stay where he was, wherever that might be, added to the mere imagination of the repelling force that might possibly have met him in the quarter whence the attractive one was also acting.

The truth I believe to be, that Hazlitt literally never quitted the chair on which he placed himself when he rose in the morning, and, but for the absolute necessity of providing for the physical wants of his nature by his own exertions, never *would* have quitted it, in search of any social intercourse or excitement whatever, — unless moved to do so by some inducement in which *female* attraction had a chief share. When alone with his own thoughts — and I judge from having repeatedly and purposely suffered him to remain alone with them for hours together, when I have been sitting with him after some long and exciting batch of talk — when thus alone, I say, he would sometimes subside into an entire self-absorption, an utter abstraction from all but his own thoughts — or more probably into that vague, dreamy, and mysterious state of intellectual existence, half repose, half enjoyment, which follows high intellectual excitement of any kind in which the pleasurable has predominated — a calm, so pure and serene, that it seemed like a sin to call him from it to that actual reality which had, for him, so little to compensate for the change.

The only other house which Hazlitt visited, which I can speak of from actual observation, was my own ; and to that, if I am entitled to judge at all, and may be supposed to have the materials for judging in an uninterrupted intercourse of fourteen years, I should say that he came in less fear of having to regret that he had come (for he never went anywhere without *some* fear of this kind), stayed with more unmingled comfort and satisfaction, and went away in a better humor with himself and the world, than he did in any other case whatever. And the reasons for this were simple and obvious, and of such a nature that they may be stated without the risk of their being supposed to include any invidious comparisons as to the feelings and conduct of other people in their intercourse with this extraordinary man — who assuredly brought upon himself all the ills that he was compelled to endure in his intercourse with others, and perhaps (in the ordinary sense of the word) *deserved* them all. That I, and those belonging to me, did not think so — in other words, that we honored, admired, and loved

7

the nobler and finer parts of his character, and therefore could
not hate or despise the weaker ones with which they were inextricably mingled, affords the simple explanation of the fact
I have stated, if I may believe it to be one. We saw in William Hazlitt as noble a nature as any with which even books
had made us acquainted, and of which, in actual experience,
we saw few, if any other examples. And because the beautiful qualities of his mind and heart (which we scarcely saw
anywhere else) were allied with a few of those deteriorating
and debasing weaknesses which constitute the sum and substance of most *other* hearts and minds, we saw the owners of
these latter think, and speak of, and treat him, as if *he* were
of unmixed baseness, and *they* were immaculate ! Because,
when angered in his personal feelings, or outraged in his
sense of right and justice, he spoke, or wrote, or acted under
the natural impulse thus created, instead of cunningly waiting
till his actual feelings were cooled or passed away, and his
sense of personal wrong forgotten, and *then* speaking, or writing, or acting, so as to reconcile a rankling desire for petty revenge with a due consideration for worldly interest, as is the
wont of nine-tenths of the world — because of *this*, we heard
him spoken of, and saw him treated, as one not fit to form a
part of human society. Because, with a finer sense of the
graces and elegances of personal manner and appearance,
and a juster estimation of the virtue and value of these, than
almost any other man living, and a knowledge of their causes,
sources, and results, that would have put to shame the tact
and teaching of the most accomplished of May Fair Exclu-
sives, he was, in his own person, awkward, embarrassed, and
strange, to a degree that, if represented on the stage, would
have been deemed a clever caricature of those qualities — because of these deficiencies (which arose in a great measure
from his exquisite sense of their opposites, and the high but
just value which he placed on them in a social point of view),
we saw him treated as a low-bred, vulgar cockney, or a savage
and saturnine recluse. Because he was (with perhaps no exception whatever, among men of first-rate talent at the time I

speak of) the only man who dared to hold by and express in plain and uncompromising terms those political sentiments and opinions which, at the early part of the first French Revolution, he had adopted in common with almost all the intellectual men of the day, his friends, teachers, and seniors — the Wordsworths, Coleridges, Southeys, etc. ; because, holding by these opinions to the last, in spite of their ill success and the politic putting of them off by those who helped to instill them into him, he dared to express them in terms, if stronger, yet not more violent than those in which half the world expresses.them now that they can keep each other in countenance ; because of this, we saw him put out of the pale of critical and social courtesy, denounced as an outlaw, not entitled to the usages of civilized warfare, and only to be hunted down as a savage or a wild beast.

In pursuance of this latter plan, for instance, precisely *because* he was the most original thinker of his day, we heard him held up as a mere waiter upon the intellectual wealth of his literary acquaintance — a mere sucker of the brains of Charles Lamb and Coleridge. Precisely *because* his face was as pale and clear as marble, we saw him pointed at as the " pimpled Hazlitt." Precisely *because* he never tasted anything but water, we saw him held up as an habitual gin-drinker and a sot !

Not to multiply instances of this treatment of Hazlitt, we saw further, what is perhaps more to the point than all else,— that these things, instead of passing by him unregarded or unnoticed (as they would have done by many) were daily and hourly acting with the most deadly effect, not merely on his feelings and habits, but on his personal character, half making him the monster that they represented him.

We saw these things in regard to Hazlitt ; we saw and felt the miserable mischiefs they were working in his mind and temper ; the intellectual martyrdom he was suffering from them, but with anything but a martyr's patience ; and we sought, not to compensate him for the injustice he was receiving elsewhere, but merely to avoid adding to the weight of that injustice, by uniformly treating him in a manner to make it impossible for him to even suspect that our feelings in regard to him were, in the smallest degree, affected by the treatment he was constantly receiving in certain quarters.

Not indeed that he feared any such effect among the *male* literary friends with whom he associated ; nor would he have cared much, even had he seen cause for such fear among *them*. But he scarcely believed it possible that women could fail to be influenced by the purely personal attacks that were made on him. And the consequence was that for days, and even weeks after the appearance of any of these pretended criticisms on the writings that he was so frequently putting forth at the time I speak of, he scarcely dared to go near any one of even his most favorite resorts, lest he should see, or fancy that he saw, " Quarterly Review," or " Blackwood's Magazine," written on the very face on which he went to gaze in silent or in eloquent admiration.

Nay, he carried his dread of the supposed personal and private results of these attacks to a pitch that, while it lasted, amounted to a sort of monomania, — many of the effects of which would have been perfectly ludicrous, had they not been so painfully the opposite to the object of them. For instance, — during the first week or fortnight after the appearance of (let us suppose) one of " Blackwood's " articles about him, if he entered a coffee-house where he was known, to get his dinner, it was impossible (he thought) that the waiters could be doing anything else all the time he was there, but pointing him out to other guests, as " the gentleman who was so abused last month in ' Blackwood's Magazine.' " If he knocked at the door of a friend, the look and reply of the servant (whatever they might be) made it evident to him that he or she had been reading " Blackwood's Magazine " before the family were up in the morning ! If he had occasion to call at any of the publishers for whom he might be writing at the time, the case was still worse, — inasmuch as there his bread was at stake, as well as that personal civility, which he valued no less.   Mr. Colburn would be " not within," as a matter of

course ; for his clerks to even ascertain his pleasure on that
point beforehand would be wholly superfluous : had they not
all chuckled over the article at their tea the evening before ?
Even the instinct of the shop-boys would catch the cue from
the significant looks of those above them, and refuse to take
his name to Mr. Ollier. They would "believe he was gone
to dinner." He could not, they thought, want to have anything to say to a person who, as it were, went about with a
sheet of "Blackwood's" pinned to his coat-tail like a dish-
clout !

Then at home at his lodgings, if the servant who waited
upon him did not answer his bell the first time — ah ! 't was
clear — she had read "Blackwood's," or heard talk of it at
the bar of the public-house when she went for the beer ! Did
the landlady send up his bill a day earlier than usual, or ask
for payment of it less civilly than was her custom — how
could he wonder at it ? It was "Blackwood's" doing. But
if she gave him notice to quit (on the score, perhaps, of his
inordinately late hours) he was a lost man ! for would anybody take him in after having read "Blackwood's ? " Even
the strangers that he met in the street seemed to look at him
askance, "with jealous leer malign," as if they knew him
by intuition for a man on whom was set the double seal of
public and private infamy; the doomed and denounced of
"Blackwood's Magazine."

This may seem like exaggeration to the reader of 1854.
But I assure him that it falls as far short of the truth as it
may seem to go beyond it ; that not one of the cases to
which I have alluded above but has been in substance detailed to me by Hazlitt himself, as (according to *his* interpretation of it) a simple matter of fact result of the attacks
in question !

DISLIKE OF WRITING.

Hazlitt almost always wrote with the breakfast things on the
table ; for, as I have said before, they usually remained there
till he went out at four or five o'clock to dinner. He wrote

rapidly, in a large hand, as clear as print, made very few cor-
rections, and almost invariably wrote on an entire quire of
foolscap ; contriving to put into a page of his manuscript exactly the amount (upon an average) of an octavo page of print ;
so that he always knew exactly what progress he had made,
at any given time, towards the desired goal to which he was
travelling — namely, the end of his task.

Unless what he was employed on was a review, he never
had a book or paper of any kind about him while he wrote.
In this respect, I imagine he stood alone among professional
authors.

With respect to Hazlitt's actual method of composition, he
never, I believe, thought for half an hour beforehand, as to
what he should say on any given subject ; or even as to the
general manner in which he should treat it ; but merely,
whether it was a subject on which he *had* thought intently at
any previous period of his life, and whether it was susceptible
of a development that was consistent with the immediate object he might have in view, in sitting down to write on it.
Having determined on these points, and chiefly on the latter,
his pen was not merely the mechanical, but (so to speak) the
intellectual instrument by which he called up and worked out
his thoughts, opinions, and sentiments, and even the style and
language in which he clothed them ; it was the magician's
wand with which he compelled and marshaled to his service
the powers of his extraordinary mind, and the stores of illustrative materials which his early life had been spent in ac-
cumulating and laying by for use or pleasure. He never considered for more than a few moments beforehand the plan or
conduct of any composition that he had undertaken, or determined to write — whether it was a mere magazine paper, or a
considerable work ; he merely thought for a brief space more
or less, till he had hit upon an opening sentence that pleased
òr satisfied him ; and when that was achieved, he looked upon
the thing as done: for everything else seemed to follow as a
natural consequence. In short, his pen had become, during
the last ten or twelve years of his life, a sort of inspiration to

him ; and he was as sure of its answering to his claims upon it, whenever he chose to make them, as if he had got all the materials on which it was to work ready arranged, labeled, and catalogued for use, in "the book and volume of his brain."

This certainty and facility were, in some degree, the result of habit and practice, no doubt ; and they are, to a certain extent, enjoyed by most writers who are much accustomed to composition. But the total want of premeditation with which Hazlitt could produce, in a singularly short space of time, an essay full of acute or profound thought, copious, various and novel illustrations, and perfectly original views, couched in terse, polished, vigorous, and epigrammatic language, was quite extraordinary, and is only to be explained by the two facts, first, that he never by choice wrote on any topic or question in which he did not, for some reason or other, feel a deep personal interest ; and secondly, because on all questions on which he did so feel, he had thought, meditated, and pondered in the silence and solitude of his own heart, for years and years before he ever contemplated doing more than thinking of them.

When Hazlitt was regularly engaged on any work or article, he wrote at the rate of from ten to fifteen octavo pages at a sitting ; and never, or very rarely, renewed the sitting on the same day, except when he was at Winterslow — where, having no means of occupation or amusement in the evening part of the day, he used, I believe habitually, to write after his tea. And, doubtless, one of his motives for going there when he had any considerable work to get through, was the knowledge that by that means alone he could persuade himself to "work double tides."

This brings me to observe that Hazlitt hated writing, and would never have penned a line, and indeed never did, till his necessities compelled him to do so. To think was, and ever had been, the business and the pleasure of his intellectual life — though latterly it had become, on many topics, a fatality and a curse. But to promulgate his thoughts to perverse, or incapable, or unattending ears — to —

"Wear his heart upon his sleeve,
For daws to peck at "—

seemed to him at best but a work of supererogation — the result of a silly vanity, or a shallow and empty egotism. But to
do this as he did, for "certain sums of money " — to "coin
his brain for drachmas," and even to feel himself tempted, as
he often did, to put off false and base coin instead of the true
and good, because the latter would not pass current — daily to
hawk about for sale "the immortal part of, him," merely to
supply the sordid wants of the mortal part — this was one of
the troubles that (unconsciously to himself, I believe) perpetually preyed upon his mind, and helped to make him the unhappy man he was.

Hazlitt's judgment and tact as to what would suit the public taste was such, that what he wrote was sure of certain sale,
in various quarters, and at a liberal price. So that the labor
of a couple of mornings in the week, upon the average, would
have amply supplied all his wants, had he chosen to employ
himself regularly with that view. Yet nothing could ever
persuade him to set to work till his last sovereign was gone,
and his credit exhausted with his landlady and his tavern-
keeper; and I have repeatedly known him to leave himself
without a half crown to buy him a dinner, or what was still
more a necessary of life to him, a quarter of a pound of tea ;
and this at a moment, perhaps, when he had just committed
some escapade, in the way of revenge for some supposed injury or slight, which had left him without a friend to whom he
could persuade himself to apply for the loan of one.

And what made this habit of procrastination the more remarkable was, that he had an almost childish horror of owing
money, and was always ready to pay it away, even to the last
guinea, the moment he received the proceeds of any considerable work. I do not mean that he had any particularly
strict notions as to the relations of debtor and creditor ; but
his dread of the personal consequences to which a debt to a
stranger made him liable, amounted to a pitch of haunting
terror and alarm, under which he could not live. Let me add,

also, that he had a grateful and honorable sense of any unusual forbearance exercised towards him in this particular,
which made it. a pleasure to him to pay the claim in question
the moment he had the means of doing so. He was also
scrupulous in remembering and returning any trifling sums
that he might have been induced to borrow of a friend, under
any momentary pressure of the kind alluded to above — always provided the kindness was done in a manner that was
agreeable to his notions of the true art of conferring obligations.[1]

With the exception of his early metaphysical work, and his
"Life of Napoleon," all Hazlitt's productions were written
with a double view — that of their appearance in a periodical
work in the first instance, in parts or numbers, and their subsequent collection into volumes. So that he got a double remuneration for nearly all of them. The whole of the " Spirit
of the Age," and the greater part of the " Table Talk " and
the " Plain Speaker," were written for and appeared anonymously in the " New Monthly Magazine." Consequently the
articles were written at long intervals from each other, and
without any one in the work having a necessary reference to
any of the others. They were also all written under the pressure of the moment, and scarcely at all altered when·they appeared in a collected form. This will account for the numerous marks of haste, oversight, and even radical error, which a
critical examination of all Hazlitt's productions may detect,
and which his own infallible tact would have discovered to a
larger extent than that of any one else, had he been able to
read them over with attention. But this he was totally incapable of doing ; and it was a remarkable peculiarity of his mental habits and temperament. He never took the smallest
pleasure in reading over, in print, anything that he had written ; on the contrary, he felt it to be a task and a trouble to
do so, and never did it but " on compulsion ; " ⁓taking all the
consequences (and they were by no means trifling ones to
him) of escaping from the task.

[1] See his masterly essay on *The Spirit of Obligations.*

It must not be supposed from this fact that Hazlitt was indifferent about his literary reputation in the high and perma-
nent sense of that phrase. He had that anxious and restless
yearning for it which is perhaps indispensable to the very existence of such a reputation. And this was one of the chief
causes of his bitter anger and resentment at the innumerable
attacks that were made on his pretensions as a writer, knowing, as he did, the extensive effect which these must necessarily produce on the progress of any reputation, much more of
one which was subject to so many disadvantages and drawbacks, even from within its own springs and sources.

But Hazlitt's intellectual temperament had been so miserably shaken and shattered by the events of his past life, that it
was physically impossible for him so to gird up his mind to
the duties it owed to itself, as to enable it to take that deep
and sustained interest in its own operations and movements,
in the absence of which no actual and substantive literary
reputation of the highest grade can ever be achieved. Hazlitt
(like Coleridge) was looked upon during his life, and will, perhaps, hereafter be looked upon, much more with reference to
what he might have done under happier or more favorable
circumstances, than to what he actually accomplished. It
will be be felt, no less by posterity than it was by his contemporaries, that the writer of the "Essay on the Principles of
Human Action," *might have been* among the greatest metaphysicians of age or country ; that the author of the "Table
Talk" and the "Plain Speaker" *might* have given to the
world a body of moral truth. and wisdom that has at present
no substantive existence ; that the critic of Shakespeare and
the Elizabethan writers *might* have supplied, more effectually
than any other writer we have yet had among us, that digested
and enlightened estimate of our own literature which we have
hitherto been left wholly without ; that the critic of the
"British Picture Galleries" *might* have set forth the true
principles of Art in a manner and to an effect that has never
yet been accomplished, and in the absence of which we can
scarcely hope to see Art rise above that elegant mediocrity at
which it stands throughout Europe in the present day.

I will only add on this subject, that Hazlitt's method of composition, even on subjects which he was accustomed to treat the most profoundly — moral or metaphysical questions — was rapid, clear, and decisive ; so much so in the latter respect, that his MS. was like a fair copy, and he scarcely thought it necessary even to read it over before sending it to the press.

What is still more remarkable is, that his power of composition was but little affected by the general state of mind he might be in at the time of sitting down to his work. If he could but persuade himself to *begin* writing on any subject which he had himself chosen for discussion, he could so abstract his thoughts from all topics but *that*, as to be able to escape for the time from even the most painful and pressing of external circumstances.

As a proof of this, I may give a passage from one of his letters, written to me when he was in Scotland, whither he had gone on a matter which affected and troubled him almost to a pitch of insanity, and never relaxed its hold and influence upon his thoughts and feelings for a single moment, except when he was engaged in writing for the press. Before his departure from town, he had arranged with Mr. Colburn for a volume of " Table Talk," which was to consist of four hundred octavo pages, and of which not a line was written when he left London. From the day he quitted home his mind had been in a state of excitement bordering (as I have said) on disease, in consequence of circumstances that I may probably refer to more particularly hereafter. Yet four or five weeks after his departure he writes me as follows, at the end of a long letter, the previous part of which offers the most melancholy evidence of what the state of his mind must have been during the whole period of his absence : —

" You may tell Colburn when you see him that his work is done magnificently ; to wit : I. On the knowledge of character, 40 pp. II. Advice to a school-boy, 60 pp. III. On patronage and puffing, 50 pp. IV. and V. On Spurzheim's theory, 80 pp. VI. On the disadvantages of intellectual su-

periority, 25 pp. VII. On the fear of death, 25 pp. VIII.
Burleigh House, 25 pp. IX. Why actors should not sit in the
boxes, 35 pp. — In all 340 pages. To do by Saturday night:
X. On dreams, 25 pp. On individuality, 25 pp. — 390 pages."
He says, in a postscript, " I have been here a month yes-
terday." [1]

During this same period, too, he had written a considerable
part of another work, which was afterwards published under
the title of the " Liber Amoris," of which he speaks as follows
in the above-named letter : " On the road down I began a
little book of our conversations, *i. e.* mine and the statue's. It
is called ' The Modern Pygmalion.' You shall see it when I
come back."

The three or four hours a day employed by Hazlitt in composition enabled him to produce an essay for a magazine, one
of his most profound and masterly Table Talks, in two or
three sittings ; or a long and brilliant article of thirty or forty
pages for the " Edinburgh Review," in about a week. But
when he had an entire volume or work in hand he invariably
went into the country to execute it, and almost always to the
same spot — a little way-side public-house, called " The Hut,"
standing alone, and some miles distant from any other house,
on Winterslow Heath, a barren tract of country on the road to
and a few miles from Salisbury. There, ensconced in a little
wainscoted parlor, looking out over the bare heath to the distant groves of Norman Court, some of his finest essays were
written ; there, in utter solitude and silence, many of his least
unhappy days were spent ; there, wandering for hours over the
bare heath, or through the dark woods of the above-named
domain, his shattered frame always gained temporary strength
and renovation.

I have sometimes regretted that I did not go down to this
place when he was there, and spend a week with him, as he

---

[1] As this letter fixes the date and place of the above-named essays, several of
which are among the finest of his compositions, it may be interesting to add that it
is dated from " Renton Inn, Renfrewshire," and it bears the post-mark of March,
1822.

two or three times pressed me to do. But I have as often
pleased myself by thinking that he was much better alone at
those times ; for he was then comparatively happy, being
absent from all the scenes and circumstances which were at
least the proximate causes of his misery, and surrounded by
every personal comfort and respect that a profuse expenditure
could command from people wholly unaccustomed to such
guests, and to whom his advent must have seemed like a godsend : for " The Hut," though it was kept by reputable people,
and afforded every needful comfort, was (as I have said) a
mere way-side public-house, situated on a barren heath, and
was frequented only by a few pedestrian travellers, and by the
guards and coachmen of the public conveyances going that
road — the high-road from London to Salisbury. ·

The admirable things which Hazlitt wrote at this place, and
the tone of mind in which some of them have evidently been
composed — particularly the essay " On Living to Oneself " [1]
— might justify one in hoping that here at least he tasted of
that intellectual peace and contentment which, of all men
living, he was the best able to appreciate, and (as it should
therefore seem) to enjoy. But I doubt if such was really the
case, and whether the utmost and the best that Hazlitt could
do, even here, either for himself or for others, was to imagine
and describe and yearn after such a state of being. To feel
and enjoy it was not within his capacity. Even had every con-

---

[1] The following are the opening passages of this essay : —
" I never was in a better place or humor than I am at present for writing on this
subject. I have a partridge getting ready for my supper ; my fire is blazing on the
hearth ; the air is mild for the season of the year ; I have had but a slight fit of in-
digestion to-day — (the only thing that makes me abhor myself) ; I have three good
hours before me ; and, therefore, I will attempt it." . . . . " As I look from
the window at the wide bare heath before me, and, through the misty moonlit air,
see the woods that wave over the top of Winterslow,

' While Heav'n's chancel vault is blind with sleet,'

my mind takes a flight through too long a series of years, supported only by the patience of thought, and secret yearnings after truth and good, for me to be at a loss
to understand the feeling I intend to write about."

It appears by a foot-note that this delightful essay was " written at Winterslow
Hut, January 18th, 19th, 1821."

ceivable external appliance and means for such enjoyment
been at hand, the (so to speak) *physical* taste for it was wanting ; the *palate* was dead, and the most exquisite flavors and
most exciting viands conveyed no pleasure to the defeated
and interdicted sense. Not that his sense of intellectual enjoyment had been jaded and palled by over-indulgence, or dis-
ordered by ill-applied stimulants. On the contrary, nothing
could be more pure, simple, and natural than Hazlitt's intellectual tastes and desires, so far as they preserved their existence at all. But they seemed, as it were, benumbed and paralyzed into a condition of torpidity and suspended animation,
that nothing could awaken into life but those violent agents
which, like that of the galvanic power applied to the dead
limb, animate only to convulse and distort.

The truth is, that although Hazlitt was by nature better
fitted for solitude than most men, he could not, under the actual condition and circumstances of his mind and temper, have
existed for any length of time out of London, or some other
great metropolis, where the world of life and action, of hope
and enjoyment, that he saw about him, might be turned into
passive instruments of hope and action and enjoyment to himself, in that secondary and intermediary sense in which alone
he could use such instruments, or any others, to such a purpose.

I should be doing injustice to Hazlitt's reputation if I were
to quit this part of my subject without noticing a fact of which
many of his literary friends must have been aware, and which,
whatever may be thought of it as regards his writings themselves, and the motives and inducements of their author in
producing them, should remove or nullify much of the adverse
criticism that has been put forth respecting them. The truth
is, that among the few faults which have been justly found
with Hazlitt's style, and the mode in which he has treated his
subjects, nearly every one of them was introduced advisedly,
and with the perfect knowledge of the writer that they were
justly liable to the remarks made on them. His plea was, that
those faults were indispensable to the reception and success

of what he wrote — to that immediate popularity, without the attainment of which he could not have written at all, because he could not have got paid for what he wrote.

Whether he was right or wrong in this theory is another question. But it was one on which ·he uniformly acted — at least after he had adopted literature as a profession : for the work to which he himself chiefly looked and referred with pride and pleasure — the " Essay on the Principles of Human Action " — though his earliest work, is almost wholly free from the faults imputed to his after productions. But the consequence, as he has a hundred times declared, is that it has not been read by anybody, and is to this day almost entirely unknown.

CONVERSATIONAL AND SOCIAL POWERS.

As I have spoken of Hazlitt's conversational powers and social qualities, I will here illustrate them by a few passages from my diary.

EXTRACTS FROM DIARY.

May 21, 1822. — On Sunday, while we (Hazlitt and myself) were with John Hunt,[1] he (Hazlitt) related two or three nice things about Jeffrey. One was a reply of his to Owen (of New Lanark), who had been relating to him something of a person who, on visiting his (Owen's) place, seemed disposed chiefly to notice those of his people who were good-looking ; on which Owen said, " Now, *my* plan is exactly the reverse of this. I notice in particular those to whom nature has not been so bountiful as she has been to the rest." " Ah," said Jeffrey, " nature smiles on one, and Owen on the other."

On another occasion, when Owen was teasing Jeffrey about his system, Jeffrey said, " But Mr. Owen, according to all this that you are telling me, *you*, who are the founder and inventor of this system, on the supposition of its being capable of working these effects, ought to be the best man in the world. Now, to tell you the truth, I don't see that you are

---

[1] Then confined in Coldbath Fields Prison for a political offense.

any better than many other people that I know. And what,"
added Jeffrey, "do you think he had the impudence to reply
to this ? Why, he bade me name the persons to whom I alluded ; and when I did so he took exceptions to them, as persons *not* so good as himself."

Speaking of Mrs. Siddons and Miss O'Neil, Hazlitt said it
was idle to compare them together ; for however excellent Miss
O'Neil might be, Mrs Siddons was *above all excellence.* He
added that he had said this to a party of Scotchmen at Edinburgh, and that they did not understand what he meant ; they
did not seem to see that there was anything in what he had
said characteristic either of Mrs. Siddons or of himself ; and
he related the story as being perfectly characteristic of *them*
— that, however acute they (the Scotch) may be to a certain point, beyond that they cannot feel or appreciate anything.

Speaking of Walter Scott, he said that when he was in
Edinburgh, Jeffrey had offered to introduce him (Hazlitt) to
Scott, but that he declined. He said to Jeffrey, " I should be
willing to kneel to him, but I could not take him by the hand."
Alluding to Scott's political opinions and his supposed con-
nection with the "Beacon " and "Blackwood's Magazine."

He afterwards said of Walter Scott, " He seems to me to
hang over Scottish literature just as Arthur's Seat hangs over
Edinburgh, like a great hulking lion." [1]

Dined at ——'s with Hazlitt. He told some capital things
of A——. When A—— was manager of the Italian Opera,
the King (George IV.) went one night, accompanied by Lord
Hertford, and A—— and Taylor lighted them, as usual, to the
royal box. On ascending the stairs Lord Hertford (who was
growing very infirm at this time) slipped and hurt himself,
and had nearly fallen down, but evidently wished it not to be
noticed, and jumped up again, and pretended that nothing had
happened. When they reached the royal box, A——, instead
of taking this cue, which the marquis had given to all in attendance, addressed him, and "hoped his lordship had not

---

[1] I think he afterwards used this comparison in print.

injured himself by the little accident on the stairs ? " The marquis, evidently hurt at this notice, replied, " Accident — accident ? what accident ? What do you mean ? "

It was A—— himself who related this story of his own blundering impertinence, but related it purely as an instance of court manners — of the want of gratitude in the marquis for the kind interest that he (A——) had taken in his infirmities. " As if," said Hazlitt, " it were the place of the manager of a theatre to see any deficiencies in a marquis ! "

He told another story of A—— having taken some people to see Harlow's copy of the Transfiguration (which Hazlitt described as very bad), and showing it to them as a prodigiously fine thing ; but on one of the party (who told the story to Hazlitt) saying that he thought one of the heads pointing to it, a very bad one, he (A——) replied, " Oh, I don't mean to say that the heads are good. I 'm not praising the Transfiguration. I don't think anything of *that ;* it is the *copy* that I speak of as inimitable. Its faults are the faults of the original."

He related another story of the same person (whom he described as a singular embodiment of self-sufficient impertinence). On entering a room at a friend's house, where two or three persons were collected round a picture, seemingly intent on admiring it, A—— walked towards the picture, but before he had got half way to it, stopped and looked : " Aye," said he, " I see — a copy, evidently. I can see that from the cracks in the varnish." " Thus," said Hazlitt, " throwing out his impertinence before him, as a herald of his approach, and, as is not uncommon with him, pitching upon as a mark of the picture's youth precisely that which, if it indicated anything, indicated its age."

Speaking of having just called on Andrews about a volume of Maxims that he was writing, he said Andrews had spoken of his (Hazlitt's) article about the Fight (between Neate and the Gas Man) in the " New Monthly," and seemed to think it was unrivaled in its way. P—— said, jokingly, " You mustn't reckon too much on his opinion ; for it may have a rival be-

8

fore long ; " alluding jestingly to one that he (P.) was writing on the same subject. " Why," he said, " I am not going to write another ! "

He had just dined with Haydon, and related one or two things told by him (Haydon) that passed at a dinner at C——'s, where Y——, the tragedian, was present. Speaking of a recent performance of his, which, by his own account, he had got through very indifferently, he said quite seriously, " But, in fact, I have a kind of feverette upon me now." He (Y——) afterwards told what he considered as a very interesting story, of his having actually been addressed *by name by a perfect stranger*, while travelling in the Highlands of Scotland — a fact which he seemed to regard as the summit of human celebrity.[1]

Speaking of the American character, Hazlitt related a story told him by ——, illustrating their coolness under uncommon circumstances. He was spending an evening with an American family, when a young man was shown into the room. On his entering, the master of the house got up and went to him, saying, " Ah, George, how do you do ? " The young man replied that he was very well, and then took his seat among the rest of the persons present. After a little while something was said showing that the young man who had just joined the party was related to the family, and had lately been absent from home. This led to inquiries from the English visitor, and it turned out that the youth was the son of the host, and had just arrived from China, and that this was the first meeting after a separation of ten years !

January 15, 1825. — To-night (at the Southampton), Hazlitt told some capital things about Dawe the painter.[2] Describing

---

[1] Hazlitt afterwards related these two stories of Y—— to Northcote, and has reported (in the *Boswell Redivivus*) N.'s characteristic commentary on the latter of them. " Good God !" exclaimed N., " did he consider this as a matter of wonder, that, after showing himself as a sign for a number of years, people should know his face ? If an artist or an author were recognized in that manner, it might be a proof of celebrity ; but as to an actor, a fellow who had stood in the pillory might as well be proud of being pointed at."

[2] Who was at this time at St. Petersburg, whence he afterwards returned with a fortune of near half a million of money

his essential and ingrained meanness of character, he said, " He had a soul like the sole of a shoe ; " and he related some things illustrative of this character. He said Dawe used to lend out every farthing of his own money at usurious interest, and then borrow money of his friends at no interest at all to get on with ; and that once he quite abused, and almost quarreled with John Lamb, who used to lend him money, because on one occasion, Lamb asked him for an acknowledgment for it in case of death. Lamb wanted a stamped receipt which would have cost a few pence, and Dawe thought this an enormity.

He described a capital scene that had taken place at Dawe's. There was a man named K——, who was reckoned to be like Dawe in personal appearance (both of them being remarkably ugly), and this K—— had often asked Hazlitt to introduce him to Dawe, — he (K.) having a great wish to see a likeness of himself. Dawe, too, had often heard of this resemblance. At last Hazlitt took K—— to Dawe's house. There was a glass over the chimney-piece in Dawe's painting-room, and on Hazlitt introducing K——, he described each as first giving a furtive glance at the glass and then at each other.

Hazlitt. This is Mr. K——, Mr. Dawe.

Dawe. Very happy to see Mr. K—— (looking first at K. and then at himself in the glass, and giving a sort of inward smile of self-congratulation, as much as to say, " I don't see any great resemblance "). I think they say we are like each other, Mr. K——. I can't say I — exactly — see — any great similarity — (looking in the glass again). There is a little — something — to be sure — about the mouth — a sort of —

K——. Why, no ; I don't see much resemblance myself. There may, perhaps, be a little something in the forehead — a kind of —

In short, each evidently piqued at the unsatisfactory nature of the portrait of himself, and each wondering how anybody could possibly think *him* like so ugly a person as the other. Hazlitt made out the scene capitally ; you could see each party coquetting, as it were, with his own similar in the glass,

and comparing it, with infinite self-satisfaction, with the living
object before him.

There was a portrait of Holcroft which Dawe had painted,
and which belonged to Mrs. Holcroft, and was to be engraved
by Dawe for a Life of Holcroft, which Hazlitt was writing.
Hazlitt said that he and Mrs. Holcroft went about it one day
to Dawe's rooms, and caught him in the act of making a dupli-
cate of it.

He described very admirably a scene he had witnessed at
the M——'s between Mrs. M—— and Dawe, illustrating the
contrast between the flowing, graceful, queen-like style and
manner of the one, and the little, peddling, pimping, snipped
manner of the other. Mrs. M. was speaking of a picture she
had just seen of Sir Joshua's, of a lady, which she described
in her fine way. " The face, Mr. Dawe, was remarkably fair
— almost of a marbly *whiteness*, and on the cheek, to relieve
this, there was a slight tinge of color. The lady wore a perfectly *white* dress, and she was walking in a sort of garden
scene, with a *white* wall behind her ; and overhead there was
floating along one *white* cloud, and by her side was growing
one *white* lily."

The *contrast* to all this was furnished by the little snipped
and cut-up interruptions of Dawe, thrown in between every
stately pause in the description. " Ah ! — Yes ! — Indeed !
— Yes, very nice — aye, indeed."

Speaking of Haydon to-night, he said he had just been
at O——'s, and that Mrs. O—— had told him how it was
that her husband (who was at that time in very slender circumstances) had been compelled to lend him (Haydon) fifty
pounds. She said, " Oh, sir, my husband *could not help*
lending it to him — he *would* have it. Why, sir, he came
round here, behind the counter, followed my husband up to
the very window, and said he *must* have it — he could not do
without it, and almost seemed as if he would have *taken* it if
it had not been given to him." " And so," said Hazlitt,
" O—— was obliged to lend it to him, to prevent his taking
it out of the till ! "

The following was intended by Hazlitt to form part of one of his Conversations with Northcote (*Boswell Redivivus*) in the "New Monthly Magazine," but was suppressed by the editor. It relates to Haydon, the historical painter.

"He then asked me if I had seen anything of H——? I said, yes ; and that he had vexed me ; for I had shown him some fine heads from the Cartoons, done about a hundred years ago (which appeared to me to prove that since that period those noble remains have fallen into a state of considerable decay), and when I went out of the room for a moment, I found the prints thrown carelessly on the table, and that he had got out a volume of Tasso, which he was spouting, as I supposed, to let me understand that I knew nothing of art, and that he knew a great deal about poetry.

"I said I never heard him speak with enthusiasm of any painter or work of merit, nor show any love of art, except as a puffing-machine for him to get up into and blow a trumpet in his own praise. Instead of falling down and worshiping such names as Raphael and Michael Angelo, he is only considering how he may, by storm or stratagem, place himself beside them, on the loftiest seats of Parnassus, as ignorant country squires affect to sit with judges on the bench. He told me he had had a letter from Wilkie, dated Rome, with three marks of admiration, and that he had dated his answer 'Babylon the Great,' with four marks of admiration. Stuff! Why must he always 'out-Herod Herod?' Why must the place where he is always have one note of admiration more than any other? He gave as his reasons, indeed, our river, our bridges, the Cartoons, and the Elgin Marbles — the two last of which, however, are not our own. H. should have been the boatswain of a man of war : he has no other ideas of glory than those which belong to a naval victory, or to vulgar noise and insolence ; not at all as something in which the whole world may participate alike. I hate 'this stamp exclusive and professional.' He added that Wilkie gave a poor account of Rome, and seemed, on the whole, disappointed. He (Haydon) should not be disappointed when he went, for his expectations were but moderate. 'Aye,' said Northcote, 'that is like the speech of a little, crooked, conceited painter of the name of Edwards, who went to Italy with Romney and Humphreys, and when they looked round the Vatican, he turned round to Romney and said, 'Egad, George, we're bit.' •

" I said that when I heard stories of this kind, of even clever men who seemed to have no idea or to take no interest except in what they themselves could do, it almost inclined me to be of Peter Pindar's opinion, who pretended to prefer taste to genius : 'Give me,' said he, 'one man of taste, and I will find you twenty men of genius.' N. replied, 'It is a pity you should be of that opinion, for all your acquaintances are great geniuses ; and yet, I fancy, they have no admiration for anybody but themselves.' "

HAZLITT AT A PRIZE-FIGHT.

The most favorable circumstances under which Hazlitt could be seen were those under which he was the most entirely himself — that is, during a few hours or days spent with him in a country ramble, at a distance from all his accustomed haunts and associations. It was then that his spirit had free leave to move and meditate at its own will, and to set forth all its finer qualities and attributes, undeteriorated by any of those peculiar habits of feeling and of thought which had been engendered by a life, the last twenty years of which had been spent in a manner anything but congenial to the tone and tendencies of its nature.

I passed much time with Hazlitt under these favorable circumstances, and will briefly refer to one or two of these passages in his life ; because they will show him in a very different light from that in which he was ordinarily seen, even by his most intimate associates ; but a light, if I mistake not, in which he would always have appeared, had not the untoward events of his early years cast him forever out of that steady current of mingled thought and action and emotion, which might and ought to have formed " the even tenor of his way " to a wise, honorable, and happy manhood, and a calm and lengthened old age.

Probably most of the readers of these Recollections are aware that Hazlitt was intended for an artist, and had studied and practiced for some few years with this view. Had he persevered steadily in this line of pursuit, there can be little doubt that he would have been all that I have supposed above ; and that, in being thus, the world would not have lost any material portion of those of his literary works that are worth preserving, and would have gained into the bargain one of the greatest painters that ever lived. Those artists and lovers of art who are acquainted with the half-dozen or so of extraordinary portraits from Hazlitt's pencil that still exist, and that were painted at the very outset of his brief career as an artist, will, I am sure, absolve me from the charge of exaggeration in the latter part of the above proposition : and those who knew the character and constitution of his mind will, I think, agree with me in opinion that, whatever else he might have been, he *must* have been a great and distinguished writer. This latter was a necessary consequence, from his unequaled capacity for the perception of *the truth* in whatever presented itself to his notice, added to his irrepressible passion for setting it forth as he saw it. In this age of writers, Hazlitt could not have helped being a writer ; and his writings would probably not have possessed a single one of the faults that they do possess, if he had not been a writer by profession — a writer for his daily bread.

But this last fact was not only the fertile cause of all the errors of his writings ; it was the source of all the misery of his life. Witness his two Essays on " The Pleasures of Painting." They alone — coupled with the fact that the performances to which they so beautifully and interestingly refer, are in their way first-rate works of art — are sufficient to bear me out in both the propositions I have hazarded above. They show at every page a heart and mind made for the reception and enjoyment of those " calm pleasures and majestic pains " which constitute the sum and substance of a wise and good

man's life, and which make the very material on which they
live and grow.

That exquisite sensibility to the beauties of external nature
and of high art which Hazlitt so eminently possessed, and
that sympathy with and delight in them which, however, are
not its necessary accompaniment, would alone have sufficed to
carry him smoothly and happily down the stream of life, without the necessity for resorting to those artificial sources of
excitement which do but recruit and multiply the ills they momentarily assuage.

The unfailing recurrence of occupation, both mental and
bodily, which his intended profession would have furnished to
him, might have wholly prevented that unwholesome ponder-
ing over its own thoughts, which was the error and the foible
of Hazlitt's mind. From having in early life nothing to do
but to *think*, he used to brood over the embryo offspring of
his contemplations, beyond the natural and healthful term of
gestation, till they at last came forth maimed of their fair
proportions, or were overlaid and killed by too much care and
cherishing.

The subsequent necessity of providing by his pen for his
daily wants cured him of this error, so far as related to the
various subjects on which he wrote ; and all his best things
were written under the actual and immediate pressure of this,
his only motive for writing — at least latterly. But the radical
error alluded to stayed by him to the last, in regard to all that
concerned his merely personal opinions. He thought about
things and people till the very faculty of thought left him,
and he could only *feel;* and he always felt according to his
fears, never according to his wishes or his hopes.

But I was about to speak of Hazlitt at those periods — " few
and far between " — when he was, so to speak, his own man —
when he was all that Nature and Contemplation had made
him ; and when all that Passion and Circumstance had grafted
upon his natural character remained dormant, or was laid
aside.

The first time that I obtained this favorable view of him

was at a very early period of our acquaintance ; and I believe
it contributed greatly to fix and confirm that feeling of regard
and interest towards him which all that I had heretofore seen
of him had called forth, while all that I had *heard* of him was
calculated to persuade me that his character was incapable of
exciting any but an opposite impression.

I had, at the period in question, the prevalent passion for
prize-fighting strong upon me. (Gentle reader, it is a long
while ago, and I know better now. Howbeit, it is the prize-
fighters themselves who have cured me — not the preachers
against them.) The famous fight between the Gas Man and
Neate was to be fought in a few days, and it was the talk of
the town. Hazlitt had never seen a prize-fight, and in talking
with him on the subject a few nights before the appointed
time, I happened to say (on his expressing curiosity on the
matter) that, if ever he meant to see one, now was his time ;
for that there had never been such a one before, and never
would be such another. I told him that I was going ; and
added (half in joke, half earnest) that he could not do a better
thing than go with me, and make an " article " about it for the
New Monthly. I little thought that he would take me at my
word ; for the time was the depth of winter, the place of meeting at least sixty miles from London, and on account of the
extraordinary interest that was excited about the event, all
sorts of extra difficulties and obstacles were in the way of the
undertaking. Moreover, what at that period were to me (a
very young man) only pleasant stimulants to the enterprise,
must, as I supposed, appear to *him* insurmountable impediments. He talked, indeed, of going, and I promised to let
him know the exact place and time. But that a man who
would certainly not have stepped across the room to see a
coronation, and who would often sit silent and motionless over
his breakfast-things till seven or eight o'clock at night, from
pure incapacity to take the trouble of moving off his chair
and putting on his shoes to go out, should, under any inducement, even think of travelling sixty or seventy miles on a winter's night, with the almost certainty of meeting with no com-

fort or accommodation when he got there, and no probable
means of getting back again, perhaps, for two or three days —
to say nothing of the expense, the previous trouble of arrangement, etc. — seemed out of the question.

However, on the morning of the day before that fixed for
the fight, I let him know my arrangements ; and he still said
he *thought* he should meet me at the time and place I named,
which was, I remember, the Golden Cross, Charing Cross, at
ten o'clock at night, to start by the Salisbury night-coach,
which arrived at the nearest town to the appointed spot at
about five o'clock in the morning.

As I expected, he did not make his appearance ; and after a
perishing ride of seven hours — a nap of two or three, on the
coffee-room *table* (for not even a chair was to be had) of the
inn where the coach put me down — with my feet (to keep
them warm) in the great-coat pockets of one of the six or
seven "strange bedfellows" with whom prize-fighting, like
misery, makes a man acquainted — a hasty but hearty and
healthy breakfast — and a walk of five or six miles to the spot
of meeting — who should I see among the first persons I recognized on the ground but William Hazlitt ! He had wisely
calculated that it would never do to arrive houseless and sup-
perless at five o'clock on a winter's morning ; so he had
lounged into Piccadilly at eight o'clock over night, found a
vacant place in the Bristol mail — got into it — somehow or
other lighted upon a comfortable bed at the same town where
I had stopped — slept and breakfasted comfortably — and there
he was, lively as a bird, gossiping gayly with his friend, Joe
Parkes, whom he had just met on the ground — and as "eager
for the fray" as the most interested and knowing of " the
fancy."

I was too anxious about the "great event" I had come
seventy miles to see to take much notice of its effects upon
Hazlitt while it was going on. But after it was over we joined
company ; and I then found that he had taken the most profound metaphysical as well as personal interest in the battle ;
and I never heard him talk finer or more philosophically than

he did on the subject — which he treated — and justly, I think
— as one eminently worthy of being so considered and treated.
As a study of human nature, and the varieties of its character
and constitution, he looked upon the scene as the finest sight
he had ever witnessed ; and as a display of animal courage he
spoke of the battle as nothing short of sublime. I found that
he had paid the most intense attention to every part of the
combat, had watched the various chances and changes of its
progress with the eye and tact of an experienced amateur, and
could have given (and, in fact, afterwards did give in the
" New Monthly Magazine ") an infinitely better, because a
more characteristic and intelligible, account of its details, than
the professional reporters employed for that purpose.

If I mistake not, *this* was the faculty in which Hazlitt ex-
ceeded any other man that perhaps ever lived — the faculty in
which his *genius* consisted. A practical musician can play
anything " at sight," as the phrase is. But Hazlitt could perceive and describe " at sight " the characteristics of anything,
without any previous study or knowledge whatever, but by a
species of intellectual intuition. Other men become acquainted
with things progressively, and with more or less quickness and
precision, according to their capacity and to the attention they
bestow. But Hazlitt *felt* them at once. They did not gradually engrave themselves upon his perceptive faculties, but
struck into them at once as by a single blow. This peculiarity
was of universal application in respect to Hazlitt, and it was
the secret of his unequaled critical faculties ; for if his criticisms themselves were often (perhaps always) more or less
defective, on account of the comparatively little of steady attention that he gave to the subject of them, his critical *faculties* have perhaps never been surpassed.

Our journey home from the fight offered one of those instances which few of Hazlitt's friends can even have conceived
possible, and fewer still have enjoyed — that of seeing him for
eight and forty hours together as happy as a boy or a bird ; as
free from all seeming consciousness of the ills which *his*
" flesh," above that of all other living men, was " heir to." as

if some kind genius had charmed his memory and imagination to sleep. Yet that no such process had taken place was clear, from the delightful manner in which both those faculties were called into play, in the Table Talk in which the pleasant hours were passed.

Having settled to proceed together on our journey home, we started immediately after the business of the day was concluded, with the intention of sleeping at a neighboring town, if we could get comfortable accommodation there, and if not, of proceeding onwards towards London, and taking the chance of anything that might present itself on the way.

We soon found that the latter was the only course ; and having reconnoitred, and made our way out of the town, which resembled nothing but a place just entered pell-mell by a besieging army, the whole of its length being one mass of vehicles jammed together in a motionless state, and all the pathways and interstices filled up by pedestrians, every individual of the whole living mass presenting in their faces, more or less, evidence of the excitement of the hour, — we got upon the London road, and, soon giving the go-by to *the* subject, which we had now (for the present) had enough of, relapsed into that natural and self-suggestive talk which is the only thing deserving the name of " conversation," and in which Hazlitt excelled all men I have ever known, provided he had (as in my case) a good listener, and one who could give the cue when it was wanting, without ever desiring to keep the ball in his own hands for a moment longer than was necessary to preserve it from falling to the ground.

It was a beautiful sunshiny afternoon, I remember, with a mild sharpness in the air, which Hazlitt seemed every now and then to drink in and snuff up with a boyish delight, while he gazed and remarked on the pleasant scenery we were passing through, as if the feeling and sight of " the country " had restored to him those times and associations which it seemed to be the sole business of his ordinary every-day life (not to forget, but) to brood over with a melancholy and mortal regret. Here, however, they seemed to come back like " angel " rather

than demon visits, and to bring with them nothing but a grave
and quiet satisfaction.

Some remark of his on the curious manner in which *smells*
bring back to us the scenes with which they have been associated in years long past, called for a remark from me which I
was surprised to find was entirely new to him, but the truth of
which he immediately admitted, namely, that certain *tastes*
produce this effect in a still more remarkable manner. I said
that to that day (and it is the same at this) I could never taste
green mustard and cress without its calling up to my mind, as
if by magic, the whole scene of my first school-days, when I
used to grow it in my little bit of garden in the inner play-
ground ; that every individual object there present used to
start up before me with all the distinctness of actual vision,
and to an extent of detail which no effort of memory could accomplish without this assistance ; and that *nothing but the
visible objects* of the scene presented themselves on these occasions.

Hazlitt illustrated the fact by several instances in his own
case, connected with smells ; and he said that the observation
had been first suggested to him by Mr. Fearn, in whose metaphysical work, he said, the fact was first brought to bear on
our mental operations. And he instanced, I remember, Mr.
Fearn's remark, that certain associations of ideas brought
back to him, as if it were actually existing, *the smell of a
baker's shop at Bassora*, as one of the finest examples on record of the far-reaching powers of the human senses when
duly connected with the imagination. He spoke, too, I remember, in the very highest terms of Mr. Fearn's powers of
metaphysical investigation, describing them as second to none
that had ever been employed on the subject.

In talk like this, ranging from the dizzy heights of

" Fate, free-will, foreknowledge absolute,"

down to the level of those merely " personal themes," in discussing which Hazlitt was equally happy and at home, we
passed pleasantly over the first five or six miles of our home-

ward journey, by which time a return chaise overtook us, and
the dusk coming on, we got into it, and, in an hour more, were
snugly housed for the night at one of those most " comfortable "
of all public domiciles, a third-rate country inn ; and here, in a ,
little wainscoted parlor on the ground floor, we were soon
warmly and cosily ensconced by a blazing fire, with the tea- ।
things on the table, the curtains let down, an early supper
ordered of roast fowl and apple-pudding (of all things in the
world — but we had had no dinner), a "neat-handed Phyllis "
to wait on us (which was always a great point of comfort with
Hazlitt), and an interminable evening before us, destined to
engender a volume of Table Talk, at least as pleasant and instructive (on one side, I mean) as any of those that have followed it in a more tangible form ; for, as I have hinted before,
Hazlitt's familiar talk, when he was in the proper cue for talking, had all the merits of his published writings, some which
those never included, and not one of their faults — the greatest
of which merits (let me add), and the source of all the others
that are *peculiar* to this kind of talk was, that not a phrase of
it would bear to be set forth in the trim array of printers'
types.

One little circumstance, however, I will mention, because I
think it is peculiarly characteristic of that wise and happy
balance between all his various faculties and mental endowments, which so greatly contributed to give that almost oracu-
lar character to Hazlitt's decisions on moral and intellectual
questions, which, when unbiased by personal feelings and
prejudices, they possessed beyond those of any man that I ever
knew. Almost all the evidences of mental weakness that we
observe in distinguished men, and often much of their mental
strength also, arise from some one class of faculties prevailing
and predominating over all the rest. The understanding, the

imagination, the sensibilities, the passions — one or other of
these hold almost undivided sway in the great majority even
of highly gifted and highly cultivated minds ; and they not
merely give the tone and color, but modify the form and substance. of all their conceptions and operations. But with Hazlitt all these qualities were so equally blended and balanced,
that they enabled him to see and appreciate, with a most
"learned spirit of human dealing," the relative value and virtue even of the opposite qualities and attributes that presented themselves to his notice and observation.

But I am making a magnificent preface to a tale that many
of my readers may deem not worth the telling. What I was
going to relate was, that, during a momentary interregnum in
our talk, I had taken from my pocket and laid on the table a
volume of — what does the reader imagine, of all books in the
world, to make one's travelling companion to a prize-fight ?
The " Nouvelle Héloise ! "

Gentle reader ! let me repeat, as before, it is a long while
ago, and in the one case equally as in the other, the passion
has become a thing of memory merely. I do not go a hundred
miles to see a prize-fight now ; and, if I did, the " Nouvelle
Héloise " would not be the book I should take with me.

I put the book aside, — not thinking of looking into it ; for I
had removed it from my pocket only because it incommoded
me. But Hazlitt asked, " What's that ? " I handed the
book to him, with a smile ; and I shall not forget the burst of
half-comic, half-pathetic earnestness with which he read the
title — the " Nouvelle Héloise ! " And then his countenance
fell as he turned over the pages silently, and the tears came
into his eyes as he looked, for the first time, perhaps, for
twenty years, on words, thoughts, and sentiments on which
his soul had dwelt and banqueted in its early days, with a
passionate ecstasy only equaled by that in which they had
been conceived and written ; for the " Nouvelle Héloise " was
the idol of Hazlitt's youthful imagination, and he himself resembled its writer more curiously and remarkably than, perhaps, any one distinguished man ever resembled another.

But what I was chiefly about to remark was, the delight Hazlitt expressed at meeting with the work under *such* circumstances, and at the sort of feeling which *he* must have for it who could make it his companion to such a scene as we had just left. "Why, then," he said, "you actually had the 'Nouvelle Héloise' in your pocket all the while you were watching those fellows this morning, mauling and hacking at each other, like devils incarnate ! Well, I confess, that's a cut above me. I can 'applaud the deed;' but to have done it is beyond me. In putting the book into my pocket, I should have had some silly scruples — some indelicate feelings of delicacy, come across me, and I should have left it at home. It's the highest thing I remember — a piece of real intellectual refinement, by G—d ! and I congratulate you upon it."

That this was to consider the matter too curiously, the reader will perhaps think, as I thought then, or the incident would not have made so strong an impression on me. I am not so sure I think so now. If not, however, it is, perhaps, that our thoughts grow ripe as our feelings fade away.

The above incident led, I remember, to some beautiful remarks of Hazlitt on the "Nouvelle Héloise," and on the intellectual and personal character of Rousseau ; but I shall not even attempt to detail them, for the same reason which has excluded almost all similar details from these Recollections — namely, that it is morally impossible to relate them without blending them (whether consciously or not) with the feelings and opinions of the relator, in a way that must divest them of all specific character, and also of that authenticity which constitutes the only real value of such details, or keeps them from degenerating into a deception and an impertinence.

I shall conclude my, perhaps, too lengthened notice of this excursion, by adding that, after a hearty supper, an early bed (which was a novelty to both of us), and a gossiping breakfast the next morning, we mounted the first coach that passed for London, arrived there in the evening, and Hazlitt (at my suggestion) wrote in the next "New Monthly" a capital description of "The Fight," signed "Phantastes." I mention this, as the paper does not appear among his collected Essays; the title and subject being deemed unsuitable to the "ears polite" of Mr. Colburn's book customers, and only to be tolerated in the ephemeral pages of a periodical miscellany.

AT FONTHILL AND BURLEIGH HOUSE.

On another occasion, I passed eight or ten days with Hazlitt, among scenes of peculiar interest, but not exactly of a nature to keep him in that good humor with himself which made his society so delightful, and in the absence of which, though his company was always in the highest degree interesting and instructive as a moral and intellectual study, it was not what one would have chosen purely for the sake of the companionship it afforded.

The place where I met him on this occasion was no other than Fonthill Abbey, which had just been thrown open to the public curiosity, after having remained up to that time a sealed book from the day of its mysterious creation. I was, by the favor of its new proprietor, staying in the house (with a view to a detailed description of its treasures of art, and of the beautiful domain surrounding it, which I was preparing for the pages of a periodical work); and I found that Hazlitt was also staying there, but was absent at the time of my arrival.

We met the next day, and were much together during the time we stayed; and though he was anything but at ease and at home in those scenes of artificial luxury and overstrained refinement which surrounded us here, yet the locality happened to be one with which many of his early associations were connected; and we made several excursions in the neighborhood, which afforded some of the most pleasant and profitable hours I ever spent with him.

Hazlitt particularly piqued himself on his skill in ciceroneship; and when he was in good health and spirits, there was nothing pleased him better than to accompany a friend to some celebrated collection of pictures, with which he himself was familiar, but which the party accompanying him had not seen before; and the first place he proposed that we should

9

go to see was Sir Richard Colt Hoare's, which is situated a
few miles from Fonthill.

On these occasions it was very curious and characteristic
to observe the manner in which the mere feelings and impressions of his youthful enthusiasm were blended with the
critical knowledge and judgment of his after years, — each
moulding and modifying the other into forms which neither
could have assumed of themselves, and which, if they did not
offer a very just estimate of the objects to which they were
applied, offered that which was infinitely more characteristic
and interesting, as illustrations of the mind and spirit in which
they were generated.

Not that the actual *criticisms* which Hazlitt pronounced on
these occasions — when he pronounced such at all — were in
any material degree impaired in value by the mere *impressions*
which had preceded them in his mind. But it was these latter
that he loved chiefly to recur to, and which, to my thinking,
were even more instructive and valuable than his formal criticisms ; because, with him, the *first impression* was always
the germ and the foundation of all that he might afterwards
have to say or to write on any topic of this kind. It was in
the astonishing depth and quickness of his first insight into
any object of art, that his unequaled critical faculty consisted ;
and all his written criticisms on actual objects of art consisted
of the impressions thus received, long before he ever thought
of becoming a critic at all. Nor did he much care to modify
the impressions, by any after accessions of knowledge that
might have come to him from other sources ; which will account for many instances that might perhaps be pointed out
in which his criticisms are erroneous or exaggerated, and
some in which they must be wholly unintelligible except to
those who are acquainted with the manner in which they have
been produced. Conceive, for instance, a man writing a detailed notice of a picture that he had not seen for twenty
years — that he then saw only once, and that he saw at a
period and under circumstances when, for him, all things were
attired in " the glory and the freshness of a dream ; " but

which he was to describe when every ray of that freshness
and beauty had not merely "faded to the light of common
day," but was changed into mortal clouds and shadows, that
overhung the Present like a pestilence, and blotted out the
Future as if it were a thing not to be !

The truth is, that Hazlitt's extraordinary critical powers
were available to him only by the light of the Past. His impressions on contemporary art were as little to be depended
on as those on contemporary literature. The pictures that he
had seen at the Louvre during the Peace of Amiens, and in
the private galleries of England about the same period, he
could describe with a more intimate sense of their merits and
beauties than any other man ; and he could convey to others
that sense more vividly than even actual observation would
have presented it — especially when he had the objects before
him to renew his impression of those individual details by
which the general impression was first created in his mind.
But to all other objects of a similar kind, if he did not willfully
close his eyes, at least he opened them only to look with that
vague and vacant gaze in which the perceptive powers, instead
of projecting themselves outward in tangible communion, as
it were, with the thing looked upon, seem to rest idle or paralyzed within us, and convey no distinct impressions to the sen-
sorium. He saw, yet saw them not.

In going through the various apartments at Sir Richard
Colt Hoare's, and afterwards at Burleigh House, I shall never
forget the almost childish delight which Hazlitt exhibited at
the sight of two or three of the chief favorites of his early
days, and the way in which he expressed that delight, not so
much to me as to the attendant who showed us the pictures,
and on whom he seemed to look with a sort of superstitious
respect, — as if the daily looking upon objects which were
nothing less than sacred in Hazlitt's eyes, had transferred
something of their sanctity to *him.*

On another day, while at Fonthill, we walked over to Salisbury (a distance of twelve miles) in a broiling sunshine ; and
I remember, on this occasion in particular, remarking the ex-

traordinary physical as well as moral effect produced on Hazlitt by the sight and feel of "the country." In London the
most inobservant person could scarcely pass him in the
street without remarking the extreme apparent debility, almost
amounting to helplessness, of his air and manner. He used
to go drooping and faltering along, like a man just risen from
a bed of sickness, seeming scarcely able to support himself
without holding by the railings or leaning against the walls ;
and invariably looking prone upon the ground, to which he
seemed ready to fall at every step. But in the country,
especially upon a vast open plain or heath, like that over which
our path on the present occasion chiefly lay, he was like a
being of another species ; his step firm, vigorous, and rapid ;
his look eager and onward, as if devouring the way before it,
and his whole air and manner buoyant and triumphant, as
if a new sense of existence and new bodily powers had been
breathed into him by the objects around.

He spoke on this occasion of having repeatedly walked
from forty to fifty miles a day in that fashion formerly, and
said that he could do so now with perfect ease and pleasure.
Yet in London (as I have hinted elsewhere) he would sit, as
if nailed to his chair, from morning till late at night, day after
day, for weeks together — merely creeping out to the theatre,
or the Southampton at ten or eleven o'clock at night, and
there taking his seat silently again, and sitting till he was
fairly warned away by the extinguished lights and the closing
doors.

Another of our excursions was to that gem of English vil-
lages, Stourhead, adjoining the seat of Sir Richard Colt Hoare.
I have never seen anything in its way so pretty as this village.
Indeed it was *too* pretty, for it gave one the idea, not of a real
country village, but of the imitation of one in some prince's
or nobleman's park ; and, knowing it *not* to be so, the effect
was odd, and, in some degree, unpleasant. It reminded one
of a village beauty, too well dressed to admit the belief that
she had been her own tire-woman ; or, in another way, it
looked like one of those pretty Paris *grisettes* who sit for half

an hour under the hair-dresser's hands before they show themselves in their shops in the morning. All the houses looked
as if they had just been newly colored and painted. The windows glittered like crystal, the little green in the centre was
like the *lawn* of a Londoner's villa, and the whole picture
was set in the framework of a superb laurel hedge, of immense height and depth, which ran in an unbroken line round
the adjoining pleasure-grounds of Sir R. Hoare. We found,
too, an exquisite little inn, with a landlady as trim and *point-de-
vice* in all about her as the village over which she seemed to
preside. Here we slept, breakfasted the next morning, and
then returned to the Abbey.

It was during this stay at Fonthill Abbey that I had occasion to remark one among many other instances in Hazlitt, of
that peculiarity which he himself so often observed and smiled
at in Charles Lamb — unconscious, I believe, that it existed in
at least an equal degree in himself, though modified by another
feature in his personal character. Whenever he showed special signs of favor towards any one in a menial stage of life,
it was sure to be some out of the way being, who was the
laughing-stock or the pity of everybody else; and among the
people of the late immense establishment of Mr. Beckford
who had been retained in the service of the new proprietor of
the place (Mr. Farquhar) was a lout of a foot-boy, who was in
special favor with Hazlitt. He had recently been promoted
from the plough-tail to the servants' hall, and had been appointed to take up Hazlitt's breakfast to his room in the morning, and to give him any information he might need connected
with the object of his visit to the place, which was similar to
mine. Now, a personal civility to Hazlitt won his heart at
once; and in the case of menial servants he always took care
to lay the foundation for this (when he could afford to do so)
by a liberal gratuity *beforehand.* And he had done this in
Tom's case so effectually that the lad took him for nothing
less than a lord in disguise, and treated him accordingly; at
the same time perceiving, by a sort of menial instinct, that
his benefactor was in fact not much more lordly or urbane in

his mere "complement extern" than he himself was, and
thereupon assuming a most lackey-like superiority over him,
in virtue of the information which he (Tom) possessed and
the other party wanted. He used to direct Hazlitt as to the
various localities of the neighborhood ; show him about the
grounds ; and in one or two instances, I remember, ventured
to go the forbidden length of naming the name of the late
lord of the Abbey. Among other things, he told Hazlitt that
he had *once* (during an almost life-long servitude on the spot !)
actually caught a sight of the visible presence of the said
mysterious being, who, in his solitary wanderings about the
grounds of the Abbey, having encountered the unlucky apparition of Tom in those sacred precints where he had no
business, instead of ordering his instant dismissal from the
service (which was the understood rule in such cases), in his
infinite magnanimity merely desired him to "get out of the
way."

The change which had come over the spirit of Tom since
the downfall at the Abbey of this more than eastern mystery
and despotism, had worked an amusing alteration in him, the
outward effects of which it was that took Hazlitt's fancy ; and
he used to take every opportunity that offered of talking with
him on subjects connected with the late and present state of
the place. While Tom, on his part, thus elevated to a companionship with "gentlefolks," and seeing those spots which
had heretofore scarcely echoed to a human footstep suddenly
changed (nobody could tell why) into a bear-garden and a public thoroughfare, was so completely mystified and moved from
his propriety as to have become, for the nonce, a "character"
well worth observation and study.

One great·practical point in Tom's favor with Hazlitt, I remember, was, that he used, by hook or by crook, to procure him
an inordinate quantity of cream for his breakfast and tea : and,
in order to excuse himself from any improper imputation on
his honesty in the affair, he used to confess, or rather to
boast, with great *naïveté*, that all "that sort of thing" was
now the understood privilege and "parquiset" of the estab-

lishment. " Lord bless'ee, zur, we all does it now, since Nabob 'a been gone away, and nobody be'nt the wòrse nur the wiser for it. Muster Phillips ¹ is master now, and we does just as we likes." In fact, what Hazlitt admired in Tom was the simple honesty of his roguery. There was nothing Tom would not have done for him — such as stealing the best fruit from the hot-houses — harnessing the pet white ponies to the pony-phaeton, and driving him round the grounds, etc., etc. — excusing it all with a " Lord bless'ee, zur, there 's no harm in it — nobody won't know nothin' about it ! " The only immorality, in Tom's eyes, was — to be found out.

EVENINGS AT THE SOUTHAMPTON.

If I were required to name the person among all Hazlitt's intimates in whose society he seemed to take the most unmingled pleasure — or I should perhaps rather say, with whom he felt himself most at ease and " comfortable " — I should say it was the late William Hone, author of the celebrated " Parodies," etc. With almost everybody else Hazlitt seemed to feel some degree of restraint on some point or other. With some (as with Northcote for instance) he seemed to feel himself bound to listen more than he liked to listen ; with others he felt called upon to talk more than it pleased him to talk. With one class of persons — the professed literati of the day — he tried to shine ; with another class — the opposite of the above — he tried *not* to shine, but, on the contrary, to be and to seem not a whit superior to those about him. In the company of females, whoever they might be, or of whatever class — even with those few who were uniformly kind and cordial in their reception and treatment of him, and of whose respect and good-will he could not reasonably doubt — there was always apparent a dash of melancholy and despondency ; and also a resentful feeling, which showed itself from time to time, not in anything he said, but in the fearful expression which used to pass across his face, and which he never even at-

¹ The " eminent" auctioneer under whose direction the property was preparing for the public sale, which shortly afterwards took place.

tempted to suppress or conceal — an expression that can only
be described by saying that it gave the look of an incarnate
demon's to a face that, in the absence of that look, indicated
the highest and noblest attributes of the human intellect and
character. In speaking of this look, I may remark that,
though no *obvious* cause was ever apparent for it, I never remember to have once observed it without being able immediately to assign the cause, even though I may inadvertently
have given it myself — for it was always something touching
more or less remotely or nearly the *personal* condition and circumstances of the man ; and I might add, it was almost always connected with one of three topics — the downfall of
Napoleon — the abuse of some deserving writer from party
motives — and (in the case where females were present), in
reference to the passion of Love. On each of these topics
there existed a morbid part in Hazlitt's mind, which no one —
friend, foe, or perfect stranger — could touch, or even approach, without exciting a feeling of mingled agony and resentment, that showed itself as I have just described. These
topics were strings in the noble instrument of his mind which
had been so early and violently overstrained, that nothing
could ever restore them to their healthful temperament, or
cause them to give out tones capable of making anything but
"harsh discords," or music the pathos of which was lost in
the pain.

But in the company of females, the dreadful look I have
spoken of (for such it was) used to come over Hazlitt's face
much more frequently than at any other time ; because the
great source of those agonized feelings which called it forth
was connected with that habitual and almost insane fear I
have before alluded to, that no woman could look upon him
without a feeling of mingled terror and distaste at least, if
not disgust.

If I have been tempted to notice more at length than it
may seem to deserve this singular feature in Hazlitt's social
and personal character, it is because it was fraught with an almost painfully pathetic interest, that has perhaps never been

equaled, either in kind or degree, even in fictitious narrative, except in that divine Eastern story of Beauty and the Beast.

It has been my lot during the last fifteen years to associate more or less familiarly with a large proportion of the most intellectual men of an age which perhaps deserves to be characterized as the most intellectual that the world ever knew ; and I confess that no part of such intercourse has connected itself with more perfectly pleasant recollections and associations than do the three or four evenings that I remember to have spent with Hazlitt and Hone, in the little dingy wainscoted coffee-room[1] of the Southampton Arms, in Southampton Buildings, Chancery Lane. There, after having dreamed and lingered at home over his beloved tea from five or six o'clock till ten or so at night, Hazlitt used to go every evening, for years, to take his supper (or dinner, as the case might be), of either cold roast beef or rump-steak and apple tart ; for he rarely tasted anything else but these — never by choice, unless it were a roast fowl, a pheasant, or a brace of partridges, when his funds happened to be unusually flourishing. And there you were sure to find him, in his favorite box on the right hand side of the fire-place, sitting (if alone) upright, motionless, and silent as an effigy, brooding over his own thoughts, and, at the same time, taking in and turning to intellectual account every word that was uttered by the few persons who used at that time habitually to frequent the house, and to most of whom he was known ; at the same time, casting furtive glances at the door every time it gave intimation of opening, partly in the hope, partly in the fear, that the in-comer might be some one of his own particular intimates, who came there, as he knew, solely to seek him.

I say that he looked for a companion under these circumstances with a mixed feeling of hope and fear. In fact, it was always a moot point whether Hazlitt liked better to be alone with his own thoughts and imaginations, or interchanging

---

[1] Since "improved from off the face of the earth," for all purposes of old local association.

them with those of other people ; nor do I believe that he
himself could ever have decided the point satisfactorily to
himself in any given case. But when accident decided it, the
result seemed sure to be the right one — always provided the
party disjoining him from himself did not happen to be one of
those three or four unlucky individuals towards whom he felt
a sort of constitutional antipathy — as some men do to cats.
But such was his humane sense of the forbearance and toleration we owe to each other, and his delicate consideration in
exercising these, that even the persons in question were sure
to go away with the impression that they had made themselves peculiarly agreeable to him. And even if the truth
happened to be so exactly the other way that he could bear
the infliction no longer, the worst he used to do was to plead
illness (as he safely might — for this sort of thing disturbed
his whole system for a day or two), get up, and go away to the
theatre — begging they would come and sit with him some
other night !

There was something in the social and intellectual character
of William Hone peculiarly suited to the simple, natural, and
humane cast of Hazlitt's mind — using the latter epithet in its
broad and general sense, as implying a sympathy with all the
qualities of our nature — its weaknesses no less than its
strengths. His manner (I speak of him when in Hazlitt's society — where alone I was accustomed to see him) united the
most perfect freedom, familiarity, and *bonhomie*, with that
delicate deference and respect which the extraordinary intellectual powers of Hazlitt were calculated to excite in all who
were capable of duly appreciating them. He also never failed
to keep Hazlitt in that active good-humor with himself which
was so indispensable to his personal comfort, and to that of
all who conversed with him. And he effected this by a species of flattery which is not merely innocent in itself, but is
the just meed of high intellectual superiority, and is never
withheld from it but by those who either envy its pretensions
or dispute them — a flattery which consists in the instant recognition and allowance of any new light thrown upon the topic

of converse, or any false one dispelled, in place of that petty
and paltry disputation for disputation's sake which is the miserable characteristic of all ordinary English conversation —
even of that which formally claims that name ; in short, that
flattery which consists in the delighted admission and reception of the Truth the instant it is made apparent to us, instead
of the dogged denial of it on that very account, and because
we ourselves have hitherto been blind to it, or have seen its
semblance in error and falsehood.

There was also about Hone a buoyancy and joyousness of
spirit which, wherever Hazlitt met with it, acted upon his
memory and imagination in a beautiful and affecting manner.
Himself the very type of intellectual dejection and despondency, the mere sight of the opposites of these in others, instead of aggravating the malady, as it does in most cases,
utterly dispelled it for the moment, and made him feel, not
joyous himself, but as if he could become so if he chose by
the mere force of those fine sympathies with his fellow-beings
which kept the constitutional melancholy of his temperament
from sinking into that fatal disease which it so often assumes.
For the effect I speak of was not a mere association of ideas,
carrying him back in imagination to the time when he himself
was buoyant and happy ; it was a complex action, arising, as I
conceive, chiefly out of his deep and universal sympathies with
human nature, but modified and blended, no doubt, by and
with his unconscious recollections of that period of his life
when "he too was an Arcadian." It was an association that
not merely "played round his head," but " touched his heart "
also.

In illustration of this sort of complex association of ideas,
and its effect upon a mind made up, like Hazlitt's, of almost
equal proportions of our intellectual and our sentient natures,
I will here refer to a simple fact that many of his associates
must have observed as well as myself, and which never occurred without exciting in me an interest almost painful, yet
blended with a peculiar and touching pleasure, precisely corresponding with that which we derive from unexpected touches

of nature in lyrical or pastoral poetry. I have already stated
that, from the time of my first acquaintance with him, Hazlitt
had been a determined water-drinker. No temptation ever
induced him to trangress his rule of life in this respect ; the
only rule he ever prescribed to himself, or could have been
likely to keep if he had. But this rule had been imposed upon
him by the moral certainty that his life would be the cost of
neglecting it ; for, in the early part of his literary career in
London, he had been led into an intemperate use of stimulants, which had at length wholly destroyed the healthful tone
of his digestive organs, and made the utmost caution necessary
to prevent those attacks, under one of which he died.

Of course, in our evening meetings at the Southampton and
elsewhere, a glass of grog, or something of the kind, was not
wanting to give that *social* flavor to our table-talk which was
one of its most pleasant qualities. Indeed, Hazlitt himself
could never bear to see the table wholly empty of some emblem of that " taking one's ease at one's inn," which was a
favorite feeling and phrase with him ; and immediately his
supper-cloth was removed (for *his* corporeal enjoyment on
these occasions was confined to the somewhat solid but brief
one of a pound or so of rump-steak or cold roast beef), he
used to be impatient to know what we were each of us going
to take ; and, as each in turn determined the important point,
he would *taste* it with us in imagination. It was his frequent
and almost habitual practice, the moment the first glass was
placed upon the table after supper, to take it up as if to carry
it to his lips, then to stop for a few moments before it reached
them, and then to smell the liquor and draw in the fumes, as
if they were "a rich distilled perfume." He would then put
the glass down slowly, without uttering a word ; and you
might sometimes see the tears start into his eyes, while he
drew in his breath to the uttermost, and then sent it forth in a
half sigh, half yawn, that seemed to come from the very depths
of his heart. At other times he would put the glass down with
a less dejected feeling, and exclaim in a tone of gusto that
would have done honor to the most earnest of *gastronomes*

over the last mouthful of his *actual* ortolan, " That 's fine, by
G—d !" literally exhilarating, and almost intoxicating, himself
with the bare imagination of it. He used almost invariably to
finish this movement by falling back into a brief fit of dejection, as if stricken with remorse at the irreparable injury he
had committed against himself, in having, by an intemperate
abuse of a manifest good, forever interdicted himself from the
use of it ; for no man ever needed more the judicious use of
stimulants, or would, if he could have borne them, have found
more unmingled benefit from them. But to him that which
could alone have medicined his mental ills, was nothing less
than deadly poison to his body.

I might here offer the reader some pleasant reminiscences
connected with those evenings at the Southampton to which I
have incidentally referred above. But the theme is so tempting, that, if I were to enter upon it formally, it would lead me
too far from what I desire to keep before me as the chief object of attention. Besides which, Hazlitt himself has treated
of those evenings in so delightful a manner (in his paper on
" Coffee House Politicians," in vol. ii. of the " Table Talk")
that I may not venture to touch them after him. But there
are three or four individuals who used to form part of those
pleasant *symposii*, to whom the nature of these Recollections
calls upon me to refer more particularly than in a passing
paragraph. The most distinguished of these was the amiable
and gifted poet, so universally known to the reading world
under the name of Barry Cornwall. This gentleman used
but seldom to grace our simple feasts " of reason," or of
folly, as the case might be) ; but when he did look in by accident, or was induced by Hazlitt's request to come, everything went off the better for his presence ; for, besides the
fact of Hazlitt's being fond of his society, and, at the same
time, thinking so highly of his talents as always to talk his
best when he (Procter) was a partaker in the talk, there is an
endearing something in the personal manner of that exquisite
writer, an appearance of gentle and genial sympathy with the
feelings of those with whom he talks, which has the effect of

exciting towards him that *personal* interest from which it
seems itself to spring, and in the absence of which the better
feelings and mental characteristics incident to social converse
are seldom if ever called forth.   In Procter Hazlitt always
found a man of fine and delicate intellectual pretensions, who
was nevertheless eager and pleased to listen, with attention
and interest, to all the little insignificant details of his daily
life which so often made up the favorite theme of his conversation, and which must have seemed, to ordinary hearers,
the most utter and empty commonplace ; but from which
Hazlitt (when encouraged by the interest I have spoken of, or
not stilled into silence by its absence) used to extract materials
for constructing the most subtle and profound theories of the
human character, or themes for conveying the most deep-
thoughted wisdom, or the most pure and touching morality.
And, above all other themes, to Procter, and to him alone
(except myself) Hazlitt could venture to relate, in all their
endless details, those "affairs of the heart " in one of which
his *head* was always engaged, and which happily always (with
one fatal exception) evaporated in that interminable talk about
them of which he was so strangely fond.
    Not that Hazlitt confined his confidences on this head to
Procter and myself.   On the contray, he extended them to
almost every individual with whom he had occasion to speak,
if he could, by hook or by crook, find or make the occasion of
bringing in the topic.   But, in general, he did this from a sort
of physical incapacity to avoid the favorite yet dreaded theme
of his thoughts ; and he did it with a perfect knowledge that
his confidential communications were a *bore* to nine tenths of
those who listened to them, and consequently that the pleasure
of the communication was anything but mutual.   In fact, it must
be confessed that the details of Hazlitt's dreamy *amourettes*
had as little interest for anybody but the dreamer, as those of
any other dreams have.   But still they were *his* dreams, related
and expounded by his own subtle and profound intellect ; and,
for my own part, I must say that I never listened to his accounts of them without learning something new and worth

knowing of the human mind or heart, and often not without gaining glimpses and guesses into the most secret and sacred of their recesses, that I might have sought in vain elsewhere, or under any other circumstances whatever. I am therefore the less disposed to doubt, that the interest which Proctor seemed to take in the same study was not an assumed one, merely put on to please the humor of one who, in the particular now in question, was looked upon and often treated as a child, even by some of his most admiring friends. The truth is, that Hazlitt *was* a child in this matter; yet at the same time he was a metaphysician, a philosopher, and a poet: and hence the (in my mind) curious and unique interest which attached to his mingled details and dissertations on this the most favorite of all his themes of converse, at least in a *tête-à-tête;* for he rarely, if ever, brought up the subject under any other circumstances.

Another of Hazlitt's favorite companions at the Southampton was a Mr. Mouncey, of whom he has made such pleasant mention in the essay noticed above, on "Coffee House Politicians;" among which latter class, however, Mouncey was by no means included. Mouncey was (and is, I hope) a solicitor, of good practice, residing in a neighboring Inn of Court, who never failed, when in town, to escape at night from the grave vacuity and bustling nonentity of the law, to enjoy, in his own quiet little box at the Southampton, over his interminable *goes* of gin-and-water, the occasional converse that the chances of the evening might offer; and it was there that Hazlitt became acquainted with him, and their acquaintance never extended beyond the scene of its origination. Yet Hazlitt had a great respect and even personal regard for Mouncey, and always seemed to take pleasure in addressing and listening to him, which, however, he did invariably from the opposite side of the room, and, in nine cases out of ten, without the possibility of making out one half of what M. said, partly from the very low tone of voice in which he was accustomed to speak (as if addressing himself or his glass of gin-and-water), but chiefly on account of the hour of Hazlitt's arrival being usually late enough to have allowed the aforesaid *goes* to effect their desiderated end, of so blending together into a pleasing confusion the confines of dream-land and reality, that the happy borderer used to murmur inwardly precisely like a man who talks in his sleep.

For my own part, often as I have talked and listened to Mouncey with unmingled pleasure, I have no recollection of having clearly understood a single sentence that he ever uttered. . Yet when you did catch a glimpse of opinion or a glance of meaning, it was invariably of a nature to impress you with that personal respect for the speaker which is one of the rarest of all the results of desultory conversation — most of all, of coffee-house conversation. In fact, Mouncey was a singular example of that *rara avis* in the Inns of Court, a man of the purest simplicity and the strictest honesty of mind, directed by sterling good sense, and modified by those high sentiments of personal honor, and that humane and liberal consideration for the feelings of others, which constitute the better part of the true " gentleman."

Another of the circumstances which made the society of this person so agreeable to Hazlitt, was the fact of his having been formerly acquainted with the friends and associates of Hazlitt's early life — Southey, Wordsworth, and Coleridge, — his (M.'s) family having lived, and being then still living, I believe, in the neighborhood of the Cumberland lakes. The opportunity thus afforded Hazlitt of comparing notes, as it were, on the personal characters of those distinguished men, with one who had no *literary* prejudices either for or against them (for Mouncey made no pretensions to a literary taste), was what he had never met with elsewhere ; and he used it often and freely.

Another of the Southampton companions of Hazlitt, during my acquaintance with him, was a Mr. W——e, of the India House, a friend also of Charles Lamb's, and therefore associated by Hazlitt with some of his most pleasant recollections of that *coterie* the breaking up of which he so often regretted. W——e was (and I hope still is) a man of much shrewdness

of observation, and considerable delicacy of taste, in matters
both of literature and art; but so fastidious in his demands
for every sort of perfection, that Hazlitt looked upon an evening spent with him as a kind of discipline of his critical faculties and judgment. For W——e had no more respect for
an opinion or a dictum merely because it was Hazlitt's, than
if it had been anybody else's. If it struck him as just and
true, he at once admitted and appreciated it; but if not, he
contested it as freely and pertinaciously, coming from the first
critical authority of his day (as he believed and acknowledged
Hazlitt's to be — perchance with a modest mental reservation
in favor of *one* other person!) as if it came from a mere novice
or a nobody. And this habit of social intercourse, instead of
piquing Hazlitt, pleased and often excited him to an earnestness of discussion and illustration that we might else have
been without. Accordingly, I have never heard Hazlitt talk
better — by which I mean at once more amusingly and more
instructively — than when W——e formed one of the talkers
and listeners. W——e, too, had a taste (*of his own*, like all
his other tastes and opinions) for pictures — which often furnished occasion for the display of Hazlitt's exquisite judgment
in respect to the higher branches of art, and his profound insight into the principles on which their power of affecting us
rests. W——e's fastidiousness, too (for he was the " Man of
Refinement " of our little knot of talkers), was not seldom a
pleasant topic of examination in his absence; though it was
never treated of in terms that he himself might not have been
present to hear.

This latter fact reminds me to remark on what was deemed
by many of Hazlitt's friends a crying defect in his intellectual
character; I mean his disposition to discuss, in their absence,
the qualities and characteristics of his friends and acquaintance, with a freedom, and even severity, of criticism, which
were in no degree modified by the fact of the parties treated
of being numbered among his intimate associates. This complaint against Hazlitt was, I am afraid, founded on something
worse than a mistake. It was the result of a *self*-deception,

10

at the best; in some cases it originated in a desire meanly to deceive others. Those who call speaking the truth of our friends behind their backs an act of treachery, and consider the treating of their vices, errors, and weaknesses as if they were facts or abstract propositions, as a *traducing* of them, will not be likely to see anything worse in inventing or propagating falsehoods of them for our sport or profit. Hazlitt discussed the characters of his friends and acquaintance simply *as if* they were *not* his friends and acquaintance, and *because* they *were* so ; in other words, because they were the only persons whose characters he *could* discuss with any foundation of fact and truth to go upon. If we desire to know and to make known the human heart and mind, are we to study it only in the dark, and state what we learn of it only when everybody is out of hearing ? It is only our friends and acquaintance of whom we can by possibility know anything, of our own actual knowledge and observation : and

"What can we reason but from what we know?"

Hazlitt carried this open and free discussion of the moral and intellectual qualities and characteristics of our friends and intimates to a pitch that perhaps it never before reached : but I do not call to mind that he ever carried it beyond the legitimate bounds which it has a right to claim for itself. He used it purely as an instrument of mental exercise and entertainment ; he never sacrificed what he believed to be the truth in the use of it. Moreover, he used it in reference to friends and foes alike ; he used it as readily in favor of those to whom it referred as against them ; and he never expected or desired that anybody should feel any scruple in using it, to the utmost extent of the truth, about himself.

At all events, what nobody who knew Hazlitt will deny is, that of all the various sources of social converse that he was accustomed to open and draw upon, no other furnished so admirable a mixture of instruction and amusement as the one in question. Get him to talk upon these "personal themes," and his fund of facts and illustrations was only surpassed by the unequaled sagacity and acuteness with which he applied them.

A VISIT WITH HAZLITT TO JOHN HUNT.

There was one man, and one only, towards whom Hazlitt seemed to cherish a feeling of unmingled personal affection and regard : that man was the late Mr. John Hunt, the elder brother of Mr. Leigh Hunt. Of him only Hazlitt was accustomed to speak uniformly in terms of unqualified admiration and esteem, as related to his personal character, no less than to his sound judgment and singular good sense. He used to say that if there was an honest man in the world, it was John Hunt. Nor did I ever hear him speak disparagingly of him in even the smallest particular of either character or conduct, except on one occasion. "Look here," said he, as I went in one morning as he was sitting at his breakfast, reading a letter he had just received — "Look here ! " — handing me the letter, and pointing to the seal of it, on which was a showy crest or coat-of-arms — "what d'ye think of that from John Hunt — from the reviler of aristocratic distinctions — the sturdy democrat — the only honest leveler and republican of them all — and the only one among them all who would die a martyr to his opinions, if he could propagate them by doing so ? "

As some of my earliest and most vivid Recollections of Hazlitt are connected with this gentleman, I shall recur to them here.

The first evidence Hazlitt gave me of a disposition to cultivate my society — or rather to accept it — for he cultivated no one — his mind and genius were essentially contemplative, and disposed to that loneliness which contemplation asks — was his inviting me to accompany him one Sunday morning in a visit to Mr. John Hunt, who was then confined in the Coldbath Fields Prison, for a political libel which had appeared in the "Examiner" newspaper, of which the Hunts were the sole proprietors.[1] We went, and found Mr. Hunt

---

[1] I have given, in a previous section, some details respecting the conversation which took place on this visit, but no description of the visit itself.

walking in the garden of the prison ; and I shall not forget the impression his appearance and manner made on me — corresponding so precisely as they did with the previous notion I had entertained of his personal character. I have never seen in any one else so perfect an outward symbol or visible setting forth of the English character, in its most peculiar and distinguishing features, but also in its best and brightest aspect, as in Mr. John Hunt. A figure tall, robust, and perfectly well-formed ; a carriage commanding and even dignified, without the slightest apparent effort or consciousness of being so ; a head and a set of features on a large scale, but cast in a perfectly regular mould ; handsome, open, and full of intelligence, but somewhat · hard and severe ; an expression of bland benevolence, singularly blended with a marble coldness of demeanor almost repulsive, because almost seeming to be so intended : such were the impressions produced on me by the first *abord* of John Hunt, as I saw him within his prison walls.

As I afterwards ·became acquainted with Mr. John Hunt and his accomplished brother, and had all my first impressions confirmed about the former, I cannot let slip this occasion of testifying my belief, that the wholesome and happy change that has taken place in our political and social institutions since the. period above referred to, and is still in happy progress, is owing in no small degree to the excellent individuals just named ; for I verily believe that, without the manly firmness, the immaculate political honesty, and the vigorous good sense of the one, and the exquisite genius and varied accomplishments, guided by the all-pervading and all-embracing *humanity* of the other, we should at this moment have been without many of those writers and thinkers on whose unceasing efforts the slow but sure march of our political, and, with it, our social regeneration as a people mainly depends. Of this I am certain — that without the writings of Mr. Leigh Hunt himself, we should have missed a large measure of that high and pure tone of political and of social feeling from which everything is to be hoped in the way of progress.

towards future good; and (having which) nothing need be feared in the way of retrogression towards past evil. Many causes may interfere to retard the coming on of that fair pageant of political and social amelioration which already shines palpable and visible in the future, even like the coming on of the heavenly host in the "Paradise Lost." But there, in the "clear obscure" of the distance, the embodied splendor shines, and nothing can ever again abolish or blot it out.

Returning to my visit with Hazlitt to Mr. John Hunt, in the Coldbath Fields Prison, — after walking and conversing for some time in the prison garden, where we found Mr. Hunt, he led us to his apartment. Here the first thing that struck me was a picture over the mantelpiece, of an old country-woman in a bonnet, which, it immediately occurred to me, was one I had heard spoken of as Hazlitt's first attempt as an artist. Hazlitt pointed to it with great apparent satisfaction, and asked me if I had ever seen it before, or knew what it was; but he seemed to shrink from distinctly saying *what* it was, and I was left to learn this from inquiry of Mr. Hunt himself. The picture; I found, belonged to Hazlitt himself. He kept it as a precious relic, not of his success, but of his *failure*, as a painter — to which art he had at one time intended to devote himself. The reader will, probably, call to mind some beautiful reminiscences of this picture in his essay "On the Pleasures of Painting." The picture itself is a striking production, evincing remarkable powers of pictorial effect, and not inferior in the force of its light and shade to some of Rembrandt's efforts of a similar kind. I have never seen the picture since, and yet it is one of those very few which dwell in my memory, as if they were actually present to the bodily sight. It represented the head and shoulders merely of a very old country-woman, in a plain black bonnet, which shaded the upper half of the face, so as to leave the features almost black, and only to be distinguished by fixed attention; while the lower half of the face was in a full light. The expression (which was perfect in its way) was that of the utter stillness, and vacuity of extreme old age. The skin was

greatly elaborated, but so as to produce the general and uniform effect, and the oneness, of nature and of Rembrandt, not
of the dry and hard detail of Denner or Holbein. But the
peculiarity of the picture consisted in the extraordinary effect
of the light and shade. The handling by which this effect
was produced was coarse yet elaborate — bold and forcible,
yet perfectly undecided, and that of a novice. But the whole
was natural and true, in a remarkable degree, and it proved to
demonstration that if Hazlitt had devoted and applied himself
steadily to the art, he would greatly have distinguished himself in it. It proved, too, that he would have distinguished
himself in precisely that way in which the leading features of
his mind enabled him afterwards to shine as a writer — namely,
in the perception and setting forth of the actual and simple
truth, in relation to whatever he might take in hand ; but especially of the truth as to human character.

The extreme apparent diffidence of Hazlitt in pointing my
attention to this picture, reminds me to observe here, that it
was the same in respect to everything else that he did. He
had in his possession, at this time, two noble copies, made by
himself, from two of Titian's finest portraits in the Louvre —
the Young Venetian Nobleman with the Glove ; and the Hyp-
polito di Medici. They used to hang in or stand about his
rooms, without frames, and covered with dirt : and I had seen
and spoken of them several times, before I learned (which I
did by mere accident), that they were painted by himself. Not
that he underrated, or took a slight interest in them. On the
contrary, he made no scruple of declaring them to be the best
copies of Titian that he had ever seen ; and they were the
only things to which I ever knew him attach any value, or feel
the least desire to retain a property in. With the exception
of these pictures, he never, during the whole of my acquaintance with him, possessed a single object of *property* — not
even a favorite book. But these he cherished with a personal fondness that seemed to give them in his eyes all the
character of living objects ; they seemed necessary to his very
existence, and to preserve, as it were, that personal identity

with his early life, in the absence of which he would scarcely
have felt that he continued to live at all, at least, to any of the
real and valuable purposes of life. They were like *keepsakes*
given to him by those twin brides of his soul, the *Ideals* of
Truth and Beauty, which he had wedded in his youth, only to
love and worship for a day, and then to be widowed from forever, and weep over their grave for the rest of his existence.
For such was, in fact, the secret cause of that profound melancholy which hung upon Hazlitt's mind like an incubus, and
was the mortal disease that sunk him to a premature grave.

I afterwards possessed these two pictures, having purchased them at a sale of the property of Haydon, who valued
them, and had purchased them of Hazlitt, when the latter had
been forced, under some momentary pecuniary pressure, to
sell them.

I do not remember anything in my intercourse with Hazlitt
which gave me so much pleasure, as being thus enabled to
preserve and restore these pictures to him. He used every
now and then to come to me on purpose to look at them, as
he had done in the case of Haydon when they were in his
possession. I remember he would stand and gaze on them
with a look of deep sadness, not unmixed with pleasure, and
almost with tears in his eyes — as one may imagine a fond
parent gazing on the grave of his buried hopes — but he
never said anything about wishing to have them, otherwise I
should have offered them to him immediately. I, on the other
hand, never thought of offering them spontaneously, knowing
that, with all his frankness and delicacy in appreciating an act
of good-will of this kind, he would not have been able to
avoid attributing it in part to the want of my setting a due
value on the pictures. At last he came one day, and after
looking earnestly at the pictures for some time, he began, in
that roundabout, awkward, and hesitating way, which he always fell into when he was not quite sure of his ground : —

" I say, Patmore, do you care about those pictures ? "

. " How do you mean ? " said I, though I anticipated what was
coming.

"Why — I mean" — said he, hesitatingly — "that is — would you like to part with them?"

"Part with them?" I said, repeating his words, and not knowing very well how to reply without the risk of hurting his self-love one way or the other — and there is nothing like awkwardness for engendering its like — "Part with them? Why, I " — and I hesitated about coming to the point as much as he did.

"Aye," — continued he — "that is, not unless you like — only I " — (and here he seemed to get farther than ever from the mark) "I — that is, I think I can get you a good sum for them if you 've a mind to part with them."

"If *that 's* what you mean," I said, "I have *not* a mind to part with them. I thought, perhaps, you wanted them for yourself."

"Why, that 's it," said he. "The fact is, so and so (naming some one whom I now forget), has been speaking to me about them. He 'll give you forty or fifty pounds down for them, I think; and will let me have them back again when I like. What do you say?"

I said, "I 'll not *sell* them — if that 's what you mean — but *you* may have them if you like."

"Well," said he, "what shall I give you for them?"

"Nonsense!" I replied; "nothing — or anything you like" — for I did not like to press his acceptance of them after he had told me what he thought of doing with them.

"Well — shall I give you ten pounds for them 'out and out,' on the chance of getting fifty?"

"Yes — if you like."

"But I 've got no money."

"Well — give it me when you like."

"No — I 'll give you a bill at two months (I think it was). I shall have money then."

I could hardly help smiling at · this proposal; but I did not dare to do so, as he was very sensitive on points of this kind.

"But may I take them with me now?" he asked, hesitatingly — "I 'll bring you the bill by and by."

"To be sure," I said, fairly smiling out at the idea of the bill, but not venturing to refuse it.

Accordingly, he took away his two favorites under his arm·; evidently delighted to have them once again in his possession; for he had more regard for them than for all his writings put together.

The next day he brought me a promissory note duly drawn — and which of course was *not* duly paid. That it was paid ultimately, I need not say. Had it been otherwise, the reader would have heard nothing of the details, at least, of this little story. About seven or eight months afterwards, when I had almost forgotten the bill he had given me, he called on me, and, holding out a ten-pound note, said, "Have you got that bill?" and ·I believe he never parted with a bank-note so readily as he did on this occasion.

Returning for a moment to our visit to John Hunt, in Cold-bath Fields Prison, I remember, as if it had happened but yesterday, the precise spot on which we met him in the prison garden; the dreary and prison-like look of the garden itself, without a tree or a shrub in it; with nothing alive but long rows of sickly cabbages and lettuces, that seemed to be pining for the free air that passed hundreds of feet above their heads — an "unreal mockery" of a garden — that seemed, to a true garden, what the melancholy "liberty" of walking in it was to liberty itself. I remember, too, the extreme cleanliness of the narrow and interminable passages through which we passed to the prisoner's cell, and that it struck me as something shocking — like the unnatural tameness of the birds and animals in the island of Juan Fernandez — a species of refinement in cruelty. The cell itself, too, I see before me as I write — with its lofty ceiling, which made the area look twice as small as it really was; its square iron-barred window, on the right-hand wall as you entered, raised out of the reach of any access either from within or without; the little blank fire-place opposite to the door; and the no-furniture, consisting of a table and two chairs. Being an optimist, I have often thought since that the statesmen of that day were the people

of all others to inculcate the blessings and the love of political liberty. To imprison for two years in a place like this one
of the most honest, honorable, and pûre-minded men that
ever lived, for expressing a political opinion that *they* did not
approve, was a pretty sure way of making him a patriot and
an advocate of freedom, if he had not been so before. There
is nothing like Evil for teaching the value and the virtue of
Good — nothing like Wrong for demonstrating and confirming
Right.

OPINIONS AND CRITICAL ESTIMATES.

It often used to occasion me no less surprise than regret to
find that Hazlitt did not duly appreciate the genius and writings of Mr. Leigh Hunt ; or rather let me confine the remark
to Mr. Hunt's *writings* for his genius and talents were not
underrated by Hazlitt. That their results were sometimes
disparaged, or their merits overlooked, is to be attributed to
various causes, arising out of the personal character of the
two men, and their intimacy with each other. If Hazlitt had
not been in habits of personal intercourse with Hunt, he would
have estimated his literary efforts justly. But, with Hazlitt,
"to know a man truly, was to know *himself*," and therefore
not to know that which is but an offset and emanation from
him. Probably no man ever formed a just critical estimate of
the writings of his personal intimate. It is scarcely possible
to do so even of one's contemporary, though he may be personally unknown to us. There never was a more just and enlightened critical spirit abroad than that which prevails in the
present day. Yet not one of our estimates of contemporary
genius will be exactly confirmed by posterity — which is the
only final and infallible judge in such matters. But for a man
to estimate the literary character of his personal intimate, or
his personal enemy, is not in human nature. He might almost
as reasonably hope to estimate his own. And yet we are apt
to think we know more about our friends — not to mention
ourselves — than strangers can possibly do. And so, perhaps,
we do. We know too much, and therefore do not know any

part accurately, still less the whole — which, to be seen and measured justly, must be seen at a certain distance, and *as* a whole.

Hazlitt saw in Mr. Leigh Hunt's writings — and saw with an almost preternatural acuteness of vision — what we have no right to see at all, and what none but his personal intimates do or can see — the secret workings and results of those personal feelings (call them failings if you please — their owner is too wise as well as too liberal in his self-knowledge to be offended at the phrase) which more or less beset and modify the mental operations of every deep and original thinker, and still more of one (as in the instance before us) whose personal feelings blend with and give color to all his meditations.

At a very early period of Mr. Leigh Hunt's literary career, his remarkable social qualities had gathered round him a *coterie* of that class of admirers who are too apt to take the form of adulators, and who, in this latter phase of their character, are not merely inclined, but impelled, to overlook the loftier qualities and attributes of their idol, in order to monster his smaller merits, or metamorphose his errors and short-comings into beauties and virtues.

The consequence for a time was, that the young and happily-constituted writer

> " To *persons* gave up what was meant for mankind ; "

never wholly deserting or misusing his high calling, but not seldom postponing its duties to the delights of social success and individual admiration ; confiding (as every man of genius is impelled and bound to do) in his own judgment and his own consciousness, as to the uses and applications of those fine qualities and capacities of his mind which his adulators failed to see or to comprehend ; but believing in and abiding by *them* in all the rest.[1]

This state of things — a happy one perhaps for him whom they touched most nearly, but a sad one for those who already

---

[1] I gather these details and impressions from Hazlitt. I had not the pleasure of Mr. Leigh Hunt's acquaintance at the time referred to.

looked to him for the due exercise of his high and rare powers
of affording mingled instruction and delight to his fellow-creatures — has long since given place to one more consonant to
the nature and tendency of those powers, and their just claims .
to the distinctions which they confer on their possessor ; and
I•only recur to it now to account for the insufficient impression
which Hazlitt entertained of the writings of Mr. Hunt, and
their future influence on the moral and intellectual character
of the age.   Hazlitt saw and grieved at the state of things I
have described ; then grew vexed and angry at it (these latter feelings being not wholly unmixed, I am afraid, with a
touch of personal envy at the "earthlier happy" condition of
his friend as compared with his own); till at last his personal
feelings blended and interfered with all his impressions respecting the writings of his friend and fellow-laborer, and
gave to his judgment that sinister bias which it was so apt to
take, or rather so incapable of escaping, on all questions of
contemporary merit and distinction.

It is true that Hazlitt has in numerous instances, and in
various quarters, used the influence of his pen and his critical powers to disseminate opinions, just, as far as they go,
respecting the literary pretensions of this delightful and accomplished writer.   He, perhaps, did more for Mr. Hunt's
reputation in this respect than any other writer of his day.
But, besides having done this more as a set-off against the
gratuitous calumnies of his enemies and maligners than as a
spontaneous tribute to the merits of the man, he has fallen
miserably short, as I conceive, of conveying a clear and full
impression of Mr. Hunt's intellectual pretensions, and still
more so in estimating the actual, and anticipating the future,
results of those pretensions upon the social character and condition of this country.

But it will, I fear, be felt that I am transgressing the true
limits of my design.   Returning to more purely personal
matters, I may say, that though Hazlitt took great pleasure in
Mr. Hunt's society, it was not the kind of social intercourse he
best liked.   It was one in which each party sought to shine

in the eyes of each other, or of the persons present, if any. And though this desire is perhaps more successful in producing the power and the result it aims at than any other means, yet to *shine* in conversation is not to *enjoy* it ; to talk brilliantly, or to hear brilliant talk, is not to talk or to listen with the heart ; it includes and supposes none of that effusion of individual feeling, and that exercise and interchange of human sympathy — none of that "flow of soul" in the absence of which, talk (be it even that of the brightest wits and choicest spirits of the time) is but "as a tinkling cymbal," or as the tittle-tattle of club-compelled exquisites and tea-drinking Abigails.

How delightful is the kind of talk I have alluded to ! It is, of all intellectual enjoyments, at once the most perfect and the most ennobling ; because it is of all others the least impaired by those debasing contradictions and weaknesses which blend more or less with all our pleasures — even with this — and cloud their brightness, while they weaken their force and fullness. This welling forth of the springs of affection and of passion in the human heart has always seemed to me precisely analogous to the singing of birds ; a spontaneous and involuntary effusion from the hidden and mysterious sources of delight ; rising in beauty and in melody with the character of its utterer, from the poor twittering of the sparrow on the housetop, to the intense and passionate warbling of the nightingale in the deep recesses·of a solemn wood at midnight ; but in each case created, called forth, and modified by something external from its source ; sinking into and growing out of that, as the waves in water, or the sounds of a wind-swept lute ; and in no case to be thoroughly enjoyed except (as with the birds) between co-mates in kindness and in love. When the nightingale, in the antique story, sought to rival the music of the human minstrel, she put forth miracles of bright sounds, but her heart burst in the unnatural struggle. And thus it is with us "human mortals." One man may rouse and stir an assembled nation by his eloquence ; another may teach a great multitude by his knowledge ; a third may " keep the table in

a roar " by his wit ; a fourth may lap his hearers in Elysium
by his fancy or imagination ; and so forth. But there is no
real enjoyment of talk except in a *tête-à-tête* between friends
or lovers ; no free pouring forth of the feelings and affections
that make up our intellectual being, except where there exists
· that frank interchange of sympathy which prompts us to listen.
with as eager an interest as we feel in speaking, and which at
the same time satisfies us that *we*, in our turn, are listened to
with a corresponding pleasure.

If there was any general subject on which the critical opinions of Hazlitt were to be distrusted, it was that of the merits
and defects of his distinguished contemporaries in literature
and art. In fact, most of what he had to say on these topics
was so moulded and modified by the personal feelings and prejudices engendered by his early associations, and by the position in which those placed him in reference to the rest of the
world, that they scarcely deserve the name of *deliberate* opinions. During the latter years of his life Hazlitt labored
under a total incapacity of reading any work, however brief,
consecutively and completely. He had spent, he used to say,
the first half of his life in doing nothing but read ; and it was
hard if he might not employ the remainder in turning his reading to account. He used to say, too, that after he began to
write, reading became a task instead of an enjoyment ; and
he never pretended to do anything voluntarily but what it
pleased him to do.   .

This was all very well for a man of leisure, and competence
to afford that leisure ; but it was an awkward propensity for
one to indulge in who undertook to review the writings of
those who did not begin to write till their reviewer had left off
reading.

I do not believe Hazlitt ever read the half of any one work
that he reviewed — not even the Scotch novels, of which he
read more than of any other modern productions, and has
written better, perhaps, than any other of their critics. I am
certain that of many works that he has reviewed, and of many
writers whose general pretensions he has estimated better

than anybody else has done, he never read one tithe; and
even what he did read was not the most characteristic portion,
or that best calculated to afford ground for a fortunate guess.
No wonder then that his " Spirit of the Age " should be dis-
figured by such a copious mixture of false criticism and personal prejudice. But then, on the other hand, where else is
to be found, in the same space and on a similar subject, such
an amount of happy illustration, sound criticism, and searching truth.

The fact is that Hazlitt's half-random guesses, founded on
a furtive and momentary glance, went nearer to the pith of
the matter in question, whatever it might be, than the elaborate and lengthened examinations of ordinary men. And
in this respect there was a remarkable conformity between his
mental and his bodily perceptions. He never fairly *looked* at
anybody ; and yet, having once seen a person, he not only
never forgot him afterwards, but could describe him to others with all the effect of an actual picture, and could trace
" the mind's observance in the face," with a sagacity almost
superhuman. I never knew him mistaken even in his physiognomical *guesses*, much less in his deliberate estimates, —
on which, by the bye, if on anything, he especially piqued
himself. " I am infallible (I have heard him say), in reading
a face."

The only one among his contemporaries with whose writings Hazlitt was really acquainted was Sir Walter Scott ; and
for him he felt a degree of admiration as a writer, that, so far
from being equaled, was scarcely shared, even in kind, by
that called forth in the case of any other writer of the present
or the last age. Indeed, Scott only needed to have been born
a hundred years ago to have held, in Hazlitt's estimation, a
rank second only to that of Shakespeare ; for in that case he
would not have been compelled to mix up with his feelings of
love and admiration those counteracting ones arising out of
Scott's politics, and their results upon his position in society.
He would only then have seen in him what the world will see
a hundred years hence — a Shakespeare in the universality of

his sympathies with human nature and human life, though not in the profounder points of his poetry and his philosophy. As it was, Hazlitt saw what there was for love and admiration, but he saw it in the pet of the Tories, the patron of " Blackwood's " and the "Beacon," the upholder of the divine right of kings, the disparaging biographer of Napoleon, and ("though last, not least in his dear *hate* ") the Scotchman.

There was something singularly interesting, and even affecting, in the perpetual struggle which took place in Hazlitt's mind on the subject of this great man — who was now scarcely below a divinity, and the next hour almost a shame and a blot upon humanity, according to the view from which he was contemplated ; now drawing all human hearts together in one bond of mutual sympathy — now trampling upon the best feelings and affections of them all for the imaginary benefit and aggrandizement of one, or half a dozen ! — squandering the "birthright " of the human race for the miserable " mess of pottage " that was to keep alive for a little longer the bedridden dotage of "divine right " and " legitimate " authority !

True it is that Scott did not

" To party give up what was meant for mankind ; "

he did but give up the tithe to his party, devoting the great body of the harvest of his intellect to the instruction, delight, and benefit of the whole human race ; nay, putting forth as beautiful and subtle an effort of his genius to vindicate the right of a poor fish-wife to enjoy her dram as ever he did to make good the title of a legitimate monarch to his throne. Yet Hazlitt hated him for reserving that tithe almost as much as if he had bestowed the whole. But he did this on the principle, that a single ill word from a wise and good man does more to injure a character or a cause, than a whole volume from the pen or the lips of a knave.

With the exception of those living writers, and, indeed, of those particular passages in their works which touched him privately and individually, Hazlitt scarcely ever referred to a contemporary work unless as a matter of business, or opened

its pages except as a task ; and of no one of those writers, except Scott, had he (as I have said), read a tithe of their productions. Yet he has written elaborate critical estimates of
about twenty of the most distinguished, in his " Spirit of the
Age." And if you take those estimates only for what they
are worth, and with that degree of qualification with which *all*
his critical writings must be taken, it will be found that they
are, at the very least, as complete and satisfactory as any
others that are to be met with elsewhere, touching the same
writers.

But the truth is, that in no case whatever could Hazlitt's
estimates of *persons* be taken implicitly ; because it was impossible for him to prevent — and he never for a moment
tried to prevent — his own intense personal feelings from
blending with and giving a color to such estimates. And of
living persons — of those who came, as it were, into hourly
intellectual contact with him, by breathing the same air and
treading on the same earth — he could not even form, much
less set forth, a fair and unbiased opinion. What I have to
say, therefore, as to his personal opinions of his contemporaries is offered purely for what it is worth, and as illustrative of
his own personal character, not of theirs — as a thing curious
and interesting to know, but not to be brought against the
reputations to which it refers, as a set-off from the just award
they had received at the hands of the most enlightened public
opinion that any age has boasted within the compass of human annals — at least in literary matters.

Having, in justice to others no less than to Hazlitt himself,
premised thus much, I shall state a few of his personal opinions, or rather feelings, about the most conspicuous among his
contemporaries, whether personal acquaintances of his own or
not ; and this without inquiring how far those opinions may
agree with or differ from his published ones on the same subject respectively.

Hazlitt looked upon Lord Byron as — a lord ! — a clever
and accomplished one — but nothing more. He considered
that Byron occupied the throne of poetry by the same sort of

11

"divine right" by which "legitimate" kings occupy *their* thrones. His poetry he regarded, for the most part, as a sort of exaggerated commonplace — the result of a mixture of personal anger and egotism, powerful and effective only from the excess of *passion* it embodied — of passion in the vulgar sense of that word. He was "in a passion" with himself, and with everything, and everybody about him; and being under no personal or moral restraints of any kind, the exhibition of this emotion became sufficiently striking and interesting to amount to the poetical.

I remember having occasionally played at whist with a person who, on any occurrence of extraordinary ill-luck, used to lay his cards down deliberately, and bite a piece out of the back of his hand! This person was, under ordinary circumstances, the very ideal of a "gentleman" — bland, polished, courteous, forbearing, kind, and self-possessed to an extraordinary degree; and his personal appearance in every respect corresponded with his manners and bearing; so that the occasional exhibitions of passion that I have alluded to were perfectly awful. Hazlitt's own passions sometimes produced similar results. I have seen him more than once, at the Fives Court in St. Martin's Street, on making a bad stroke or missing his ball at some critical point of the game, fling his racket to the other end of the court, walk deliberately to the centre, with uplifted hands imprecate the most fearful curses on his head for his stupidity, and then rush to the side wall and literally dash his head against it! The sight in both these cases was terrific; but, then, *anybody could have produced it* by using the same bodily action.

Now, Hazlitt seemed to think that Lord Byron's poetry was something on a par with these merely physical exhibitions of bodily passion. He was in one habitual passion — with his poverty, with his lameness, with his loss of caste in society, and, above all, with the "Edinburgh Review," for having told him the truth about his boyish verses; and, accordingly, his whole life and conversation were one continuous "unpacking of his heart with words," for want of daring or being able to use sharper weapons against himself and his fellow-beings. *Anybody might have written his poetry* (so Hazlitt thought and said) if they could only have worked themselves up to an equal amount of personal rage and hatred against himself and all mankind.

Such was Hazlitt's general opinion of Byron ; and there is no denying that it is true of a certain part of his poetry — of the bad part of it — in other words, of that part which is not poetry at all ; of the blasphemy, the profligacy, the indecency, the utter and elaborate wickedness, the "malice prepense" against all the human race, — all of which are so painfully conspicuous in almost every part of that shame and scandal of the age — "Don ,Juan." And it is not very far from the truth of much of that portion of his works which embody (however blended with other things) his own individual character. But it is scarcely needful to say how utterly false and unfair it is when applied to his poetry as a general proposition — how ridiculously inapplicable it is to the lofty grandeur and severe beauty of his tragedies (hitherto wholly unappreciated) ; to the profound and subtle philosophy, and the burning passion (using the word in its poetical sense), of the " Manfred ; " to the sublime imaginations and beatific visions of many parts of the supernatural Dramas ; to the unequaled descriptions and imagery of the " Childe Harold ; " to the soul-melting pathos and perfect purity of the " Stanzas to Thirza," the "Dream," etc. It is in virtue of these, and in spite of the mere personal egotism and vulgar malice of much of his writings, that Byron enjoys and deserves his high reputation, and will continue to enjoy it while Milton and Shakespeare maintain theirs.

To the powers of Shelley, and to their poetical results, Hazlitt did as little justice as to those of Byron. And in this instance I could never very clearly account to myself for the personal cause of his dislike, — which in every other similar instance there was no difficulty in doing. Scott was a Tory ; Byron was a lord ; and it will be seen hereafter, that in the various other cases in which he withheld the due meed of

honor from his distinguished contemporaries, there was some
personal feeling or other capable of explaining, if not of excusing, the injustice. But in the case of Shelley, I could
never make out any better reason than that *he had seen him
and did not like his looks !*

> " I do not like thee, Doctor Fell,
> The reason why I cannot tell ;
> I do not like thee, Doctor Fell."

This was a favorite mode with Hazlitt of forming his personal opinions ; and one which, in his case, was not a very
dangerous one, on account of his intuitive skill in reading
"the mind's observance in the face." But there can be no
doubt that in this instance he grossly and strangely deceived
himself. If ever any human being was gifted with " the vision and the faculty *divine*," Shelley was so gifted. Yet all that
Hazlitt chose to see in him were certain supposed corollaries
from his personal appearance and physical conformation. Shelley's figure was tall and almost unnaturally attenuated, so as
to bend to the earth like a plant that has been deprived of its
vital air ; his features had an unnatural sharpness, and an un-
healthy paleness, like a flower that has been kept from the
light of day ; his eyes had an almost superhuman brightness,
and his voice a preternatural elevation of pitch and a shrillness
of tone ; all which peculiarities probably arose from some
accidental circumstances connected with his early nurture and
bringing up.[1] But all these Hazlitt tortured into external
types and symbols of that unnatural and unwholesome craving
after injurious excitement, that morbid tendency towards interdicted topics and questions of moral good and evil, and
that forbidden search into the secrets of our nature and ultimate destiny, into which he strangely and inconsequentially
resolved the whole of Shelley's productions. His vast and
vivid insight into the possible future, as springing out of and
moulded by the present and the past ; his gorgeous and glow-
ing imagination ; his universal philanthrophy — the patriotism
of one whose all-embracing spirit could know no country but

---

[1] This description is Hazlitt's, not mine: I never saw Shelley.

the world ; his daring yet devout faith in good, as the necessary offspring and end of evil ; his intense sympathy with all
natural beauty, as the living type, the visible image, of that
which is intellectual ; his wonderful affluence and pomp of
language, — altogether unrivaled by any other writer, ancient
or modern : all these Hazlitt seemed to overlook in Shelley.
There is but one intelligible explanation of this ; and it is
that, in fact, Hazlitt had *read* little or nothing of all the various
poetical wealth to which I have referred. And such I believe
to have been the case ; for though I have often heard him speak
disparagingly of Shelley as a poet, I never heard him refer to a
single line or passage of his published writings.

For Hazlitt's dislike and disparagement of the author of
" Lalla Rookh," there is not much difficulty in accounting.
He (Moore) was understood to have discouraged, and ultimately broken off, Lord Byron's connection with Leigh Hunt
and Hazlitt in " The Liberal ; " an undertaking which, had it
been cordially taken up by Byron and his friends, might, Hazlitt thought, have produced great results. Hazlitt attributed
the strangling in its birth of this promising offspring of the
new " Spirit of the Age " to the personal envy, and consequent
ill-offices, of Moore — and he never forgave him — though
more, I believe, from a public than a private and personal feeling on the matter.

But what Hazlitt could forgive less was an insulting reference which Moore has made (in his " Rhymes on the Road ")
to one of Hazlitt's intellectual idols, Rousseau, who, with the
heroine of the " Confessions," Madame de Warens, he (Moore)
calls " low people." Referring to *" Les Charmettes,"* he says
of its former celebrated inhabitants, —

> " And doubtless 'mong the grave and good,
> And gentle [1] of their neighborhood,
> If known at all, they were but known
> As strange, low people, low and bad,
> Madame herself to footmen prone,
> And her young *pauper* all but mad."

[1] Meaning well-born.

This outrage upon Hazlitt's early associations was more than he could bear. It drove him "all but mad ;" and he never after lost an opportunity, public or private, of venting his indignation against the perpetrator of it. Nor would it be easy to repel the cannonade of argument and invective by which he sought to demonstrate that it *was* an outrage, no less against fact and justice than against feeling and common honesty.[1]

I must not refrain from adding my belief, that Hazlitt's indignation, though not engendered, was in some degree heightened, by his Rousseau-like suspicion that the poet's sneer at Rousseau *was partly intended to point at himself*—a suspicion not wholly without plausible grounds at the time, considering that he was convinced (whether justly or not I have no means of knowing) that his (Hazlitt's) connection with "The Liberal" had just been dissolved by the remonstrances of Moore, *on the very grounds urged against Rousseau,* namely, that it was "discreditable" to his "noble" friend to have to do with people who were so "poor" as to make the connection desirable to them in a pecuniary point of view ; so "low" as to lodge in a second floor; and so "bad" as to have been seen speaking to "improper" females by the light of the gas-lamps.

It is very painful to me to put on record the personal opinions and feelings of Hazlitt respecting his early friends and associates, Coleridge, Southey, and Wordsworth, particularly the two latter, men from whose writings I have received more delight and instruction than from those of any other two living men, or indeed from all others united, Hazlitt alone excepted ; men also for whose personal characters I have ever cherished a degree of respect amounting to reverence. But I must not shrink from my purpose, nevertheless. And I need not fear that its execution will in the smallest degree affect either the literary or the personal estimation of the distinguished men to whom it refers, even in the eyes of those who are disposed to treat Hazlitt's decisions as oracles ; because the reasons for the disparaging opinions I am about to record of them will ac-

[1] Particularly in his Essay in the *Plain Speaker* on "The Spleen of Party."

company and explain those opinions, and throw the odium of
them (if any there be) where it really ought to rest.

But my task is not the less painful on this account, but
rather the more so, since its faithful execution must necessarily expose the miserable weaknesses and errors of a man of
whose intellectual powers I thought no less highly than I do
of the men they were employed to disparage, and with a view
to the redemption of whose personal character from the un-
merited odium which has been heaped upon it, these pages
have partly if not chiefly been written.

The truth is that, in the case of Coleridge, Southey, and
Wordsworth alone, Hazlitt seemed to have willfully repudi-
ated that guiding and pervading spirit of his personal character, the love of truth and justice for themselves alone. And
what made the matter in appearance worse was, that he had
seemed to do this from a personal feeling alone ; so, at least,
the case was represented by those who made it part of the
business of their lives to *mis*represent the motives, feelings,
and actions of this much-maligned and ill-appreciated man.
Many extravagant and ridiculous stories were related, or
rather whispered about vaguely, all of them more or less discreditable to the personal character of Hazlitt, as the *immediate* cause of his alienation from the distinguished friends of
his early life : and in the most discreditable of them all there
was, I have been led to believe, some truth. I allude to a
story relating to Hazlitt's alleged treatment of some pretty
village jilt, who, when he was on a visit to Wordsworth, had
led him (Hazlitt) to believe that she was not insensible to his
attentions ; and then, having induced him to "commit" himself to her in some ridiculous manner, turned round upon him,
and made him the laughing-stock of the village. There is, I
believe, too much truth in the statement of his enemies, that
the mingled disappointment and rage of Hazlitt on this occasion led him, during the madness of the moment (for it must
have been nothing less), to acts · which nothing but the supposition of insanity could account for, much less excuse. And
his conduct on this occasion is understood to have been the

immediate cause of that breach between him and his friends above-named (at least Wordsworth and Southey), which was never afterwards healed.

But I am bound to declare that their treatment of him on this occasion was *not* the cause of his subsequent feelings towards these distinguished men, or of his treatment of them as arising out of those feelings. It was not the petty anger arising out of a sense of some trifling personal injustice (even if he entertained any such feeling, which he scarcely could in the case in question), that could make Hazlitt either blindly insensible to the claims of such men as Wordsworth and Southey, or willfully unjust to those claims, whether personal or intellectual.

But there was *one* offense — call it a crime — for such it was in his estimation — which could make him both blindly insensible and almost deliberately unjust to the claims, whatever they might be, of those whom he deemed guilty of it. He felt an almost boundless sympathy with the weaknesses of our nature, and an equally unlimited toleration for almost all their natural results. But there was one of those results for which, believing it to be in some *un*natural, he entertained a hatred that can scarcely be conceived by those who have not been accustomed to witness and watch the consequences of violent passions, when habituated from earliest youth to work their own will, without a touch of restraint or self-assistance. Against the man who could steal from his fellow-man to preserve his own life, or even to gratify his passing desires, Hazlitt could feel little, if any, of that anger and resentment which honest men are expected, and for the most part accustomed, to look upon almost as one of their social duties. But against the man who could deliberately set himself to assist in robbing THE HUMAN RACE of its birthright, merely in consideration of the "mess of pottage" that *he* was to get for his pains — against the individual who could (reversing the deed of the immortal Roman), plunge his country into the gulf to preserve or benefit himself — in a word, against the political apostate, Hazlitt cherished a hatred so bitter and intense, that it blended with the very springs of his life, and colored every movement and affection of his mind. And such men he considered Coleridge, Southey, and Wordsworth to have been, when they deserted the principles of the French Revolution, and set themselves, heart and soul, to oppose its " child and champion," Napoleon Bonaparte. But when they showed themselves (as the two former did in an especial manner) the most powerful, persevering, and effective of all the literary opponents of that idol of Hazlitt's hopes and admiration, his anger and resentment against them amounted to a degree of rage, that made him reckless of all justice, and of all consequences — a fanaticism of hatred, which can only be compared to, and has, perhaps, only been paralleled by, that *odium theologicum* which has at intervals desolated the nations with flame and bloodshed, in behalf of a religion of peace.

In Coleridge, — on whom, from the very dawning of his intellectual faculties, Hazlitt had been accustomed to look almost as the heaven-appointed apostle of human liberty, sent forth to preach its doctrines and promulgate its beauties and virtues in words of more than mortal eloquence, — he suddenly beheld the Pitt-appointed editor of the " Morning Post ' newspaper — the writer of daily diatribes, which not merely advocated and advised, but at last actually caused and created,[1] that Tory crusade against freedom which ultimately consigned it to twenty years more of outrage and violence, and ended by debauching and debasing its noblest champion into its deadliest foe.

This was bad enough for Hazlitt ; though the peculiar character of Coleridge's intellect, and the " transcendental " changes to which it was liable, might have prepared him for the possibility at least of something of this kind, — especially when it is borne in mind that Coleridge had already aban-

---

[1] Such, at least, was the deliberate opinion of one of the greatest statesmen of his day, Charles Fox, who declared in his place in the House of Commons, that the war against France had been caused by the *Morning Post* — the dictum being exclusively directed to Coleridge's writings there

doned (on a point of conscience), the profession to which he
had been bred — the church — and had no means but his pen
of escaping from absolute destitution.   But when Hazlitt saw
the severe, the single-hearted, the simple-minded Southey — a
man whose almost ascetic habits preserved him from the possibility of want, and, on the other hand, whose varied and
available talents and acquirements, and his singular industry,
gave him the certain means of satisfying wants tenfold beyond
any that he could even comprehend as such — when he saw
this man suddenly, from the minstrel of Joan of Arc and the
immortalizer of Wat Tyler, emerge into the most fertile, the
most ingenious, the most persevering, and the most efficient of
all the literary supporters, advocates, and apologists (as the
case might be), of those recognized abuses on which corrupt
power at that time rested its sole hope of continuance and
perpetuation ; in short, when he beheld, in the late fanatic to
liberty, the furious denouncer of Reformers as " worse than
housebreakers," — when he saw the late scorner of all kings,
and despiser and maligner of courts, changed into the special-
pleading advocate of divine right and legitimacy, the bower-
down at levees, and the poet-laureate and panegyrist of George
the Fourth, it half unseated his reason, and rendered him, on
these topics, scarcely accountable for what he wrote or said.
     But it must be especially stated, that even under these cir-
cumstances, and inflamed as he was against Southey with a
feeling of something like personal revenge, for his desertion
of a cause, for *his* (Hazlitt's) consistent devotion to which he
was suffering a daily martyrdom of mingled obloquy and privation, he never once, to the best of my recollection, either in
print or otherwise, treated Southey as a dishonest man, but
only as a weak, a vain, a self-willed, and a mistaken one.   He
sometimes wrote and oftener spoke of Southey with a degree
of contempt and disparagement that amounted to the ridiculous, when compared with his great natural powers, his noble
acquirements, and the vast literary results which have proceeded from them.   But if pressed (though not otherwise, I
confess), he admitted a saving clause in favor of his sincerity

and love of truth. Whereas, in the case of Coleridge, his feelings carried him to the opposite extreme ; for while he ex- aggerated his estimate of the intellectual powers of that ex- traordinary man to an almost superhuman pitch, he treated the chief public uses which he made of those powers as the results of the most shameless hypocrisy and the most despic- able cant.

With respect to Wordsworth, Hazlitt's estimate of him, both as a writer and a man, was much nearer to the truth than in either of the other two cases ; for the worst that Words- worth had done in the way of political apostasy was, to accept an obligation from a party he despised, and thus cut himself off from the will as well as the power to use his pen against them. He never used it *for* that party ; nor did Hazlitt ac- cuse him of having ever gone a single step from the pure, even, and dignified tenor of his way, either to gain or to keep the good that he chose to accept from evil hands. On the contrary, the worst that Hazlitt had to say of Wordsworth was, that he was a poet and nothing more ; meaning thereby that he was incapable of taking any personal interest in the actual wants, desires, enjoyments, sufferings, and sentiments of his fellow-men ; and that, so long as he could be permitted to wander in peace and personal comfort among his favorite scenes of external nature, and chant his lyrical ballads to an admiring friend, and make his lonely excursions into the mys- tic realms of imagination, and enjoy unmolested the moods of his own mind, the human race and its rights and interests might lie bound forever to the footstools of kings, or be half- exterminated in seeking to escape thence, for anything that he cared, or any step that he would take to the contrary, — unless it were to write an ode or a sonnet on the question, and keep it in his desk till the point had settled itself. In short, Hazlitt seemed to look upon Wordsworth as a man purged and ethe- realized, by his mental constitution and habits, from all the every-day interests and sentiments with which ordinary men regard their fellow-*men*, and incognizant of any claims upon his human nature but such as have reference to *man* in the abstract ; and that, while he could secure leisure to dream and dogmatize and poetize on this latter theme, the living world and its ways were matters wholly beneath his notice.

The pertinacity with which Hazlitt used to insist on this pretended *selfism* of Wordsworth — this alleged repudiation, and even hatred, of interests and sympathies external from those engendered by his own contemplation of his own mind, — and the malicious pleasure with which he used to dwell on and recur to anecdotes which he deemed illustrative of this characteristic, were very remarkable. One anecdote, in particular, I remember to have heard him repeat many times, and always with a feeling of bitterness and *acharnèment* which was evidently the result of a strong and cherished personal dislike. It merely related to some disparaging observation which Wordsworth was said to have made (for Hazlitt did not pretend to have heard it himself — so that the whole story was probably a fabrication or a blunder of the relator) on somebody's admiring and pointing Wordsworth's attention to a cast from some beautiful Greek statue in Haydon's painting-room ; the ridiculous and wholly gratuitous inference being, that Wordsworth hated to look on anything beautiful or admirable that did not bear the impress of his own mind, and that he desired everybody else should do the same ; in short, that he hated everything in the world but his own poetry, and that he never enjoyed a moment of personal satisfaction but when he was (as Hazlitt used disparagingly to phrase it), " mouthing it out " to the gaping ears of ignorant worshipers, and fancying that all the human race would soon be doing the same.

It may seem something more than superfluous — almost impertinent — for me to deprecate the idea that my own impressions regarding the illustrious man above-named were in the smallest degree affected by what I have now related. But I cannot help doing so nevertheless. Had my debt of personal gratitude to Wordsworth as a poet been less deep than it is, I might perhaps have been in some degree influenced by Hazlitt's disparaging notions of him as a man ; for I knew nothing of Wordsworth myself; and we are but too apt to take a malicious pleasure in seeing reduced nearer to our own level the general character of those whom we admit to soar above us in some particular. Even had Wordsworth been only the *greatest* of modern poets, I might perhaps have yielded my belief to Hazlitt's pertinacious exhibitions of him as anything but great as a man. But, happily, the beauty, the charm, and the virtue of Wordsworth's poetry is, that it for the most part affects the reason as a personal thing — that it touches us as if it were a matter between the poet and ourselves, and thus engenders a feeling little, if at all, differing in spirit and effect from that individual gratitude which even the worst of mankind are proud and pleased to owe and to pay, in return for personal benefits and obligations. Almost all other poets may be appreciated and enjoyed without any other benefit than that appreciation and enjoyment ; but it is impossible to appreciate and enjoy Wordsworth without being wiser, better, and happier after the enjoyment has ceased. And the man who makes us permanently happier than we could have been without his aid, has our personal gratitude as much as if he had effected the object by a personal boon. The man whom Wordsworth's poetry has lifted from the debasement and despondency of spirit in which it may have found him, and endowed him with the "riches fineless " of a heart and mind capable of creating their own wealth by the happy alchemy of a purified and purifying imagination (and there are many such men living), feels himself as much bound to the poet by personal ties of gratitude and love, as if he had lifted him from actual poverty, and given him the means of worldly competence and comfort. And that the poet who has done this in innumerable instances could be the man Hazlitt believed and sought to represent Wordsworth, is not to be conceived on any recognized principle of the human mind, or any experience that we possess of its qualities and operations.

Moreover, I do not recollect a single instance in which Hazlitt's depreciating stories of Wordsworth were drawn from his own personal experience. They were founded on the mere idle or malicious gossip of people who could see nothing in Wordsworth but his reputation, and who gathered their notions of that from the early pages of the " Edinburgh Review ; " and they were turned, by Hazlitt's perverse ingenuity, to those self-tormenting purposes to which he was so prone, whenever his personal feelings took part against his better knowledge and judgment.

The writings of Bulwer had not attracted Hazlitt's attention till just before his death. As I have said before, he never read a line of any living writer, except when called upon to do so as a matter of business — either with a view to an article in the "Edinburgh Review," or when a new work was sent to him to criticise for any other periodical. At last, on my repeatedly urging him to do so, he read " Paul Clifford," and he thought so highly of it, that he at once made up his mind to read all Bulwer's novels, with the intention of discussing their merits in the "Edinburgh Review." And I believe he wrote to Mr. Jeffrey proposing the subject — as he always did in similar cases before going to work.

So the matter rested for some time — Hazlitt, in the *interim,* often expressing his anxiety to get "the job," as he called it — if it were only that he might have a sufficiently strong inducement to read the works of which " Paul Clifford " had given him so attractive a foretaste. Shortly after this period, Mr. Jeffrey retired from the ostensible management of the " Edinburgh Review " — which was confided to Mr. Macvey Napier ; and on that gentleman visiting town, Hazlitt proposed to him personally the subject of Bulwer's novels. I saw him immediately after he had spoken to Mr. Napier on this matter ; and I found that there was a *hitch* somewhere ; though in what particular point of literary, personal, or political demerit on the part of Bulwer the difficulty turned, Hazlitt could never learn. Certain it is, however, that Hazlitt anxiously desired to write the review in question ; that he expressly proposed it to Mr. Napier (as I believe he had done to Mr. Jeffrey before — though of this I am not quite certain), and that it was positively and finally refused — the *subject* being an interdicted one.

The literary public must draw their own conclusions from this little fact in the secret history of one of our great critical tribunals. I cannot help them to any further means of arriving at the solution of the mystery ; nor should I have thought of making any allusion to it here, had it not proved what may be satisfactory to the numerous admirers of Bulwer as a novelist — namely, that even the perusal of one only of his works conveyed a due impression of his powers to the greatest critic of the day. Hazlitt also stated to me, on this curious point of literary history, that in his interview with Mr. Napier, that gentleman had mentioned to him that Mr. Campbell had more than once pointed Mr. Jeffrey's attention to Bulwer's novels, as a fit subject for a conspicuous notice in the Review, but that the same obstacle (whatever it was) had existed at that time.

Of Walter Savage Landor, Hazlitt entertained a very high opinion, even before the production of his noble work, the " Imaginary Conversations ; " but Mr. Landor's intimate connection and friendship with Southey created that personal feeling about him in Hazlitt's mind which always prevented his judgment from forming an unbiased decision. That the fierce republican, and the poet of the " Vision of Judgment," should be able to set their horses together, seemed to throw a doubt on the sincerity, as well as the stability, of the opinions of both. On the appearance, however, of the " Imaginary Conversations," Hazlitt lost all doubt of Landor's sincerity and political honesty, and attributed the contradiction in question to one of those crotchets of the brain with which genius is so apt to be haunted. The book was one after his own heart ; and some parts of it he considered finer than anything else from a modern pen. There were, however, many parts which he looked upon as pure raving, and others which seemed as if they were put forth in-that spirit of arrogant and insolent assumption of superiority over all the rest of the world, past and present, which was peculiarly obnoxious to Hazlitt's essentially diffident nature. He did not think that the fate of a nation was to be settled by a phrase, or the character of a whole people predicated in the stroke of a pen. Not that he had any respect for a name. But he hesitated to set aside the award of a whole generation ; and for that of ages he entertained what might almost have been deemed a superstitious reverence, but that it was founded on deep and accurate observation of the causes and qualities which lead to a national reputation. He believed, indeed, that a people is infallible in its decisions, on all questions of fact and of national feeling — of course, provided it have the fair means and materials for forming its decision ; and therefore, that to dispute " Public Opinion " is to dispute an identical proposition. Prove to him, for example, that the actual government of any given state is supported by public opinion, fairly and properly so called, and his inference was that *that* was the form of government fitted for the people governed by it. And so of any other question, moral, political, or literary — any question in which the imagination and the feelings take part.

It followed that Mr. Landor's dogmatic mode of abolishing a reputation of ages' standing by a breath of his mouth, or creating one by the same summary process where nobody else had ever seen a vestige of the materials for it, did not fall in with Hazlitt's notions of what was just and fitting. Hence the violent and, in some degree, unjust portions of an article which he wrote on the " Imaginary Conversations " in the " Edinburgh Review." He was, however, not answerable, he told me, for the whole of that article, alterations and additions having been made in it after it left his hands.

Subsequently Hazlitt was personally introduced to Landor, at his residence at Florence ; and he returned to England with an improved and heightened opinion of his great talents, and with all the prejudices he had formerly entertained against his personal character almost entirely removed.

Among his literary contemporaries there was none to whom Hazlitt did more justice than to the exquisite writer known to the reading public as Barry Cornwall. His personal intimacy with that writer commenced, I believe, almost immediately after the appearance of the " Dramatic Scenes ; " and it en-

dured, without breach, till Hazlitt's death — a period of pretty
nearly twenty years. I doubt if the same can be said of any
one other of his intimacies — I mean the *unbroken* continuance
of it. But there is — as in what case is there not ? — between
the writings of that delightful poet and his personal character
a beautiful correspondence and relationship, which, to those
who know him, cause them to act and react upon each other,
till the result is a pervading sense of gentle sweetness of temperament, and genial goodness of heart, which those petty
pains and discrepancies that are so apt to disturb the current
of our ordinary intercourse are incapable of suffering. To
quarrel about trifles with a man who has added to our intellectual wealth to the extent that Barry Cornwall has, is difficult under any circumstances ; but to do so when every feature
of his poetry is reflected in his personal character is impossible ; and not even Hazlitt could do it, who could quarrel
upon a look, a movement, or a shadow. I have twenty times
seen him *try* to do it — always by "making the meat" on
which his incipient anger was to be nourished. But his efforts at self-tormenting always ended where they began — in
feeling, at least, if he could not see, the error and injustice of
his suspicions.

In speaking of the justice which Hazlitt rendered to the literary pretensions of Barry Cornwall, I must be understood to
mean that comparative measure of it which alone he was in
the habit of meting out to his contemporaries, when called
upon to do so professionally as a critic, or personally when
speaking of them in conversation. In referring to the characteristics of Barry Cornwall's writings, Hazlitt was not unjust or stinting in his praise. But with the *amount* of his
beauties as a poet, he was as little acquainted as he was with
that of any other of his contemporaries — for the simple reason, as before stated, that he had not read a twentieth part of
them. What he had read he fully appreciated ; but beyond
that he had not only nothing to say, but he felt nothing. And
this is as if one should profess to understand and appreciate

12

Milton by reading his "Lycidas," or Pope by his Epistles or his Satires.

Among all Hazlitt's acquaintance and friends, there was not one more tolerant and considerate towards him, or more kind and generous to the last, than was Barry Cornwall. He was among the very few — some "two or one" — to whom Hazlitt knew and felt that he might always resort, at a moment of real need or difficulty, without fear of meeting with unkindness or repulse ; or, what was more obnoxious to him, that miserable modicum of remonstrance and " good advice " which people are so apt to dole out as an obligato accompaniment to the strain, whose music is thus turned into the elements of discord.

For Sheridan Knowles, Hazlitt felt great personal kindness and regard. He was never more entirely at ease than in the company of that natural and happily constituted man. They had met very early in life, and some of Hazlitt's least unhappy associations were connected with his intercourse with Knowles, who, having always felt an almost reverential admiration for Hazlitt's talents and writings, was accustomed to express what he felt in no stinted terms. They seldom met — Knowles living in Scotland up to the period of Hazlitt's death. But when the latter visited London they were a good deal together : and when Hazlitt was in Scotland, Knowles accompanied him in a short visit to the Highlands, and was his factotum in all matters and arrangements connected with a course of lectures Hazlitt delivered on Poetry, in Glasgow and elsewhere.

It was at Hazlitt's lodgings that I first met this distinguished dramatist and excellent man ; and the commencement of our acquaintance involved so characteristic a feature of Knowles's mind, that I may be excused for referring to it more particularly. On my looking in at Hazlitt's on the evening in question, he told me that Knowles was in town, and was coming to spend the evening with him ; and he begged me to stay. From what Hazlitt had often said to me of Knowles, I had a great wish to see him ; but it so happened that I had, not long before, written in " Blackwood's Magazine " a detailed criticism on " Virginius," which I *now* feel to have been much too severe in its unfavorable parts, and of which (as I learned from Hazlitt) Knowles believed me to be the writer. I therefore reminded Hazlitt of this fact, and prepared to take my departure at once — being as little disposed, on my own account as on Knowles's, to stand the brunt of a meeting which I believed Hazlitt to have proposed in forgetfulness of the above circumstance.

But Hazlitt would not hear of my going, and agreed to take the consequences of the meeting upon himself. Accordingly I stayed, and presently Knowles came. Almost immediately after mentioning my name, Hazlitt alluded to the criticism in question ; and I. can never forget the frank, cordial, and manly manner in which Knowles treated the thing ; for he took it up at once, as a stumbling-block necessary to be moved out of the way before we could make any approach to that hearty communion and good-fellowship which became the company in which we met. There was not a word of that cant of commonplace authorship which pretends to bow to the justice of severe criticism, and to deprecate that which is otherwise. On the contrary, he told me frankly, and at once, that until Hazlitt had told him who the article was written by, he had always looked upon it as the effusion of some personal enemy, who wished and sought to do him all the harm he could in his new career of authorship ; but that since Hazlitt had assured him that such was anything but the case, he had taken a totally different view of the remarks — that he now believed most of the censure to be just, and did not feel anything like anger or resentment on the subject.

The cordial and hearty terms and tone in which this feeling and belief were expressed made it impossible to doubt their sincerity, or to withhold one's esteem for the frank good-nature from which they sprang. Nor has a cordial acquaintance and intimacy, subsisting up to the present time, tended in any degree to change this impression ; while the subsequent writings of this distinguished man have convinced me that my first impressions of his talents as a dramatic writer did him manifest injustice in some particulars, and fell far short of his merits in others.

There was no one in whose welfare and success as a writer Hazlitt seemed to feel more personal interest than in those of Sheridan Knowles ; and this interest was heightened, rather than repressed, by an impression he entertained, that there was a singular absence in Knowles of that mental and moral correspondence between the writer and his productions which we are so apt to expect, and so disappointed and perplexed at not finding. I never knew Hazlitt wholly at fault as to the intellectual qualities of any man, or unable to assign some reasonable or plausible explanation of the results of those qualities, except in the case of Sheridan Knowles. He says, in his "Spirit of the Age : " " We should not feel that we had discharged our obligations to truth and friendship if we were to let this volume go without introducing into it the name of the author of ' Virginius.' This is the more proper, inasmuch as he is a character by himself, and the only poet now living that is *a mere poet.* If we were asked what sort of a man Mr. Knowles is, we could only say, he is the writer of ' Virginius.' His most intimate friends see nothing in him by which they could trace the work to the author."

I know of nothing more unlike Hazlitt's usual sagacity and penetration than this unmeaning and, at the same time, contradictory award. Knowles, he says, is "a mere poet ; " by which it is impossible to guess what he means. Then he is, essentially and by way of distinction, "the sort of man " that you would describe as " the writer of ' Virginius.' " And, finally, " his most intimate friends " cannot discover any correspondence between the author so designated and the work from which the designation is derived ! What follows, too, though more just, is not much more specific or discriminative. "Virginius," says Hazlitt, is " the best acting tragedy that has been produced on the modern stage ; " and " Mr. Knowles is the first tragic writer of the age ; " but "in other respects he is a common man."

What is the explanation of all this contradiction ? For if

we can find one, it will unquestionably involve a characteristic feature in the extraordinary mind that it is the chief business of these pages to illustrate. That explanation, as it seems to me, is to be found in the following words, which conclude Hazlitt's hasty glance at the author of "Virginius : " "*We have known him almost from a child*, and we must say he appears to us the same boy-poet that he ever was."

Now, Sheridan Knowles is not many years younger than Hazlitt would have been were he alive now — perhaps six or seven ; consequently, the very earliest of the associations of Hazlitt's opening intellect were connected with the idea of "the boy-poet ; " and he neither would nor could consent to dissipate those early associations, a single train of which was worth the whole sum and substance of his after life. For Knowles's benefit and pleasure Hazlitt would have had the world regard him as another Shakespeare, if it pleased. But for him (Hazlitt) Knowles could never be anything higher or better than the frank and warm-hearted friend and companion of those few opening years of his life which he could . alone recall with any feelings of satisfaction.

ORIGIN OF THE "LIBER AMORIS."

I scarcely know whether or not it will be thought that the proper time has arrived for explaining the true origin of the strange, and, to all but those who are more or less acquainted with its history beforehand, the utterly unintelligible work above named — the " Liber Amoris." The prevalent opinion on such purely personal matters seems to be, that a profound silence should be preserved on them until such time as all those who know anything about them have passed from the scene ; or, at all events, that those who can alone furnish the true materials for such records cannot be permitted to tell their tale ; while those who avowedly know nothing about the matter may talk of and discuss it to their heart's content.

Yet the world has lately begun to feel that Moore, for instance, having accepted, had almost as little right to destroy

the autobiography that Byron intrusted to his care, to be
published after his death, as he had to destroy the man himself during his life.

Hazlitt's personal reputation has suffered more, even in the
estimation of wise and good men, from the publication of the
" Liber Amoris," than from anything else that his enemies or
himself have written or said or done against him. And the
simple reason is, that the real history and origin of the book
remain to this day a mystery to all but a few individuals, some
of whom are afraid and others ashamed to speak of it ; and
that, consequently, it has been made the fertile topic on which
Hazlitt's personal enemies, and the lovers of literary scandal
in general, have propagated all sorts of ridiculous fictions and
fabrications, all more or less discreditable to the persons to
whom they relate, and none that I have ever heard having the
smallest foundation in fact.

For my own part, I should have been disposed to tell the
truth on this strange and interesting episode in Hazlitt's life,
·whatever that truth might have been ; because the design of
these pages is to furnish, so far as I possess the materials, a
true, not a favorable picture of the mind and heart to which
they relate. But seeing, as I do, in the materials of this little
history, nothing that is morally discreditable to any of the
parties connected with it, much that is honorable to all, and
(in the personal details of it, as it regards Hazlitt himself)
something as touching as anything I am acquainted with in
the actual history of the human heart, I do not feel that I have
a right wholly to suppress those materials, in deference to the
false or the pretended *delicacy* of those who never use the word
but in an indelicate sense.

The story of Hazlitt's love for the female who is the subject
of the " Liber Amoris," could he himself have delivered it to
the world in the form of "a round unvarnished tale," would
have made one of the most beautiful and affecting chapters in
the Romance of Real Life, that was ever put on paper ;
one that it would have been impossible to peruse without the
reader's heart being softened by a sense of its own weakness,

while it was elevated and purified by a perception of the moral grandeur and beauty to which its affections may lift it.

There is nothing in poetry more truly poetical, nothing more ennobling by the strength of its passion, while it is no less softening and humanizing by the depth and darkness of its pathos, than much of what is contained in a series of letters written to me by Hazlitt, during the time when he was most under the influence of the devouring passion to which I am now referring. And as to the truth and *reality* of every word there written, none who knew him will believe that anything but the very intensity of that reality could have impelled him to write them *at all.* Such was his almost physical incapacity of writing *a letter* on any subject, however imperatively his worldly occasions might require one, that I suppose all the rest of the correspondence of his whole literary life would scarcely make up the amount of what I received from him during the three months he was absent in Scotland, in consequence of circumstances arising out of the affair in question : and this during the period when he was employed on, and had actually completed in six weeks, an entire volume of his most remarkable Essays.

It is from these letters that I shall furnish some brief but sufficiently explanatory materials for the true history of the "Liber Amoris." And if any one, with these materials for judgment and scrutiny before him, can entertain towards the man to whom they relate any less kindly feelings than those arising out of pain and pity, he must have formed strange notions on the constitution of, and little sympathy with, our common nature.

As the extracts I shall give will, so far as is needful, tell their own story, I shall only premise further, that the heroine of this romance of real life was the daughter of persons of respectable character and connections, in whose house Hazlitt lodged for a considerable length of time immediately previous to the date of the following letters ; and that her personal appearance and manner were scarcely overrated, even in the lover's estimate of them which may be gathered from the letters themselves.

I give these extracts in the order in which the letters they are taken from reached me, — so far at least as this can be made out by the post-marks ; for nearly all the letters are without date.

EXTRACTS OF LETTERS FROM W. HAZLITT TO P. G. PATMORE
(DATED BETWEEN MARCH AND JULY, 1822).

"What have I suffered since I parted with you ! A raging fire in my heart and in my brain, that I thought would drive me mad. The steamboat seemed a prison — a hell — and the everlasting waters an unendurable repetition of the same idea — my woes. The abyss was before me, and *her* face, where all my peace was centred — all lost ! I felt the eternity of punishment in this world. Mocked, mocked by her in whom I placed my hope — writhing, withering in misery and despair, caused by one who hardens herself against me. I wished for courage to throw myself into the waters ; but I could not even do that — and my little boy, too, prevented me, when I thought of his face at hearing of his father's death, and his desolation in life. . . . .

"You see she all along hated me ('I always told you I had no affection for you '), and only played with me.

" I am a little, a very little, better to-day. Would it were quietly over, and that this form, made to be loathed, were hid out of sight of cold, sullen eyes. I thought of the breakfasts I had promised myself with her, of those I had had with her, standing and listening to my true vows ; and compared them to the one I had this morning. The thought choked me. The people even take notice of my dumb despair, and pity me. What can be done ? I cannot forget her, and I can find no other like *what she seemed.* I should like you to see her, and learn whether I may come back again as before, and whether she will see and talk to me as an old friend. Do as you think best."

" I got your letter this morning, and I kiss the rod, not only with submission, but with gratitude. Your rebukes of me and your defense of her are the only things that save my soul from hell. She is my soul's idol, and, believe me, those words of yours applied to the dear creature ('to lip a chaste one and suppose her wanton') were balm and rapture to me.

" Be it known to you, that while I write this, I am drinking ale [1] at the Black Bull, celebrated in " Blackwood's." It is owing to your letter. Could I think her 'honest,' I am proof even against Edinburgh ale ! She, by her silence, makes my ' dark hour,' and you dissipate it — for four and twenty hours. . . . .

" I have seen the great little man,[2] and he is very gracious to me. I tell him I am dull and out of spirits, but he says he cannot perceive it. He is a person of infinite vivacity. My Sardanapalus is to be in.[3]

" In my judgment, Myrrha is just like —— ——, only I am not like Sardanapalus.

" Do you think if she knew how I love her, my depressions and my altitudes, my wanderings and my pertinacity, it would not melt her ? She knows it all ! I don't believe that any human being was ever courted more passionately than she has been by me. As Rousseau said of Madame d'Houdetot (forgive the allusion), my soul has found a tongue in speaking to her, and I have talked to her in the divine language of love. Yet she says she is insensible to it. Am I to believe her or you ? You ; for I wish it to madness."

" The deed is done, and I am virtually a free man. . . . . What had I better do in these circumstances ? I dare not write to her — I dare not write to her father. She has shot me through with poisoned arrows, and I think another ' winged wound ' would finish me. It is a pleasant sort of balm she has left in my heart. One thing I agree with you in — it will remain there forever — but yet not long. It festers and consumes me. If it were not for my little boy, whose face I see

---

[1] He had not for years previously touched anything but water, except his beloved tea, nor did he afterwards, up to the period of his last illness.

[2] Jeffrey.

[3] An article in the *Edinburgh Review* on Byron's tragedy so called.

struck blank at the news, and looking through the world for
pity, and meeting with contempt, I should soon settle the
question by my death.   That is the only thought that brings
my wandering reason to an anchor — that excites the least interest, or gives me fortitude to bear up against what I am
doomed to feel for *the ungrateful.* Otherwise, I am dead to
all but the agony of what I have lost.   She was my life — it is
gone from me, and I am grown spectral.   If it is a place I
know, it reminds me of her — of the way in which my fond
heart brooded over her.   If it is a strange place, it is desolate,
hateful, barren of all interest — for nothing touches me but
what has a reference to her.   There is only she in the world
— 'the false, the fair, the inexpressive she.'   If the clock
strikes, the sound jars me, for a million of hours will never
bring peace to my breast.   The light startles me, the darkness terrifies me — I seem falling into a pit, without a hand to
help me.   She came (I knew not how) and sat by my side, and
was folded in my arms, a vision of love and joy — as if she
had dropped from the heavens, to bless me by some special
dispensation of a favoring Providence — to make me amends
for all.   And now, without any fault of mine but too much love,
she has vanished from me, and I am left to wither.   My heart
is torn out of me, and every feeling for which I wished to live.
It is like a dream, an enchantment — it torments me, and
makes me mad.   I lie down with it — I rise up with it — and
I see no chance of repose.   I grasp at a shadow — I try to
undo the past, or to make that mockery real — and weep with
rage and pity over my own weakness and misery. . . . .
    "I had hopes, I had prospects to come — the flattering of
something like fame — a pleasure in writing — health even
would have come back to me with her smile.   She has blighted
all — turned all to poison and driveling tears.   Yet the barbed
arrow is in my heart — I can neither endure it nor draw it
out, for with it flows my life's blood.   I had dwelt too long
upon Truth to trust myself with the immortal thoughts of
love.   *That —— —— might have been mine — and now never
can:* these are the two sole propositions that forever stare

me in the face, and look ghastly in at my poor brain. I am in
some sense proud that I can feel this dreadful passion. It
makes me a kind of peer in the kingdom of love. But I could
have wished it had been for an object that, at least, could have
understood its value and pitied its excess. . . . . The
gates of Paradise were once open to me, and I blushed to
enter but with the golden keys of love ! — I would die — but
her lover — my love of her — ought not to die. When I am
dead, who will love her as I have done ? If she should be in
misfortune, who will comfort her ? When she is old, who will
look in her face and bless her ? . . . . Oh, answer me,
to save me if possible *for* her and *from* myself !

" Will you call at Mr. ——'s school, and tell my little boy
I 'll write to him or see him on Saturday morning. Poor little
fellow ! "

" Your letter raised me a moment from the depths of despair ; but, not hearing from you yesterday or to-day (as I
hoped), I am gone back again. You say I want to get rid of
her. I hope you are more right in your conjectures about her
than in this about me. Oh, no ! believe it, I love her as I do
my own soul : my heart is wedded to her, be she what she
may ; and I would not hesitate a moment between her and an
angel from heaven. I grant all you say about my self-tormenting madness ; but has it been without cause ? Has she
not refused me again and again with scorn and abhorrence ?
. . . . 'She can make no more confidences !' These
words ring forever in my ears, and will be my deathwatch.
My poor fond heart, that brooded over her, and the remains
of her affections, as my only hope of comfort upon earth, cannot brook or survive this vulgar degradation. Who is there
so low as I ? Who is there besides, after the homage I have
paid her, and the caresses she has lavished on me, so vile, so
filthy, so abhorrent to love, to whom such an indignity could
have happened ? When I think of this (and I think of it forever, except when I read your letters) the air I breathe stifles
me. I am pent up in burning impotent desires, which can

find no vent or object. I am hated, repulsed, bemocked, by all I love. I cannot stay in any place, and find no rest or interruption from the thought of her contempt, and her ingratitude. I can do nothing. What is the use of all I have done? Is it not that my thinking beyond my strength, my feeling more than I ought about so many things, has withered me up, and made me a thing for love to shrink from and wonder at? Who could ever feel that peace from the touch of her hand that I have done; and is it not torn forever from me? My state is, that I feel I shall never lie down again at night, nor rise up of a morning in peace, nor ever behold my little boy's face with pleasure while I live, unless I am restored to her favor. Instead of that delicious feeling I had when she was heavenly kind to me, and my heart softened and melted in its own tenderness and her sweetness, I am now inclosed in a dungeon of despair. The sky is marble, like my thoughts; nature is dead without me, as hope is within me; no object can give me one gleam of satisfaction now, or the prospect of it in time to come. I wander, or rather crawl, by the sea-side; and the eternal ocean, and lasting despair, and her face, are before me. Hated, mocked by her on whom my heart by its last fibre hung. I wake with her by my side, not as my sweet companion, but as the corpse of my love, without a heart in her — cold, insensible, or struggling from me; and the worm gnaws me, and the sting of unrequited love, and the canker of a hopeless, endless sorrow. I have lost the taste of my food by feverish anxiety; and my tea, which used to refresh me when I got up, has no moisture in it. Oh! cold, solitary, sepulchral breakfasts, compared to those which I made when she was standing by my side; my Eve, my guardian angel, my wife, my sister, my sweet friend, my all. . . . . Ah! what I suffer now, shows only what I have felt before.

" But you say, ' The girl is a good girl, if there is goodness in human nature.' I thank you for those words, and I will fall down and worship you, if you can prove them true; and I would not do much less to him that proves her a demon.

" Do let me know if anything has passed : suspense is my greatest torment. I am going to Renton Inn, to see if I can work a little."

" I ought to have written you before ; but since I received your letter I have been in a sort of hell. I would put an end to my torments at once, but that I am as great a coward as I am a fool. Do you know that I have not had a word of answer from her since ? What can be the reason ? Is she offended at my letting you know she wrote to me ? or is it some new amour ? I wrote to her in the tenderest, most respectful manner — poured my soul at her feet — and this is the way she serves me ! Can you account for it, except on the admission of my worst suspicion ? God ! can I bear to think of her so — or that I am scorned and made a sport of by the creature to whom I have given my very heart ? I feel like one of the damned. To be hated, loathed as I have been all my life, and to feel the utter impossibility of its ever being otherwise while I live, take what pains I may ! I sit and cry my eyes out. My weakness grows upon me, and I have no hope left, unless I could lose my senses quite. I think I should like this. To forget — ah! to forget — there would be something in that — to be an idiot for some few years, and then wake up a poor, wretched, old man, to recollect my misery as past, and die ! Yet, oh ! with her, only a little while ago, I had different hopes — forfeited for nothing that I know of."

"I was in hopes to have got away by the steamboat tomorrow, but owing to . . . . I cannot, and may not be in town till another week, unless I come by the mail, which I am strongly tempted to do. In the latter case, I shall be there on Saturday evening. Will you look in and see, about eight o'clock? I wish much to see you, and her and John Hunt, and my little boy, once more ; and then, if she is not what she once was to me, I care not if I die that instant."

Many of the letters in the " Nouvelle Héloise " are among

the most beautiful and affecting effusions which exist in those
works of fiction that concern themselves with sentiment and
passion rather than with incident and action. But I venture
to say that there is nothing in the " Nouvelle Héloise " equal
in passion and pathos to the foregoing extracts. And the
reason is, that the latter are actual and immediate transcripts
from the human heart. In this respect, the letters from which
these extracts are taken are, perhaps, more beautiful and
touching than anything of their kind that was ever given to
the world. But I am far from doubting that innumerable
others exist, equaling them in all the qualities in which *they*
excel ; for real and intense passion levels all ranks of intellect, laughs learning and worldly wisdom to scorn, and invests
the commonplaces of life with the highest attributes of poetry
and eloquence.

Perhaps the published writings most resembling these letters
in the depth and intensity of the passion they embody and
convey, are the celebrated letters addressed by Mary Wool-
stoncraft to Imlay.

HAZLITT'S MARRIAGE.

The ceremony, so much talked and written about, at length
was solemnized on *Sunday* morning, the 1st of May, 1808, at
St. Andrew's Church, Holborn ; the married couple afterwards
breakfasted at Dr. Stoddart's, and then proceeded to Winterslow. The only persons present at the marriage, so far as I
can collect, were Dr. and Mrs. Stoddart, and Mr. and Miss
Lamb ; but I strongly suspect that there were other guests,
of whom there is no remaining record.

Lamb, in a letter to Southey, dated August 9, 1815, more
than seven years after the event, thus alludes to his having
been present : " I was at Hazlitt's marriage, and had like to
have been turned out several times during the ceremony. Anything awful makes me laugh."

It was not an every-day kind of business this, with William
Hazlitt for bridegroom, and Charles Lamb for best man, and
Miss Lamb for bridesmaid — and all of a Sunday morning !

I wonder whether Elia appeared at the altar in his snuff-
colored smalls ? I wonder whether Miss Lamb wore, after
all, the spring dress, or the China-Manning silk, or a real white
gown ? I wonder in what way Lamb misbehaved, so as to
leave so strong an impression on his own mind years after ?
To have been in St. Andrew's that day, and to have seen the
whole thing from a good place, would have been a recollection
worth cherishing; and there are plenty of men and women
living who are old enough to have done so, though of those
who mixed in that "set" so early, scarcely one.

Mrs. Hazlitt's property at Winterslow, which had been
left to her by her father, with a reversionary interest in what
he bequeathed to Mrs. Stoddart for her life, was settled
upon herself at her brother's instigation, and much to my
grandfather's annoyance. There was about 120*l*. a year altogether.

Mr. Hazlitt and the Doctor had never been very good
friends ; and the Doctor's new politics, and the new prospects in Malta, arising out of his conversion to the more
fashionable lay-creed of the day, had produced a decided
estrangement before 1806 or 1807. He had set his face
against the *threatened* alliance between the families, and was
very anxious to get his sister out of the way of temptation,
and marry her more suitably, or more in conformity with his
own personal views, in Malta.

When he had found that there was no help for it, he had
tried to behave with civility to his future brother-in-law, and
had asked him to his house, when he settled again in England.
But there was no real heartiness, I am afraid, in the friendship ; and Mr. Hazlitt was not blind to the fact. Relations
did not improve subsequently ; the breach grew wider and
wiler.

The story goes, too, that Mr. Hazlitt said of an ephemeral
newspaper speculation of Dr. Stoddart's, that if any one
wanted to keep a secret, he could not do better than put it in
the "Correspondent ! " Mr. Hazlitt himself has related the
anecdote, which is no doubt sufficiently authentic ; and of

course, if it came to the Doctor's ears, it was not a thing apt
to make their communications friendlier.

No two people could be more opposite in their characters
than the Doctor and Mrs. Hazlitt. She hated formality and
etiquette, while he was all formality and etiquette. ,

There is an anecdote rather to the purpose, which may
at this time of day, perhaps, be repeated without offense.
Lieutenant Stoddart, their father, in the old days at Salisbury,
would sometimes be drinking his grog when his children were
in the room, and he would say to John, " John, will you have
some ? " to which John would answer, " No, thank you,
father ; " than he would say to Sarah, " Sarah, will you have
some ? " to which she would reply, " Yes, please, father."

Not that she ever indulged to excess, but she was that sort
of woman. Her brother and Lord B., then Mr. B., had been
fellow-collegians at Oxford, and Mr. B. and the Stoddarts were
sufficiently intimate to warrant Miss S. (not the Doctor) in
calling him by his Christian name. When Mr. B. became
Lord B., and a high officer of state, she wrote to him to use
his influence for somebody, and she was the plain, downright,
impervious kind of woman, who did not perceive any impropriety in still keeping up the old familiarity of address. Her
letter beginning " My dear H——" had to be intercepted by
a judicious friend.

Mr. Hazlitt had rather admired these traits of character in
her, meeting her occasionally at Lamb's or her brother's, before their marriage, and it still remained to be seen whether
they would be equally acceptable to him now that she was
more than a friend to him. I have heard that her unaffected
good sense was one of the things which made him resolve he
would have her.

One evening, at Mitre Court Buildings, when my grandfather had escorted Miss Stoddart to the theatre, and had
brought her back afterwards, Charles called for warm water,
which Miss Lamb did not seem very anxious to produce. But
Miss Stoddart unconsciously hunted out the kettle, and set it
to boil, not at all to Miss L.'s satisfaction. But Mr. Hazlitt,

the tradition runs, was highly pleased, as it seemed to him to show an honesty and sterlingness of character.

This connection with the Stoddarts, thus begun in 1808, was, however, of service in more than one respect ; it certainly tended to infuse into the Hazlitt blood certain southern characteristics, among them a taste for formality and method ; for my grandmother, with all her inattention and repugnance to domestic matters, was by no means destitute of a love of order, and her brother John was a precisian. The Celtic element may have been thought by some to predominate hitherto too exclusively, to the disadvantage and sacrifice of what are understood as the conventional gentilities. My great-grand-father was an Irishman, and my grandfather after him ; nor am I quite positive that the Irish blood is extinct in us Haz-litts to this day, notwithstanding a second intermarriage with the Reynells, a quarter of a century later on.

REMOVAL TO LONDON.

In 1812, a few months after the birth of their second but only surviving child, my grandfather and grandmother removed from Winterslow to London, and rented number 19 York Street, Westminster, of Mr. Jeremy Bentham. It was a house which had belonged, as tradition said, to Milton ; from the parlor windows was a view of Mr. Bentham's own residence and garden, which backed upon the house of Milton. It is not improbable that originally the garden formed part of the poet's premises.

My grandfather came to town with very little book-knowledge, with no introductions, with very small independent resources, and with shy and unsocial habits. He had thought upon many subjects, and had committed some of his notions to paper ; but his books mere not popular, and their sale scarcely paid the printer's bills. He had renounced the profession of painting, because he had no hope of acquiring in it sufficient excellence and rank to please himself ; and here he was, about to fight his way, and win bread for three mouths, in that to him new and strange vocation, popular authorship, which de-

13

manded just what he lacked, fluent expression and brilliant commonplace. He had a very fair stock of ideas to start with ; but it was in the faculty of evolving them and clothing them in attractive phraseology that his weakness was.

These were the difficulties by which he felt that he was surrounded. Then there were certain counterbalancing advantages. His wife had a moderate competence ; he knew the Lambs, the Stoddarts, and his brother's other friends ; and his former publications, if they had brought him no money, at least brought him a share of celebrity, and introduced him to two or three of the booksellers.

He had not looked very far and wide out into the world, but he had penetrated very deeply into the recesses of his own good and warm heart, and had watched for years the subtlest operations of the human mind. With him, to know himself was to know others.

Such books as he was acquainted with, he had mastered. He had gone with the eye of an analyst through Hobbes and through Locke. He was familiar with Chaucer and Boccaccio. He was versed in the writings of Taylor and Barrow. He was at home in Fielding and Smollett, in Richardson and Mrs. Inchbald. He had " The New Héloise " by heart. But of the volumes which form the furniture of gentlemen's libraries, he was egregiously ignorant, and at any time would have cheerfully confessed his deficiency in the kind of information which is served up to the public of all countries by its authors. Mr. Hazlitt's resources were emphatically internal ; from his own mind he drew sufficient for himself ; and he had to see now, in the thirty-fourth year of his age, whether he had enough there to hold the world with, too.

The prospect did not seem, on the whole, very bright and encouraging for a man whose politics were those of the minority, who never read a book through after he was thirty, and who, in original composition, could scarcely at the outset see his way two sentences before him.

He inaugurated his change of plans, that is to say, his final settlement in the metropolis, promisingly enough. During

the first year of his residence in London he delivered, at the
Russell Institution, a series of lectures on the English philosophers and metaphysicians, ten in number. He was merely
turning to account, of course, his early studies at home, sup-
plemented and strengthened by later excursions, in the long
winter evenings at Winterslow, into the writings of Hobbes,
Locke, and other masters of the English school.

HAZLITT AS A REPORTER.

A kind of indication that the lectures at the Russell Institution were not pecuniarily remunerative, is that Mr. Hazlitt
was induced shortly afterwards to seek an engagement on the
"Morning Chronicle" as a parliamentary reporter. This was
an occupation which was calculated to suit neither his tastes
nor his health; it involved late hours, and the gallery at that
time was a hot-bed of intemperance. My grandfather's health
had never been robust, and the sedentary life of a hard student
had still further impaired it.

Like many other reporters, he was not a short-hand writer.
He had no knowledge of stenography, or at best, no competent knowledge. He took notes of a very hurried description,
restricting himself to general heads and salient points; and if
he was not able, after his *turn*, to make out what he had
written very satisfactorily, yet he had a memory which was
retentive and accurate enough for that purpose; and I doubt
whether anything worth preserving was lost through him.
The complaint which I have heard made was, that he gave
speakers credit for delivering better grammar and sense than
was really the case; and this is a complaint which has attached so far to all reporters in all times. My friend, Mr.
John Payne Collier, has a MS. copy of Coleridge's "Christa-
bel," in Miss Stoddart's handwriting, which belonged to my
grandfather, and with which were bound up, oddly enough,
some blank leaves, serving him for his reporting notes. I also
possess a volume of them; and very strange specimens of cal-
ligraphy they are, considering that Mr. Hazlitt, as a rule, wrote
a beautifully clear hand.

He ran another danger, which was that of losing the thread of the debate, while he was listening to some favorite orator. He is said to have been so fascinated once by the eloquence of Plunket, that he omitted to take any notes at all of his speech. He himself tells a little anecdote of these days : —

" I have heard Sir Francis Burdett say things there [in the House of Commons] which I could not enough admire ; and which he could not have ventured upon saying, if, besides his honesty, he had not been a man of fortune, of family, of character, aye, and a very good-looking man into the bargain ! "

His career as a reporter was soon terminated by his utter dislike to the employment, and by the injury which his constitution suffered from the use of stimulants, in which he followed what was an universal propensity in his day among the members of the press. Some carried it to a greater excess than others. It was not necessary that he should carry it very far ; his physical strength was unequal to much indulgence of any kind.

When he gave up the gallery, he did not leave the press, but transferred his services to the critical department of the " Chronicle," occasionally contributing political articles. Among these latter were the celebrated " Illustrations of Vetus," which appeared in the " Chronicle " at the close of 1813, and attracted considerable attention.

He experienced great difficulty in the first instance, when he began to write for the newspapers ; but he found that where the strong necessity for doing a thing was present to him, he managed to surmount all obstacles.

He says himself : " I had not till then [about 1812] been in the habit of writing at all, or had been a long time about it ; but I perceived that with the necessity the fluency came. Something I did *took*, and I was called upon to do a number of things all at once. I was in the middle of the stream, and must sink or swim. I had, for instance, often a theatrical criticism to write after midnight, which appeared the next morning. There was no fault found with it — at least, it was as good as if I had had to do it for a weekly paper. I only did it at once and recollected all I had to say on the spot, because I could not put it off for three days, when perhaps I should have forgotten the best part of it. Besides, when one is pressed for time, one saves it. I might set down nearly all I had to say in my mind while the play was going on. I know I did not feel at a loss for matter — the difficulty was to compress, and write it out fast enough."

He succeeded Mr. Mudford as theatrical critic on the "Chronicle," quite at the commencement of 1814. Mr. Mudford procured a place on the " Courier," of whose columns he availed himself to make known to the public that " it was impossible for any one to understand a word Mr. Hazlitt wrote." [1]

FULL OF WORK.

I find newspaper-work his mainstay during 1814 and 1815. He wrote regularly for the " Chronicle," and occasionally for the " Champion " and " Examiner." The review of Wordsworth's " Excursion " in the last is his.

Wordsworth had sent Lamb a copy of the poem, and one day, while Lamb was out, Martin Burney came and took the book away. My grandfather wanted the copy for his review, and had sent Martin in search of it. Lamb, when he found that the volume had disappeared, and learned the circumstances, was very much annoyed ; [2] and my grandfather, understanding that he had taken offense, came to his rooms and " blew up " him and Mary well. " Blow up " is Lamb's own word ; and Lamb (in a letter to a friend) adds, that he supposed it would come to a breach. Which was, in fact, the case.

In the correspondence between Lamb and Wordsworth there are several references to this affair. Lamb had been invited to write a paper on " The Excursion " in the " Quarterly," and as there was some delay about it, he explained to

---

[1] Mr. W. Mudford was at one time editor of the *Courier*. He is the author of a work on the Battle of Waterloo, and others. There is an account of him in Jerdan's *Autobiography*.

[2] Lamb was full of crotchets. He once made an extravagant outcry, because Coleridge came while he was away, and took Luther's *Table Talk*.

the author that it arose through Hazlitt's "unlucky detention of the book." At the same time he put in a word for his friend. "His remarks," he could not help saying, "had some vigor in them, particularly something about an old ruin being too modern for *your primeval nature*, and *about a lichen.*" In his next letter to the poet, he wrote: "Your experience about tailors seems to be in point blank opposition to Burton, as much as the author of 'The Excursion' does, *toto cælo*, differ in his notion of a country life from the picture which W. H. has exhibited of the same."

The criticism, which, according to Lamb, wore a look of haste, made no difference whatever in the relations between Hazlitt and Wordsworth, which had never been cordial, or, with the exception of the short visit to Nether-Stowey in 1798, and to Grasmere in 1803, at all intimate. I am afraid that Wordsworth's letters to Lamb contained sometimes severe things about W. H., and it cannot but be observed that if Lamb wants to fire off a sly epigram against W. H., he generally does so in his Grasmere parcel.

HAZLITT AND HAYDON.

My grandfather had become acquainted in 1812 with Haydon, the historical painter. He met him, one day, at Northcote's, whom he had known since his youth, and who lived at 39 Argyll Street, Regent Street.

On this occasion they left the house together, it seems, and walked some distance, my grandfather expatiating on Shakespeare's "Macbeth." This was the commencement of their knowledge of each other, but they never became intimate. My grandfather unluckily could not be induced to form a very exalted estimate of Haydon's powers, and Haydon reciprocated by attempting to paint upon paper a man whom he was incapable of understanding.

Haydon was an extraordinary egotist, and was therefore very jealous of egotism, when he observed it in other people. He congratulated himself, I find, on being a better Christian than Shelley, Keats, and the rest of that school. "Luckily for me," he says, " I was deeply impressed with the denunciations, the promises, the hopes, the beauty of Christianity ; " and again, he observes : " I never heard any skeptic, bvt Hazlitt, discuss the matter with the gravity such a question demanded." I suspect that Haydon would have found it difficult to maintain his position, if Mr. Hazlitt had confronted him with "How do you know, sir, that I *am* a skeptic ? " Perhaps Haydon may be said to have been a little too lavish of his animadversions. He was not peculiarly proof against criticism, nor very indifferent to what people said about him, and he might, with advantage to himself, have given an example of forbearance and tenderness. Besides, he should not have associated with a set whose religious opinions were so repugnant to his own ; there was the great risk that he might be mistaken for one of them. I have not seen Mr. Haydon's picture of Christ, in which he introduced Mr. Hazlitt "looking at the Saviour *as an investigator*, Keats in the background, and Wordsworth 'bowing in reverence and awe.' " It is singular enough that he should have selected two "skeptics" for such a purpose as this, even though one of them was only brought in by virtue of his critical faculty. This happened in 1817, just before the artist removed to Lisson Grove North.

A little prior to this, the notorious " Catalogue Raisonnée " of the British Institution was published, and was reviewed by Mr. Hazlitt in the " Examiner " for 1816. He called it "the most extraordinary that ever appeared in a country making pretensions to civilization," and declared that " the day after it came out, it ought to have been burnt by the common hangman." Here he had all lovers of art on his side — and Mr. Haydon. Northcote, however, was so delighted with it, that he ordered a long candle the first evening of its appearance, and went to bed to read it in ecstasy ! So he told Haydon.

Haydon's " Solomon " had succeeded' in defiance of some adverse criticisms upon it beforehand on the part of friends, much to the painter's exultation. He sent my grandfather a card for the private view.

" The greatest triumph," says he (1814), "was over Hazlitt.

My friend Edward Smith, a Quaker, had met him in the room,
and Hazlitt abused the picture in his spitish humor; but in
coming round he met me, and holding out his two cold fingers,
said, ' By God, sir, it is a victory,' [and he] went away and
wrote a capital criticism in the ' Morning Chronicle.' "

I have the strongest suspicion that Haydon's "greatest
triumph " was no triumph at all, and that the "capital criticism in the ' Morning Chronicle ' " proceeded from the writer's
natural kindness of heart, for once *at any rate,* getting the
better of his judgment. To Edward Smith he could afford to
be more candid. If Haydon had not been a struggling and
poor man, the criticism might not have been so capital, for my
grandfather's opinion of him was by no means high.

Haydon says again : " One day I called on him and found
him arranging his hair before a glass, trying different effects,
and asking [he asked ?] me my advice whether he should
show his forehead more or less. In that large wainscoted
room Milton had conceived, and perhaps written, many of his
finest thoughts, and there sat one of his critics admiring his
own features. Bentham lived next door. We used to see him
bustling away, in his sort of half-running walk in the garden.

" Both Hazlitt and I looked with a longing eye from the
windows of the room at the white-haired philosopher in his
leafy shelter, his head the finest and most venerable ever
placed on human shoulders."

The breach with the Lambs, after the *blowing up,* did not
last very long. They were at what was to have been a christening party at my grandfather's in York Street, in the September of 1814, as I collect from a passage in Mr. Haydon's
" Autobiography." Haydon was also there on the occasion,
and has recorded his impressions. He says : —

" In the midst of Hazlitt's weaknesses, his parental affection
was beautiful. He had one boy. He loved him, doted on
him. He told me one night this boy was to be christened.
' Will ye come on Friday ? ' ' Certainly,' said I. His eye
glistened. Friday came, but as I knew all parties, I lunched

heartily first and was there punctually at four. Hazlitt then lived in Milton's house, Westminster, next door to Bentham. "At four I came, but he was out. I walked up and found his wife ill by the fire in a bed-gown — nothing ready for guests, and everything wearing the appearance of neglect and indifference. I said, ' Where is Hazlitt ? ' ' Oh dear, William has gone to look for a parson.' ' A parson ! why, has he not thought of that before ? ' ' No, he did n't.' ' I 'll go and look for him,' said I ; and out I went into the Park, through Queen's Square, and met Hazlitt in a rage coming home. ' Have ye got a parson ? ' ' No, sir, these fellows are all out.' ' What will you do ? ' ' Nothing.' "

Nothing *was* done that day, but a good deal of company, including Charles and Mary Lamb, dropped in soon afterwards, and there was " good talk," but no victuals that pleased Mr. Haydon.

The christening took place, however, on the 26th of September that year, at St. Margaret's, Westminster ; it was the little boy's third birthday. Martin Burney and Walter Coulson were the godfathers.[1]

HAZLITT'S HOUSEKEEPING.

I have heard odd accounts of that York Street establishment. My grandmother was woefully undomestic, and my grandfather " hated," to use his own words, " the formal crust of circumstances, and the mechanism of society."

As for my grandfather, he had been brought up in the country by parents who were in indifferent circumstances, and who were not of a very methodical turn of mind. At an early period, he seems to have been left a good deal to his own resources and inclinations, and when very young studied painting under his brother John, who was very far from being a formalist, and at Paris, in the Louvre, where he had to shift for himself with very slender means. We know that apart

[1] While my father was quite a little fellow, he went to Mr. Black's at Millbank to spend the day, and going down to the river with a bucket to get water for Black's garden, he fell in, and was rescued by his host's dog Platoff.

from any merely sentimental and transitory attachments he may have formed, he was disappointed in love at an early age, in a manner which preyed upon his spirits afterwards, and that he never thoroughly rallied from the blow. Added to all this, he was induced to enter into a marriage which was certainly not one of choice (though it was in no way forced upon him), and the woman with whom he thus knit himself permanently was one of the least domestic of her sex. She was a lady of excellent disposition, an affectionate mother, and endowed with no ordinary intelligence and information. But for household economy she had not the slightest turn ; and she was selfish, unsympathizing, without an idea of management, and destitute of all taste in dress.

. She was fond of finery, but her finery was not always very congruous. A lady is living who recollects very well the first visit Mrs. Hazlitt paid to her family at Bayswater. It was a very wet day, and she had been to a *walking match.* She was dressed in a white muslin gown, a black velvet spencer, and a Leghorn hat with a white feather. Her clothes were perfectly saturated, and a complete change of things was necessary, before she could sit down. ·

The stiff, ceremonious ways of Dr. Stoddart and his family did not please her at all. When one of her nephews was praised in her hearing as an example of good breeding and politeness, she laughed, and exclaimed, " Oh, do you like such manners ? John seems to me like an old-fashioned dancing-master." .

The hall at York Street was a great square place like a kitchen, and the parlor where Mr. Hazlitt sat was up-stairs. It was a big, wainscoted room, with two windows, which looked upon the garden of Jeremy Bentham's house ; the mantel-piece was an old-fashioned high piece of architecture, which my grandfather had made a note·book of by covering with hieroglyphical memoranda for future essays.

There was Mrs. Tomlinson, the housekeeper, and her two daughters, of whom one was a single lady, the other was married to Private ——, of Her Majesty's —— foot.[1] This gallant soldier was frequently asked in by Mrs. T., his affectionate mamma-in-law, and there was high festival below stairs on these occasions.

Between the consumption of victuals and drink in the kitchen, and the consumption in the parlor, where the same set came to dinner about three times a week, the household expenses must have been considerable, with all the discomfort and absence of method observable in the arrangements.

HAZLITT'S MARRIED LIFE.

"I want an eye to cheer me, a hand to guide me, a breast to lean on ; all which I shall never have, but shall stagger into my grave without them, old before my time, unloved and unlovely, unless ——. I would have some creature love me before I die. Oh ! for the parting hand to ease the fall ! "

The passage above cited is in the autograph MS. of an "Essay on the Fear of Death," written in 1821, but it was omitted in the printed version in " Table Talk."

" How few," he says again, " out of the infinite number that marry and are given in marriage, wed with those they would prefer to all the world ; nay, how far the greater proportion are joined together by mere motives of convenience, accident, recommendation of friends ; or, indeed, not unfrequently by the very fear of the event, by repugnance, and a sort of fatal fascination."

These lines came about the same period from the same pen and the same heart. My grandfather had been united to Miss Stoddart for thirteen years ; but the marriage, as I had as well confess at once, was not a happy one. I should even go so far as to say that he had his individual case and fate in view, where he speaks of marriages being brought about sometimes " by repugnance and a sort of fatal fascination."

Never, I suppose, was there a worse-assorted pair than my

---

[1] Lamb's *Becky* was originally at my grandfather's. Was she a daughter of Mrs. T ? I should think so. An apt pupil, at any rate ; for she ruled the roost at Lamb's, as her mother or mistress did at 19 York Street.

grandfather and grandmother. If they had not happened to marry, if they had continued to meet at the Lambs', as of old, or at her brother's, they would have remained probably the best of friends. She would have appreciated better his attainments and genius ; while in her, as Miss Stoddart, or as the wife of anybody else but himself, he would have admired and recognized many of the qualities which endeared to him the society and conversation of Mrs. Montagu. Mrs. Hazlitt was capitally read, talked well, and was one of the best letter-writers of her time. She was a true wife tò William Hazlitt, and a fond mother to the only child she was able to rear ; but there was a sheer want of cordial sympathy from the first set-out.

They married after studying each other's characters very little, and observing very little how far their tempers were likely to harmonize ; or, more properly speaking, how far his was likely to harmonize with any woman's, or hers with any man's.

She might have been a blue-stocking, if she could have set the right value on her husband's talents, and entered into his feelings ; she might have been undomestic, if she had been more like his *Madonna*. But, unluckily for them both, she was intellectual, without reverence for his gifts ; and homely, without any of those graces and accomplishments which reconcile men to their homes.

I believe that Mr. Hazlitt was physically incapable of fixing his affection upon a single object, no matter what it might be, so that it was but one. He might worship Miss Railton, or Miss Wordsworth (if De Quincey is to be believed), or anybody else in his mind's eye, but not in his body's eye, which was at all events as potent an organ.

He comprehended the worth of constancy, fidelity, chastity, and all other virtues as well as most men, and could have written upon them better than most ; but a sinister influence or agency was almost perpetually present, thwarting and clouding a superb understanding — that singular voluptuousness of temperament, which we find at the root of much that

he offended against heaven and earth in, as well as of many
of the fine things we owe to his pen.

Mr. Hazlitt's moral constitution supplies, or seems to supply,
an illustration of the differences between the two words *sen-
suousness* and *sensuality.* He was not a sensualist, but he
was a man of sensuous temperament. A sensualist is a person in whom the animal appetite obscures and deadens all
loftier and purer instincts. In the sensuous man an intense
appreciation of the beautiful in Nature and Art is associated
and intimately blended with those potent instincts which en-
danger virtue.

His wife had not much pretense for quarreling with him on
the ground of former attachments of his still lingering in his
thoughts, and keeping his affection in a state of tangle ; for
she, too, had had her little love affairs, and accepted him only
when her other suitors broke faith. But in truth, she was not
the sort of woman to be jealous ; it was not her " way of
looking at things," as Mary Lamb used to say of her. She
used, however, to tax him from time to time with having had
a sweetness once for Sally Shepherd. Who Sally Shepherd
was, is more than I can tell, unless she was a daughter of
Dr. Shepherd of Gateacre, whose portrait he painted in
1803.

Both Mr. and Mrs. Hazlitt remained tenderly devoted to
their little son. It was a trait in their characters which must
always be admired ; it was a feature in my grandfather's which
excited even the applause of Mr. Haydon.

The child was often a peacemaker between his parents when
some unhappy difference arose ; and when it came to Mr.
Hazlitt frequently taking up his residence, after 1819, at Winterslow Hut, my father usually spent part of his time with one,
and part with the other. In 1822 he was put to school at a
Mr. Dawson's, in Hunter Street, London ; and it was just
before he was going to start for this new scene that my grandfather addressed to him the "Advice to a School-boy," a
letter full of admirable suggestion and counsel, and strongly
stamped with that impress of the writer's personal sentiments

and sufferings which has individualized so large a proportion of his works.

In this letter to a boy of ten, he *speaks at* the circumstances by which he was surrounded at the moment, and points obliquely to his own frustrated hopes — of the hopes which he nourished in his "sublime" youth, of happiness with a Railton, or a Wordsworth, or a Windham, or a Shepherd

He says : —

"If you ever marry, I would wish you to marry the woman you like. Do not be guided by the recommendation of friends. Nothing will atone for or overcome an original distaste. It will only increase from intimacy; and if you are to live separate, it is better not to come together. There is no use in dragging a chain through life, unless it binds one to the object we love. Choose a mistress from among your equals. You will be able to understand her character better, and she will be more likely to understand yours. Those in an inferior station to yourself will doubt your good intentions, and misapprehend your plainest expressions. All that you swear is to them a riddle or downright nonsense. You cannot by possibility translate your thoughts into their dialect. They will be ignorant of the meaning of half you say, and laugh at the rest. As mistresses, they will have no sympathy with you ; and as wives, you can have none with them.

"Women care nothing about poets, or philosophers, or politicians. They go by a man's looks and manner. Richardson calls them 'an eye-judging sex ;' and I am sure he knew more about them than I can pretend to do. If you run away with a pedantic notion that they care a pin's point about your head or your heart, you will repent it too late."

He was afraid that he might be taken from the little fellow, and that he might be left alone in the world. "As my health is so indifferent, and I may not be with you long, I wish to leave you some advice (the best I can) for your conduct in life, both that it may be of use to you, and as something to remember me by. I may at least be able to caution you against my own errors, if nothing else."

He wished him to know what he knew, and to learn what he had learned, that there might be no "bar of separation between them." "I would have you, as I said, make yourself master of French, because you may find it of use in the commerce of life ; and I would have you learn Latin, partly because I learnt it myself, and I would not have you without any of the advantages or sources of knowledge that I possessed — it would be a bar of separation between us — and secondly, because there is an atmosphere round this sort of classical ground to which that of actual life is gross and vulgar."

He used to give his little boy money when he went away in the morning, to spend while he was away. The great hall at York Street was his play-ground ; and on these occasions a rather promiscuous circle of acquaintances from the neighborhood used to be invited in to assist in the outlay of the silver, which papa had given with a strict injunction, like the old French gentleman in the story-book, that it should be gone before he came back — a bidding which Mr. W. H. Jr., with the help of his young friends, executed as a rule without difficulty. My grandfather wished his son to grow up with generous notions, and this was the way, in *his* opinion, to set about inculcating the principle and feeling upon his mind.

SARAH WALKER.

In the year 1820 Mr. Hazlitt had first taken apartments at No. 9 Southampton Buildings, Chancery Lane. His landlord was a Mr. Walker, a tailor by trade, and a lodging-house keeper. Walker was Mr. J. P. Collier's tailor. Whether he was Mr. Hazlitt's tailor also, and it was thus he was led to go there, I know not.

He had two daughters, Sarah and Betsy ; and it happened on the 16th August, 1820, that Mr. Hazlitt saw Sarah Walker for the first time, and was smitten by her personal attractions. Betsy Walker afterwards married a gentleman named Roscoe, and made him an excellent wife, it is said.

To him Sarah Walker was perfect loveliness. He was infatuated. He thought that he saw in her features a likeness to the old paintings of the Madonna. The girl herself must have been, at any rate, of somewhat superior breeding, if not looks. She felt, or pretended to feel, an interest in Mr. Hazlitt's works, of some of which she had copies, given to her by himself. He gave her other books, but she said that his *own* were those she chiefly prized ! She admired a statuette of Napoleon which he possessed, and he gave that to her. But she declined to receive it, and returned it to him afterwards, with the remark that she fancied he only meant she was to take care of it while he was away. In one of his conversations with Miss Walker, Mr. Hazlitt took occasion to describe to her the nice points of difference between the French, English, and Italian characters, and Miss W. pretended to feel an interest in the subject, and to express a wish to see foreign countries, and to study foreign manners, if the opportunity should ever present itself.

" *H.* But I am afraid I tire you with this prosing description of the French character, and abuse of the English ? You know there is but one subject on which I should ever like to talk, if you would let me.

" *S.* I must say you don't seem to have a very high opinion of this country.

" *H.* Yes, it is the place that gave you birth ——.

" *S.* Do you like the French women better than the English ?

" *H.* No ; though they have finer eyes, talk better, and are better made. But they none of them look like you. I like the Italian women I have seen much better than the French. They have darker eyes, darker hair, and the accents of their native tongue are so much richer and more melodious. But I will give you a better account of them when I come back from Italy, if you would like to have it.

" *S.* I should much. It is for that I have sometimes had a wish for travelling abroad, to understand something of the manners and characters of different people." . . . .

Even an honest hallucination has its respectability to recommend or excuse it. Mr. Hazlitt's was complete and sincere as any man's ever was. As to dishonorable views, I unhesitatingly affirm, once for all, that he had them not. A careful perusal of the book in which his passion is told will convince anybody of so much, who goes to the task of reading it with a correct knowledge of the writer's character.

Take another episode from this book, that of the *flageolet*. She has one, but he is not sure it is good enough for her.

"*S*. It is late, and my father will be getting impatient at my stopping so long.

"*H*. You know he has nothing to fear for you ; it is poor I that am alone in danger. But I wanted to ask about buying you a flageolet. Could I see that you have ? If it is a pretty one, it would n't be worth while ; but if it is n't, I thought of bespeaking an ivory one for you. Can't you bring up your own to show me ?

"*S*. Not to-night, sir.

"*H*. I wish you could.

"*S*. I cannot, but I will in the morning.

"*H*. Whatever you determine I must submit to. Good-night, and bless thee ! "

"[The next morning S. brought up the tea-kettle, on which, and looking towards the tea-tray, she said, 'Oh, I see my sister has forgot the teapot.' It was not there, sure enough ; and tripping down-stairs, she came up in a minute, with the teapot in one hand and the flageolet in the other, balanced so sweetly and gracefully. It would have been awkward to have brought up the flageolet on the tea-tray, and she could not go down again on purpose to fetch it. Something therefore was to be omitted as an excuse. Exquisite witch !] "

It appears that my grandfather was not the first person of position whom this " exquisite witch " had entranced. There *must have been* a good deal in her, surely ?

She confessed to my grandfather the existence of another attachment, one day, when he pressed her.

"*H*. . . . . Is there not a prior attachment in the case ? Was there any one else that you *did* like ?

"*S*. Yes ; there was another.

"*H*. Ah ! I thought as much. Is it long ago, then ?

14

"*S.* It is two years, sir.

"*H.* And has time made an alteration, or do you still see him, sometimes?

"*S.* No, sir; but he is one to whom I feel the sincerest affection, and ever shall, though he is far distant.

"*H.* But did he return your regard?

"*S.* I had every reason to think so.

"*H.* What, then, broke off your intimacy?

"*S.* It was the pride of birth, sir, that would not permit him to think of our union.

"*H.* Was he a young man of rank, then?

"*S.* His connections were high.

"*H.* And did he never attempt to persuade you to anything else?

"*S.* No; he had too great a regard for me.

"*H.* Tell me; how was it? Was he so very handsome? Or was it the fineness of his manners?

"*S.* It was more his manner; but I can't tell how it was. It was chiefly my fault. I was foolish to suppose he could ever think seriously of me. But he used to make me read with him — and I used to be with him a good deal, though not much, neither — and I found my affections engaged before I was aware of it.

"*H.* And did your mother and family know of it?

"*S.* No, I have never told any one but you; and I should not have mentioned it now, but I thought it might give you some satisfaction.

"*H.* Why did he go at last?

"*S.* We thought it better to part.

"*H.* And do you correspond?

"*S.* No, sir. But, perhaps, I may see him again some time or other, though it will only be in the way of friendship." . . .

I have thought it desirable to bring forward these passages, as I shall have to do others, in order to throw a little light on the character of Miss Walker. The difficulty is that we can only get at that through one who, though his love of truth was

so great as to lead him often to speak it to his own disadvantage
and disparagement, was in this case the dupe of one of the
most extraordinary illusions recorded in biography. The passion "led him like a little child" (to use his own phrase), and if
it was satisfied, he augured that his " way would be like that of
a little child." What is peculiarly striking is, that when he
found that she had a second admirer, for whom though absent,
and almost hopelessly lost to her, she entertained, as she told
him, a sincere and unalterable fondness, he declared that he
could bear to see her happy with this other, and would pro-
mote that object if he could ! But what he dreaded was, the
feeling that she had a repugnance to him, independently of this.
He began, perhaps, to fear that some of the "Blackwood's"
people had been to her and had told her that he was *pimpled*
Hazlitt, and the author of the books of which some account
had been given in their magazine and in the " Quarterly ! "

When Mr. Hazlitt went to 9 Southampton Buildings, he
was living separate from his wife. He had been doing so for
some little time before the autumn of 1819, but I cannot supply the precise dates.

I am without exact information as to the period when Mr.
Hazlitt proposed a formal separation under the Scottish law ;
it must have been late in 1820, or early in 1821, at all events,
some time in the latter year. There were delays and post-
ponements from some cause or other, and Mr. Hazlitt himself
does not seem to have gone to Scotland till the beginning of
1822. In January of that year he was still at Stamford, and
wrote while there an account of his conversations with Miss
Walker, which he afterwards called " Liber Amoris." The
original MS. is dated " Stamford, January 29th, 1822."

In a letter to a friend he says, " I was detained at Stamford and found myself dull, *and could hit upon no other way
of employing my time so agreeably.*"

He seems to have taken his departure very shortly after the
commencement of the new year (1822) ; for on the 17th of the
month I find a letter addressed to him by Miss Walker from
London (Southampton Buildings), in answer to one she had
received. It was as follows : —

"LONDON, *January* 17, [1822].

"SIR, — Doctor Read sent the ' London Magazine,' with
compliments and thanks ; no letters or parcels, except the one
which I have sent with the ' Magazine,' according to your directions.   Mr. Lamb sent for the things which you left in our
care, likewise a cravat which was sent with them.   I send my
thanks for your kind offer, but must decline accepting it.   Baby
is quite well.   The first floor is occupied at present ; it is
quite uncertain when it will be disengaged.

"My family send their best respects to you.   I hope, sir,
your little son is quite well.

"From yours respectfully,

"S. WALKER.

"W. HAZLITT, ESQ."

Upon his arrival at Edinburgh he opened a correspondence
with a friend, whom he had made the repository of his confidence and his secrets — at present, the sole repository, I imagine.   He wrote to Mr. Patmore [1] when he had been in Scotland three weeks nearly, and told him that he had written
twice to Miss Walker, and had had only one note from her,
couched in very distant terms.   Mr. Hazlitt's letter (or one of
them rather) was written in February, 1822 ; he sent Mr. Patmore a copy of it.

"You will scold me for this," he began, "and ask me if this
is keeping my promise to mind my work.   One half of it was
to think of Sarah ; and besides, I do not neglect my work
either, I assure you.   I regularly do ten pages a day, which
mounts up to thirty guineas' worth a week, so that you see I
should grow rich at this rate, if I could keep on so.   .   .   .   .
I walk out here in an afternoon, and hear the notes of the
thrush, that come up from a sheltered valley below, welcome
in the spring ; but they do not melt my heart as · they used :
it is grown cold and dead.   As you say, it will one day be

---

[1] If Mr. Patmore had not avowed himself in *My Friends and Acquaintance* to
be the person to whom the correspondence was addressed, I should have felt it my
duty to suppress his name.   As it is, I do not see that there can be any object in doing so .

colder. . . . . Do not send any letters that come. I should like you and your mother (if agreeable) to go and see Mr. Kean in 'Othello,' and Miss Stephens in 'Love in a Village.' If you will, I will write to Mr. T——— to send you tickets. Has Mr. Patmore called?" . . . .

The following was the reply received : —

"SIR, — I should not have disregarded your injunction not to send you any more letters that might come to you, had I not promised the gentleman who left the inclosed to forward it at the earliest opportunity, as he said it was *of consequence.* Mr. Patmore called the day after you left town. My mother and myself are much obliged by your kind offer of tickets to the play, but must decline accepting it. My family send their best respects, in which they are joined by

"Yours truly,

"S. WALKER."

It appears that this letter was franked, and Mr. Hazlitt could not make out the writing. He had asked her whether the apartments occupied by him were let yet, and she took no notice of the question. He confessed to Mr. Patmore in this letter that he half suspected her to be "an arrant jilt," yet he "loved her dearly." The evening before he left for Scotland, he had broken ground on the subject of a *platonic attachment,* but she did not quite know whether that could be. "Her father was rather strict, and would object."

The next letter to Patmore is of the 30th March, 1822. He was still alone at or near Edinburgh : nor was he quite sure yet whether Mrs. Hazlitt was coming there to have the business settled, or not. He had written to 9 Southampton Buildings, once more, but his letter remained without an answer. I shall not enter into the merely rhapsodical portions of this correspondence, because their committal to paper and appearance in print *once* must ever form a subject of regret. They are the unconnected and inconsequent outpourings of an imagination always supernaturally vivid, and now morbidly so. But he was not drawn away entirely from other matters.

These letters occasionally contain miscellaneous items of news. " It is well," says he, " I had finished Colburn's work,[1] before all this came upon me. It is one comfort I have done that. . . . . I write this on the supposition that Mrs. H. may still come here, and that I may be left in suspense a week or two longer. But, for God's sake, don't go near the place *on my account.* Direct to me at the post-office, and if I return to town directly, as I fear, I will leave word for them to forward the letter to me in London — not in S. B. . . . . I have finished the book of my conversations with her, which I call ' Liber Amoris.'   " Yours truly,
                                                    " W. H.[2]
" EDINBURGH, *March* 30.

" P. S. I have seen the great little man,[3] and he is very gracious to me. *Et sa femme aussi!* I tell him I am dull and out of spirits. He says he cannot perceive it. He is a person of an infinite vivacity. My Sardanapalus [4] is to be in. In my judgment Myrrha is most like S. W., only I am not Sardana-palus.
" P. G. PATMORE, ESQ.,
      " 12 Greek Street, Soho, London."

I have no letter between March 30th and April 7th. Mrs. Hazlitt was still expected, but had not yet arrived.

[*April* 7, 1822.]

" MY DEAR FRIEND, — I received your letter this morning with gratitude. I have felt somewhat easier since. It showed your interest in my vexations, and also that you knew nothing worse than I did. I cannot describe the weakness of mind to which she has reduced me. I am come back to Edinburgh about this cursed business, and Mrs. H. is coming down next week. . . . . A thought has struck me. Her father has a bill of mine for 10*l.* unhonored, about which I tipped her a *cavalier epistle* ten days ago, saying I should be in town this

[1] The second volume of *Table Talk.*
[2] I am quoting from the original autograph letter : in the printed copy the text differs.
[3] Jeffrey.
[4] The review of Byron's *Sardanapalus* in the *Edinburgh.*

week, and ' would call and take it up,' but nothing reproachful. Now if you can get Colburn, who has a deposit of 220 pp. of the new volume, to come down with 10*l.*, you might call and take up the aforesaid bill, saying that I am prevented from coming to town, as I expected, by the business I came about. . . . . W. H.

" P. S. Could you fill up two blanks for me in an essay on Burleigh House in Colburn's hands, — one, Lamb's Description of the Sports in the Forest : — see ' John Woodvil,'

" To see the sun to bed, and to arise, etc. ; "

the other, Northcote's account of Claude Lorraine in his Vision of a Painter at the end of his life of Sir Joshua ? . . . .

" FINAL. Don't go at all. . . . . To think that I should feel as I have done for such a monster !

" P. G. PATMORE, ESQ.,
    " 12 Greek Street, Soho, London."

THE HAZLITT DIVORCE.

On Sunday the 21st April, 1822, Mrs. Hazlitt landed at Leith. She had left London on the previous Sunday in the smack *Superb*, at 3 P. M. So it had been a week's voyage. She experienced fine, dry weather. In her Diary, which she entitled the "Journal of my Trip to Scotland," she gives the following account of her arrival : —

Sunday, 21*st* [*April*]. — At 5 A. M. calm. At 1 P. M. landed safe at Leith. A laddie brought my luggage with me to the Black Bull, Catherine Street, Edinburgh. Dined at three on mutton chops. Met Mr. Bell at the door, as I was going to take a walk after dinner. He had been on board the vessel to inquire for me. After he went, I walked up to Edinburgh. . . . . Returned to tea. . . . . Went to bed at half-past twelve.

Mr. Hazlitt casually heard of her arrival from Mr. Bell, but they did not apparently meet, though Mr. H. was at the Black Bull that Sunday, as will be seen presently. He wrote off to Mr. Patmore on the same day : —

[EDINBURGH, *April* 21, 1822.]

" MY DEAR PATMORE, — I got your letter this morning, and I kiss the rod not only with submission but gratitude. Your rebukes of me and your defenses of her are the only things that save me. . . . . Be it known to you that while I write this I am drinking ale at the Black Bull, celebrated in ' Blackwood.' It is owing to your letter. Could I think the *love* honest, I am proof against Edinburgh ale. . . . . Mrs. H. is actually on her way here. I was going to set off home . . . . when coming up Leith Walk I met an old friend come down here to settle, who said, ' I saw your wife at the wharf. She had just paid her passage by the *Superb*.' . . . . This *Bell* whom I met is the very man to negotiate the business between us. Should ·the business succeed, and I should be free, do you think S. W. will be Mrs. ——? If she *will* she *shall;* and to call her so to you, or to hear her called so by others, will be music to my ears such as they never heard [!}. . . . . How I sometimes think of the time I first saw the sweet apparition, August 16, 1820 ! . . . . I am glad you go on swimmingly with the N[ew] M[onthly] M[agazine]. I shall be back in a week or a month. I won't write to *her.*   [No signature.]

" I wish Colburn would send me word what he is about. Tell him what I am about, if you think it wise to do so.

" P. G. PATMORE, ESQ.,
    " 12 Greek Street, Soho, London."

The letters in the printed volume are very apt to mislead such readers as they may find, for they are not printed faithfully, even as regards the sequence of events. We must therefore go back to Mrs. Hazlitt's Diary, which is, I believe, perfectly accurate, and certainly most minute : —

Monday, 22d [April]. — . . . . Mr. Bell called about twelve, and I went with him to Mr. Cranstoun, the barrister, to consult him on the practicability and safety of procuring a divorce, and informed him that my friends in England had

rather alarmed me by asserting that, if I took the oath of calumny, and swore that there was no collusion between Mr
Hazlitt and myself to procure the divorce, I should be liable
to a prosecution and transportation for perjury. Mr. Hazlitt
having certainly told me that he should never live with me
again, and as my situation must have long been uncomfortable,
he thought for both our sakes it would be better to obtain a
divorce and put an end to it. . . . .

Tuesday, 23d. — Consulted Mr. Gray [a solicitor]. . . . .
The case must be submitted to the procurators to decide
whether I may be admitted to the oath of calumny. If they
agree to it, the oath to be administered, then Mr. Hazlitt to be
cited in answer to the charge, and if not defended [I told him
I was sure Mr. Hazlitt had no such intention, as he was quite
as desirous of obtaining the divorce as me], he said then, if
no demur or difficulty arose about proofs, the cause would
probably occupy two months, and cost 50*l.*, but that I should
have to send to England for the testimony of two witnesses
who were present at the marriage, and also to testify that we
acknowledged each other as husband and wife, and were so
esteemed by our friends, neighbors, acquaintances, etc. He
said it was fortunate that Mr. and Mrs. Bell were here to bear
testimony to the latter part. And that I must also procure a
certificate of my marriage from St. Andrew's Church, Holborn.
I took the questions which Mr. Gray wrote . . . . to Mr.
Bell, who added a note, and I put it in the penny post. Sent
also the paper signed by Mr. Hazlitt securing the reversion of
my money to the child, which Mr. Bell had given me, by the
mail to Coulson, requesting him to get it properly stamped
and return it to me, together with the certificate of my marriage. . . . .

Thursday, 25th April [1822]. — Mr. Bell called to ask if he
could be of any assistance to me. I had just sent a note to
Mr. Hazlitt to say that I demurred to the oath, so there was
no occasion to trouble Mr. Bell. In the afternoon Mr. Ritchie,
of the " Scotsman " newspaper, called to beg me, as a friend to
both (I had never seen or heard of him before), to proceed in

the divorce, and relieve all parties from an unpleasant situation. Said that with my appearance it was highly probable that I might marry again, and meet with a person more congenial to me than Mr. Hazlitt had unfortunately proved. That Mr. Hazlitt was in such a state of nervous irritability that he could not work or apply to anything, and that he thought that he would not live very long if he was not easier in his mind. I told him I did not myself think that he would survive me. . . . . In the evening Mr. Bell called. . . . . I then told him of Mr. Ritchie's visit, at which he seemed much surprised, and said if Mr. Hazlitt had sent him, as I supposed, he acted with great want of judgment and prudence. . . . .

Saturday, 27th April. — Gave Mr. Bell the stamp for the 50*l.* bill, and the following paper of memorandum for Mr. Hazlitt to sign : —

" 1. William Hazlitt to pay the whole expense of board, clothing, and education, for his son, William Hazlitt, by his wife, Sarah Hazlitt (late Stoddart), and she to be allowed free access to him at all times, and occasional visits from him.

" 2. William Hazlitt to pay board, lodging, law, and all other expenses incurred by his said wife during her stay in Scotland on this divorce business, together with travelling expenses.

" 3. William Hazlitt to give a note of hand for fifty pounds at six months, payable to William Netherfold or order. Value Received."

Mr. Bell said he would go that day to Mr. Gray . . . . then go on to Mr. Hazlitt's, and call on me afterwards ; but I saw no more of him.

Sunday, 28th April, 1822. — Wrote to Mr. Hazlitt to inform him I had only between five and six pounds of my quarter's money left, and therefore, if he did not send me some immediately, and fulfill his agreement for the rest, I should be obliged to return on Tuesday, while I had enough to take me back. Sent the letter by a laddie. Called on Mr. Bell, who said that Mr. Gray was not at home when he called, but that he had seen his son, and appointed to be with him at ten

o'clock on Monday morning. Told me that Mr. Hazlitt said
he would give the draft to fifty pounds at three months instead of six, when the proceedings had commenced (meaning,
I suppose, when the oath was taken, for they had already
commenced) but would do nothing before. Told me he was
gone to Lanark, but would be back on Monday morning. . . . .
   Tuesday, 30th April. — Went to Mr. Bell after dinner, who
did not know whether Mr. Hazlitt was returned or not. . . . . .
In the evening, after some hesitation, went to Mr. Hazlitt myself for an answer. He told me he expected thirty pounds
from Colburn on Thursday, and then he would let me have
five pounds for present expenses ; that he had but one pound
in his pocket, but if I wanted it, I should have that. That he
was going to give two lectures at Glasgow next week, for
which he was to have 100*l.*, and he had eighty pounds beside
to receive for the "Table Talk" in a fortnight, out of which
sums he pledged himself to fulfill his engagements relative to
my expenses : and also to make me a handsome present, when
it was over (20*l.*), as I seemed to love money. Or it would enable me to travel back by land, as I said I should prefer seeing something of the country to going back in the steamboat,
which he proposed. Said he would give the note of hand for
fifty pounds to Mr. Ritchie for me, payable to whoever I
pleased : if he could conveniently at the time, it should be for
three months instead of six, but he was not certain of that.
. . . . Inquired if I had taken the oath. I told him I only
waited a summons from Mr. Gray, if I could depend upon the
money, but I could not live in a strange place without : and I
had no friends or means of earning money here as he had ;
though, as I had still four pounds, I could wait a few days.
I asked him how the expenses, or my draft, were to be paid,
if he went abroad, and he answered that, if he succeeded in
the divorce, he should be easy in his mind, and able to work,
and then he should probably be back in three months : but
otherwise, he might leave England forever. He said that as
soon as I had got him to sign a paper giving away 150*l.* a year
from himself, I talked of going back, and leaving everything.

. . . . I told him to recollect that it was no advantage for myself that I sought . . . . it was only to secure something to *his* child as well as mine. He said he could do very well for the child himself ; and that he was allowed to be a very indulgent, kind father — some people thought too much so. I said I did not dispute his fondness for him, but I must observe that though he got a great deal of money, he never saved or had any by him, or was likely to make much provision for the child ; neither could I think it was proper, or for his welfare that he should take him to the Fives Court, and such places . . . . it was likely to corrupt and vitiate him. . . . . He said perhaps it was wrong, but that he did not know that it was any good to bring up children in ignorance of the world. . . . . He said I had always despised him and his abilities. . . . . He said that a paper had been brought to him from Mr. Gray that day, but that he was only just come in from Lanark, after walking thirty miles, and was getting his tea. . . . .

Thursday, 2d May [1822]. — Mr. Bell called to say Mr. Hazlitt would sign the papers to-morrow and leave [them] in his hand. And that he should bring me the first five pounds. When he was gone, I wrote to Mr. Hazlitt, requesting him to leave the papers in Mr. Ritchie's hands, as he had before proposed.

Friday, 3d May. — Received the certificate of my marriage, and the stamped paper transferring my money to the child after my death, from Coulson, the carriage of which cost seven shillings. Called on Mr. Gray, who said, on my asking him when my presence would be necessary in the business, that he should not call on me till this day three weeks. . . . .

Saturday, 4th May, 1822. — Mr. Ritchie called, and gave me 4*l.*, said Mr. Hazlitt could not spare more then, as he was just setting off for Glasgow. . . . .

Tuesday, 7th May. — Wrote to my little son. . . . .

Tuesday, 21st May. — Wrote to Mr. Hazlitt for money. The note was returned with a message that he was gone to London, and would not be back for a fortnight.

Wednesday, 22*d.* — Called on Mr. Ritchie to inquire what I was to do for money, as Mr. Hazlitt had gone off without sending me any : he seemed surprised to hear he was in London, but conjectured he was gone about the publication of his book, took his address, and said he would write to him in the evening.

It is necessary now to shut up the Diary, and to resume our examination of the correspondence with Patmore, where we shall find (what the Diary does not tell us) an account of Mr. Hazlitt's temporary return to town. The letter which follows the last from which I extracted the pertinent and illustrative parts, was written, it should be recollected, on the 21st April, 1822, on the very day of Mrs. Hazlitt's arrival at Leith in the *Superb.* The next has no date, but from an expression in the letter which succeeds, it may be securely assigned to the 2d of June. It was posted at Scarborough, where the steamboat put in by which Mr. Hazlitt had taken his passage to London.

[OFF SCARBOROUGH,
in the steamboat for London.]

" DEAR PATMORE, — What have I suffered since I parted with you ! A raging fire is in my heart and in my brain, that never quits me. The steamboat (which I foolishly ventured on board) seems a prison-house, a sort of spectre-ship, moving on through an infernal lake, without wind or tide, by some necromantic power — the splashing of the waves, the noise of the engine, gives me no rest, night or day — no tree, no natural object, varies the scene — but the abyss is before me, and all my peace lies weltering in it ! . . . . The people about me are ill, uncomfortable, wretched enough, many of them — but to-morrow or next day they reach the place of their destination, and all will be new and delightful. To me it will be the same. . . . The people about me even take notice of my dumb despair, and pity me. What is to be done ? I cannot forget *her;* and I can find no other like what *she* *seemed.* . . . . W. H."

The arrangement of the letters in the "Liber Amoris " is again incorrect and unfaithful to the order of time. In the series of the original autographs, from which I quote, the next letter is of the 3d June. Nothing had yet been settled, and Mrs. Hazlitt had started on a tour to the Highlands and to Ireland. She was in tolerably active correspondence during the interval with her son, Miss Lamb, Mr. Walter Coulson, and her sister-in-law, Peggy Hazlitt.

The 3d of June letter, however, contains only one passage which is at all to the purpose, and even that perhaps might be not disadvantageously omitted. It demonstrates the over-whelming force of the infatuation as well as the nervous shock, and is so far worth a place.

" Do you know," he says to his correspondent, "the only thing that soothes or melts me is the idea of taking my little boy, whom I can no longer support, *and wandering through the country as beggars !* " . . . . He finishes by saying that if he could find out her [S. W.'s] real character to be different from what he had believed, " I should be no longer the wretch I am, or the god I might have been, but what I was before, poor, plain W. H."

The next is a note, which does not occur in the printed book : —

[*Between June 3 and June 9, 1822, but undated.*]

" MY ONLY FRIEND, — I should like you to fetch the MSS., and then to ascertain for me whether I had better return there or not, as soon as this affair is over. I cannot give her up without an absolute certainty. Only, however, sound the mat-ter by saying, for instance, that you are desired to get me a lodging, and that you believe I should prefer being there to being anywhere else. You may say that the affair of the divorce is over, and that I am gone a tour in the Highlands. · . . . Ours was the sweetest friendship. Oh ! might the delusion be renewed, that I might die in it ! Test her through some one who will satisfy my soul I have lost only a lovely frail one that I was not likely to gain by true love. I am going to see K——, to get him to go with me to the High-

lands, and talk about *her*. I shall be back Thursday week, to appear in court *pro formâ* the next day. . . . .
" Send me a line about my little boy. W. H.

" 10 GEORGE STREET,
 ' EDINBURGH."

He found out K——, as he had said he should do, and induced him to accompany him to the Highlands. Their conversations appear to have been, for the most part, a mere repetition of what we are already, to confess the truth, a little too familiar with. In a letter, which he addressed to K——, afterwards, or which at least is thrown in the ' Liber Amoris ' into an epistolary shape, he reminds him of what they talked of and what they saw during this remarkable trip together.

" You remember," he says to him, " the morning when I said, ' I will go and repose my sorrows at the foot of Ben Lomond '— and when from Dumbarton Bridge its giant shadow, clad in air and sunshine, appeared in view? We had a pleasant day's walk. We passed Smollett's monument on the road (somehow these poets touch one in reflection more than most military heroes) — talked of old times. You repeated Logan's beautiful verses to the cuckoo, which I wanted to compare with Wordsworth's, but my courage failed me ; you then told me some passages of an early attachment which was suddenly broken off ; we considered together which was the most to be pitied, a disappointment in love where the attachment was mutual, or one where there has been no return ; and we both agreed, I think, that the former was best to be endured, and that to have the consciousness of it a companion for life was the least evil of the two, as there was a secret sweetness that took off the bitterness and the sting of regret. . . . . One had been my fate, the other had been yours !

" You startled me every now and then from my reverie by the robust voice in which you asked the country people (by no means prodigal of their answers) ' if there was any trout-fishing in those streams ? ' and our dinner at Luss set us up for the rest of our day's march.

" The sky now became overcast ; but this, I think, added

to the effect of the scene. The road to Tarbet is superb. It
is on the very verge of the lake — hard, level, rocky, with low
stone bridges constantly flung across it, and fringed with
birch-trees, just then budding into spring, behind which, as
through a slight veil, you saw the huge, shadowy form of Ben
Lomond. . . . . The snow on the mountain would not let
us ascend ; and being weary of waiting, and of being visited
by the guide every two hours to let us know that the weather
would not do, we returned, you homewards, and I to London." . . . .

He did not hear from Patmore, whom he had requested to
let him know how matters were going on at Southampton
Buildings, and he returned to Scotland without going to London at all.   On the 9th of June he wrote to Mr. Patmore from
an inn in Berwickshire : —

" RENTON INN, BERWICKSHIRE.
[*June* 9, 1822.]

" MY DEAR PATMORE, — Your letter raised me for a moment
from the depths of despair, but not hearing from you yesterday
or to-day, as I hoped, I am gone back again. I
grant all you say about my self-tormenting madness, but has it
been without cause ? When I think of this, and I think of it
forever (except when I read your letters), the air I breathe
stifles me. . . . . I can do nothing. What is the use of
all I have done ? Is it not this thinking beyond my strength,
my feeling more than I ought about so many things, that has
withered me up, and made me a thing for love to shrink from
and wonder at ? . . . . My state is that I feel I shall
never lie down again at night nor rise up of a morning in
peace, nor ever behold my little boy's face with pleasure, while
I live, unless I am restored to her favor. . . . . I wonder,
or rather crawl, by the sea-side, and the eternal ocean, and
lasting despair, and her face are before me. . . . . Do
let me know if anything has passed : suspense is my greatest
torment. Jeffrey (to whom I did a little unfold) came down
with 100*l.*, to give me time to recover, and I am going to

Renton Inn to see if I can work a little in the three weeks before it will be over, if all goes well. Tell Colburn to send the "Table Talk" to him, 92 George Street, Edinburgh, unless he is mad, and wants to ruin me. . . . . Write on the receipt of this, and believe me yours unspeakably obliged,   W. H."

The next letter hardly requires a preface : —

[RENTON INN, BERWICKSHIRE,
June 18, 1822.]

" MY DEAR FRIEND, — Here I am at Renton, amid the hills and groves which I greeted in their barrenness in winter, but which have now put on their full green attire, that shows lovely in this northern twilight, but speaks a tale of sadness to this heart, widowed of its last and its dearest, its only hope. For a man who writes such nonsense, I write a good hand. Musing over my only subject (Othello's occupation, alas ! is gone), I have at last hit upon a truth that, if true, explains all, and satisfies me. You will by this time probably know something, from having called and seen how the land lies, that will make you a judge how far I have stepped into madness in my conjectures. If I am right, all engines set at work at once that punish ungrateful woman ! Oh, lovely Renton Inn ! here I wrote a volume of Essays ; here I wrote my enamored follies to her, thinking her human, and that below was not all the fiends. . . . . By this time you probably know enough and know whether this following solution is *in rerum naturâ* at No. 9 S. B. . . . . Say that I shall want it [the lodging] very little the next year, as I shall be abroad for some months, but that I wish to keep it on, to have a place to come to when I am in London. . . . . If you get a civil answer to this, take it for me, and send me word. . . . . Learn first if the great man of Penmaen-Mawr is still there. You may do this by asking after my hamper of books, which was in the back parlor. . . . . Tell her that I am free, and that I have had a severe illness.   W. H.

15

"I would give a thousand worlds to believe her anything but what I suppose. . . . .   W. H.

"P. G. PATMORE, ESQ.,
   "12 Greek Street, Soho, London."

So runs this letter, crossed and crossed again, of June 18th ; there is a good deal in it which I have withheld, as irrelevant and foreign to the purpose. By comparing it with the version given in the "Liber Amoris," very important discrepancies present themselves, probably introduced by the writer subsequently, when the correspondence was returned to him for the purposes of the book. I have strictly adhered to the text as it was originally composed.

MRS. HAZLITT'S DIARY RESUMED.

Sunday, 9th June, 1822. — Sent a letter to Mr. Hazlitt to remit the money he had promised.

Monday, 10th June. — . . . . Received a note from Mr. Ritchie, to say he would come the next day and explain about money matters to me. Had also a letter from the child. . . . .

Tuesday, 11th June. — . . . . Mr. Ritchie came. . . . . Told me that Mr. Hazlitt only got 56*l.* from Glasgow, and nothing from Colburn, so that he could not give me the money I asked, but that he had told him whatever small sums of money I wanted to go on with, he would let me have by some means or other.

Thursday, 13th June [1822]. — Mr. Bell called, and said that Mr. Hazlitt had gone to Renton Inn, but that he would remit me some money, which he showed him he had for the purpose, as soon as the oath was taken, which he said he was to give him due notice of. . . . . Asked if I did not take the oath to-morrow ? I said I had not heard from Mr. Gray, but was in hourly expectation of it. . . . . The note came soon after, appointing the next day. . . . .

Friday, 14th June. — Mr. Bell called, and said he was going to Mr. Gray's, and would come back for me. Returned, and said Mr. Gray informed him he could not be admitted, as he would be called on with Mrs. Bell the next Friday as witnesses. So I undertook to let him know when the ceremony was over. [Here follows the description of the taking of the oath.] . . . . On the whole, with the utmost expedition they can use, and supposing no impediments, it will be five weeks from this day before all is finished. Went down and reported this to Mr. and Mrs. Bell : dined there. They told me that Mr. Hazlitt took 90*l.* to the Renton Inn with him. . . . . Mr. Bell undertook to send him a parcel that night with the joyful intelligence of the oath being taken, as he would get it sooner that way than by the post. . . . .

Saturday, 15*th June.* — Mr. Bell called, and wrote a letter to Mr. Hazlitt here, and made it into a parcel, not having sent to him last night, as he promised. Wrote to Peggy. Feel very faint to-day.

Sunday, 16*th June* [1822]. — . . . . Adam Bell called, while I was at breakfast, to say that Mr. Hazlitt was come back, and had been at their house the night before. . . . .

Monday, 17*th June.* — Went to Mr. Bell as soon as I had breakfasted. He told me that Mr. Ritchie was to bring me 20*l.* that day in part of payment, and that the rest would be paid me as Mr. Hazlitt could get it. That he had proposed only ten now, but that Mr. Bell had told him that *that* would not do, as I proposed taking some journey, and had no money. Said he did not know anything about the child. Went home very uneasy about him, as his holidays were to begin this day ; and I fretted that he should be left there, and thought he would be very uneasy if they had not sent him to Winterslow, and feel quite unhappy and forsaken ; and thought on his father's refusing to tell me where he was to be, till I was so nervous and hysterical I could not stay in the house.

Went down to Mr. Bell's again at one, as they told me he [Mr. H.] would be there about that time, that I might see him myself, and know where the child was. He was not come, and Mr. Bell did not like my meeting him there. I told him if I could not gain information of the child, I would

set off to London directly, and find him out, and leave the
business here just as it was. He then gave me a note to send
him [Mr. H.] about it, but I carried it myself, and asked to
see him.

They said he was out, but would return at three o'clock. I
left the note, and went at three. They then said he would be
back to dinner at four. I wandered about between that and
Mr. Bell's till four ; then, going again, I met him by the way :
he gave me 10*l.*, and said I should have more soon by Mr.
Bell. I said I did not like Mr. Bell ; I had rather he sent by
Mr. Ritchie, which he said he would.

I asked about the child, and he said he was going to write
. that night to Mr. John Hunt about him ; so that the poor little
fellow is really fretting, and thinking himself neglected. . . . .

Mr. Bell said that he seemed quite enamored of a letter he
had been writing to Patmore ; that in their walk the day before
he pulled it out of his pocket twenty times, and wanted to read
it to them ; that he talked so loud, and acted so extravagantly,
that the people stood and stared at them as they passed, and
seemed to take him for a madman. . . . . .

The next twelve days were spent by Mrs. H. in the tour to
the Highlands and to Dublin. She returned on the 28th June.

Mr. Hazlitt, upon the conclusion of the affair, with the exception of certain formalities, wrote to Mr. Patmore : —

" 10 GEORGE STREET, EDINBURGH.
[*June* 18 *or* 19, *received June* 20, 1822.]

" MY DEAR FRIEND, — The deed is done, and I am virtually
a free man. Mrs. H. took the oath on Friday. . . . .
What had I better do in these circumstances ? . . . . She
·[Miss W.] has shot me through with poisoned arrows, and I
think another winged wound would finish me. It is a pleasant
sort of balm she has left in my heart. One thing I agree with
you in, it will remain there forever, but yet not very long. It
festers and consumes me. If it were not for my little boy,
whose face I see struck blank at the news, and looking through
the world for pity, and meeting with contempt, I should soon

settle the question by my death. That is the only thought that brings my wandering reason to an anchor, that excites the least interest, or gives me fortitude to bear up against what I am doomed to feel for the *ungrateful.* Oh, answer me, and save me, if possible, for her and *from* myself. W. H.

" Will you call at Mr. Dawson's school, Hunter Street, and tell the little boy I 'll write to him or see him on Saturday morning. Poor little fellow ! See Colburn for me about the book. The letter, I take it, was from him."

[EDINBURGH, *June* 25, 1822.]

" MY DEAR AND GOOD FRIEND, — I am afraid that I trouble you with my querulous epistles ; but this is probably the last. To-morrow decides my fate with respect to *her;* and the next day I expect to be a free man, There has been a delay *pro formâ* of ten days. In vain ! Was it not for her, and to lay my freedom at her feet, that I took this step that has cost me infinite wretchedness? . . . . You, who have been a favorite with women, do not know what it is to be deprived of one's only hope, and to have it turned to a mockery and a scorn. There is nothing in the world left that can give me one drop of comfort — *that* I feel more and more. . . . . The breeze does not cool me, and the blue sky does not allure my eye. I gaze only on her face, like a marble image averted from me — ah ! the only face that ever was turned fondly to me !

" I shall, I hope, be in town next Friday at farthest. . . . . Not till Friday week. Write, for God's sake, and let me know the worst.

" I have no answer from her. I *wish* you to call on Roscoe [1] in confidence, to say that I intend to make her an offer of marriage, and that I will write to her father the moment I am free (next Friday week), and to ask him whether he thinks it will be to any purpose, and what he would advise me to do. . . . . You don't know what I suffer, or you would not be so

---

[1] The gentleman who had married the sister, and was said to be very happy in his choice.

severe upon me. My death will, I hope, satisfy every one
before long.   W. H."

A very important letter, so far as regards this very delicate
and painful subject, was received from Mr. Patmore in reply
to the above. He had made inquiries, and the result was that
there was the best authority for supposing Miss Walker to be
a person of good character and conduct, but that she was not
disposed to entertain any proposal on the part of Mr. Hazlitt,
of whom, to say the truth, after what she had seen and heard,
she stood in considerable awe. Nothing could be more candid
and blunt than the tone of Mr. Patmore's letter, and I think
that this candor and bluntness operated beneficially in the end.
But the effect was not immediate.

While Mr. Hazlitt was in correspondence with Mr. Patmore
and the Walkers about this unfortunate and extraordinary
business, his wife, as she was still, till sentence was pronounced, was occupied in her tour. On her return to Edinburgh, she found letters from Mr. Coulson, from Peggy Hazlitt,
and from her son, waiting for her.

MRS. HAZLITT'S DIARY RESUMED.

Saturday, 29*th June*, 1822. — Sent the child's letter to his
father with a note, telling him that I was just returned from
Dublin with four shillings and sixpence in my pocket, and I
wanted more money. He came about two o'clock, and brought
me ten pounds, and said he did not think he was indebted to
me my quarter's money, as he had supplied me with more
than was necessary to keep me. . . . . He had been uneasy at not hearing from the child, though he had sent him a
pound and ordered him to write. I remarked that the letter
I sent him was addressed to him, and I supposed the child did
not know how to direct to him. He said he would if he had
attended to what he told him. That he wrote to Patmore, and
desired him to see for the child, and convey him to Mr. John
Hunt's, and that in his answer he said, " I have been to the
school, and rejoiced the poor little fellow's heart by bringing

THE HAZLITT DIVORCE. 231

him away with me, and in the afternoon he is going by the
stage to Mr. Hunt's.[1] He has only been detained two days
after the holidays begun." . . . . That Mr. Prentice had
told him last night it [the business] was again put off another
fortnight ; requested me to write to Mr. Gray, to know whether
I should be called on next Friday, and if it would be necessary
for me to remain in Scotland after that time ; if not, he thought
I had better go on the Saturday by the steamboat, as the accommodation was excellent, and it was very pleasant and good
company. That he intended going by it himself, as soon as he
could, when the affair was over, and therefore I had better set
out first, as our being seen there together would be awkward,
and would look like making a mockery of the lawyers here.
Wished I would also write to the child in the evening, as his
nerves were in such an irritable state he was unable to do so.
Both which requests I complied with.

Monday, 1st July. — Received a note from Mr. Gray, to say
I should not be called on for two or three weeks, but without
telling me how long I must remain in Scotland.

Saturday, 6th July [1822]. — . . . . Met Mr. Hazlitt
and Mr. Henderson, who had just arrived [at Dalkeith Palace]
in a gig. Mr. H. said he had heard again from Patmore, who
saw the child last Tuesday, and that he was well and happy.
I told him of my last letter and its contents. . . . . [He]
adverted again to the awkwardness of our going back in the
same boat. I told him I had some thoughts of going by boat
to Liverpool and the rest by land, as I should see more of the
country that way ; which he seemed to like. Asked me if I
meant to go to Winterslow ? Said, yes, but that I should be
a week or two in London first. He said he meant to go to
Winterslow, and try if he could write,[2] for he had been so dis-
tracted the last five months he could do nothing. That he
might also go to his mother's[3] for a short time, and that he
meant to take the child from school at the half-quarter, and

[1] At Taunton.
[2] Mrs. H. had a house in the village, but Mr. H. put up at the Hut. A strangely
close juxtaposition !
[3] At Alphington, near Exeter.

take him with him ; and that after the holidays at Christmas
he should return to Mr. Dawson's again. Said he had not
been to town [London], and that we had better have no communication at present, but that when it was over he would let
me have the money as he could get it. Asked if I had seen
Roslin Castle, and said he was there last Tuesday with Bell,
and thought it a fine place. Mr. Henderson shook hands,
and made many apologies for not recollecting me, and said I
looked very well, but that from my speaking to Mr. H. about
the pictures, he had taken me for an artist. . . . . The
two gentlemen passed me in their gig as I was returning.

These extracts may appear needlessly full and lengthy, but
they are so abundant in characteristic touches that it is difficult
to deal with them more succinctly. They show, what there is
nothing else to show, Mr. Hazlitt's peculiar temperament as
developed by the present transaction, my grandmother's practical turn and dimissal of all sentimentality, and, at the same
time, the strong affection of both of them for their child — *he*
made the only common ground there was ever to be again, perhaps that there ever had been, between the husband and the
wife. In the next entry there is more about the "money."

Wednesday, 10th July [1822]. — Called on Mr. Ritchie, to
ask if he thought I should finish the business on Monday? I
told him that I wanted to know what was to be done about my
own payment, as Mr. Hazlitt now seemed to demur to the one
quarter that he had all along agreed to, and there was also the
20*l.* that I was to have as a present. He said that he was at
present very much engaged in some business which would end
in two days more, and that then, if I was at all apprehensive
about it, he would write to, or see, Mr. Hazlitt on the subject.

Thursday, 11th July. — Met Mr. Hazlitt in Catherine Street,
and asked him what I was to do if Mr. Gray sent in my bill to
me, and he said I had nothing to do with it, for that he had
paid Mr, Prentice 40*l.*, which was nearly the whole expense

for both of them. I said that was what Mr. Ritchie, to whom I had spoken about it, thought. He said Mr. Ritchie had nothing at all to do with it, and I remarked that he was the person he had sent to me about it, and that he did not think it would finish on Monday; and [I] asked if he had heard anything more ? He said no, but he thought it would be Monday or Tuesday; and as soon as it was done, he wished I would come to him to finally settle matters, as he had some things to say, and I told him I would. I was rather flurried at meeting him, and totally forgot many things I wished to have said, which vexed me afterwards.

Friday, 12th July. — On my return [from a walk to Holyrood House] I found a note from Mr. Gray, appointing next Wednesday for my attendance, and desiring a " payment of 20*l.* towards the expense." I took it to Mr. Bell's ; he and Mr. Hazlitt went out at the back door as I went in at the front. I gave the message to Mrs. Bell, who told me Mr. Hazlitt had been to Mr. Gray's. . . . .

Saturday, 13th July. — Met Mr. Hazlitt at the foot of my stairs, coming to me. He said that Mr. Gray was to have the money out of what he had paid Mr. Prentice. . . . . I told him he need not be uneasy about meeting me in the steamboat, for I did not intend to go that way. Asked him if he thought it a good collection of pictures at Dalkeith House [this is so characteristic !]; he said no, very poor. . . . .

Wednesday, 17th July. — Mr. Bell called between ten and eleven. . . . . He had come, by Mr. Gray's desire, to accompany me to the court, and was himself cited as a witness. [Mrs. H. then describes going to the court, but the proceedings were *pro formâ*, as the depositions had been arranged to be taken at Mr. Bell's private residence.] Returned, and wrote a note to Mr. Hazlitt, to have in case he was out, saying that I would call on him at two o'clock I left it. . . . . Saw Mr. Hazlitt at four o'clock ; he was at dinner ; but I stopped and drank tea with him. [!] He told me that all was done now, unless Mrs. Bell should make any demur in the part required of her. . . . . Said he would set off to London by the mail that night, though he thought he should be detained by illness or die on the road, for he had been penned up in that house for five months . . . . unable to do any work ; and he thought he had lost the job to Italy, but to get out of Scotland would seem like the road to paradise. *I told him* [1] *he had done a most injudicious thing in publishing what he did in the* [New Monthly] *Magazine about Sarah Walker, particularly at this time, and that he might be sure it would be made use of against him, and that everybody in London had thought it a most improper thing, and Mr. John Hunt was quite sorry that he had so committed himself.*

He said that *he* was sorry for [it], but that it was done *without his knowledge or consent.* That Colburn had got hold of it by mistake, with other papers, *and published it without sending him the proofs.* He asked me where I should be in town, and I told him at Christie's. He inquired what kind of people they were. I told him a very respectable quiet young couple lately married. He desired me to take care of myself, and keep up a respectable appearance, as I had money enough to do so. *He* [2] *wished he could marry some woman with a good fortune, that he might not be under the necessity of writing another line; and be enabled to provide for the child, and do something for John; and that now his name was known in the literary world, he thought there was a chance for it, though he could not pretend to anything of the kind before.* . . . .
I left Mr. Henderson with him, pressing him to accompany him to the Highlands ; but he seemed, after some hesitation, to prefer going to London, though I left the matter uncertain. He [Mr. Henderson] had been dawdling backward and forward about it for three weeks, wishing to have the credit of taking him there, but grudging the money, though he was living upon us for a week together in London.

---

[1] The italics are mine. This passage must find room here, in spite of my scruples. The affair was well known, and was soon in print in the *Liber Amoris.* To conceal it would be useless; and all that I can do is to place it in its true light before the world. Mrs. H. was a plain-spoken woman, without any false delicacy about her. She was perfectly acquainted with the whole history of the matter.

[2] The italics are mine. The *John* referred to presently was, of course, his brother. This passage is very remarkable.

Mr. Hazlitt said that, if he went to Winterslow, he would take the child, as he wished to have him a little with him ; so I thought he had better go with the first that went, as I did not think of staying in town more than two or three weeks, and then making some stay at Winterslow, and proceeding afterwards to Crediton.[1] He said we could settle that best in town.

Mrs. Dow [Mr. H.'s landlady] brought in the bill, which he just looked at and said, " Is that the whole, ma'am ? " " Yes, sir ; you had better look over it, and see that it is correct, if you please." " *That*, ma'am," he said, "is one of the troubles I get rid of. I never do it." " You are a very indolent man, sir." " There is a balance of twenty-four shillings, ma'am ; can you have so much confidence in me as to let me have that ? " " No, sir, I can 't do that, for I have not the money." " I shall be glad then, ma'am, if you will let me have the four shillings, and you may pay the pound to Mrs. Hazlitt on Saturday, as when it comes, she will be here." " Yes, sir, and Mrs. Hazlitt may look over the bill, if she pleases."

Thursday, 18th July [1822]. — She returned with the four shillings, saying she had been to two or three places to get that. . . . Went to Mr. Ritchie, who gave me the note of hand for fifty pounds at six months, dated 6th May, and the copy of memorandums signed by Mr. Hazlitt. . . . . He said he had expected him and Mr. Henderson to supper last night, but they did not come. I told him he wished to go to London by the mail, and probably had done so. . . . . He said he must repeat that he thought we had taken the step most advisable for both parties. . . . Called at his [Mr. H.'s] lodgings to inquire if he went by the mail. Mrs. Dow said yes ; he left there about eight o'clock. . . . . Called at the coach-office, and they said Mr. Hazlitt did not go by the mail. Saw the waiter at the inn door, who said he went by the steamboat at eight o'clock this morning. . . . .

[1] Where Mr. H.'s relations were settled ! This is also a curious part of the business. My grandmother was intimate and friendly with the Hazlitts to the last, and frequently visited them here.

Carried back Mrs. Bell's book. Mr. Bell said I was a great fool to have acceded to his wish for a divorce, but that it was now done, and he thought I had better get some old rich Scotch lord, and marry here. "I was now Miss Stoddart, and was I not glad of that?" "No: I had no intention of marrying, and should not do what he talked of." He said I must needs marry; and I told him I saw no such necessity. . . . .

This is the conclusion. Mrs. Hazlitt sailed on the following day, at 2 P. M., in the smack *Favorite* from Leith. I have also done with the Patmore correspondence, of which I have only two other letters, post-marked July 3 and July 8, 1822, but both destitute of interest and illustration.[1]

The divorce was a separation *a mensâ et thoro*, and my grandfather had accomplished what he desired, the severance of his connection with a lady who, he conceived, did not understand or value him, and who had her independent means of support. But it was not a parting forever. Strangely enough, there does not seem to have been any ill-will on either side in the matter. They were to meet again.

It should be remembered that they had a strong tie remaining, which they could not or would not cut. It was my father — their only surviving child. They were both fondly attached to him, Mr. Hazlitt in his way, and Mrs. Hazlitt in hers, and he was often a channel of communication between his disunited parents.

Let me leave this subject of the "Liber Amoris" for good, with one observation, that it does not seem that the passion left a very deep or lasting impression on his mind. It was a piece of Buncle-ishness, which soon evaporated, and we hear, fortunately, very little of it afterwards, and then only in casual and half unintelligible allusions. As for the dissolution of

---

[1] Yet there is a passage in one of them — where he tells Mr. P. he thinks he shall come home by the mail, and asks him to come in and see him, about eight o'clock — which I shall quote, because it demonstrates his deep affection and respect for one of the most worthy men that ever lived — John Hunt. He says: "I wish much to see you and her, *and John Hunt and my little boy* once more; and then, if she is not what she once was to me, I care not if I die that instant."

that marriage-bond, it was decidedly the best course to have taken, and it was a mere piece of diplomacy after all. There were no tears shed on either side. It was *a stroke of business.* Let it pass. *Majora canemus.*

HAZLITT'S LAST DAYS.

Mr. Hazlitt removed, about 1827, from Down Street to 40 Half-Moon Street, Piccadilly ; and here he lodged, when in town, during a couple of years.

It happened, when the MS. of the second volume of " Napoleon " was almost ready for the printer, some burglars, who had got at the back of the premises through Shepherd's Market, tried to break in, and put Mr. Hazlitt into a great state of terror. He posted off the next morning to the " Atlas " office with his MS., and begged that it might be taken care of till the printer wanted it ; and he had not even then, when the danger or alarm was all over, and his treasure was secure, quite overcome his excitement. I owe this anecdote to a gentleman who became acquainted with Mr. Hazlitt towards the close of his life, and who was an eye-witness of his arrival, MS. in hand, at the newspaper office.

To another friend, whom he met with the adventure fresh in his mind, he said, " You know, sir, I had no watch, and they would n't have believed I had no watch and no money and, by G—, sir, they 'd have cut my throat."

His industry never flagged. He was unceasingly occupied. His health was by no means reëstablished, and his spirits were sadly indifferent ; but he went on, in spite of every obstacle, with the activity and continuity of a beginner.

In 1829 he shifted his quarters from 40 Half-Moon Street, to 3 Bouverie Street, Fleet Street, where he occupied (with his son) a first floor.

There was an alarm of fire while he was here, and the business was to get their pictures away — the copies of Titian and the " Death of Clorinda." He was cross with my father (ill-health improves nobody's temper) for being so cool ; but he himself did nothing but act the by-stander with great suc-

cess. They were temporarily deposited, till the danger was
over, at the Sussex Coffee House over the way.

At Bouverie Street he wrote numerous papers in the " Atlas,"
two or three in the " New Monthly," one or more in the " Examiner," and two in the " Edinburgh Review "— Flaxman's
" Lectures on Sculpture " and Wilson's " Life of Defoe.'
The latter is in the " Review " for January, 1830.

Lamb, in the postscript of a letter to Wilson, November 15,
1829, says : " Hazlitt is going to make your book a basis for
a review of De Foe's novels in the 'Edinbro'.' I wish I
had health and spirits to do it."

It seems that it was his greatest wish to make a paper on
Bulwer's novels in the " Review," and he spoke upon the
subject to Jeffrey, and, after his retirement from the editorship, to his successor, Mr. Napier. But there was a difficulty
felt and intimated, in connection with the proposal, both by
Jeffrey and Napier. Mr. Hazlitt could never learn what it
was ; but he had to give up the notion. He regretted this the
more, inasmuch as he had read " Paul Clifford," and been
pleased with it ; and he was anxious, as Mr. Patmore has it,
to "get the job," if it was only to furnish him with a motive
for going through the others.

He was now bringing to completion his Magnum Opus,
which, since his strength had begun visibly to decline, after
his telling illness of 1827, he was fondly solicitous of seeing
off his hands and in type. The finishing touches were put to
the third and fourth volumes at the latter end of 1829, under
the roof of Mr. Whiting the printer, of Beaufort House, in
the Strand ; [1] and the second and concluding portion of the
" Life " was at length launched safely in 1830. The sale of
the former volumes had been very inconsiderable, and the
publication of the remainder did not greatly help it on, I am
afraid. It came after Sir Walter's, and did not go off at all
well.

But the author's chief aim was not present gain so much

[1] Perhaps, after the alarm of fire at Bouverie Street, he thought the MS. safer at
Mr. Whiting's.

as posthumous identification with a subject, which he considered, as time went on, would grow in interest, and would
be judged, as it deserved.

I have understood, however, that he was to have had for
the copyright a considerable sum (500*l.*), of which he received
only a portion (140*l.*) in a bill, which, when the affairs of
Messrs. Hunt and Clarke became hopelessly involved, was
mere waste paper.

Mr. Hazlitt was dreadfully harassed by this disappointment. To him, as to most literary men, especially where
there is sickness and growing incapacity for application, a sum
of some hundreds of pounds was of the utmost moment, and
the loss of it entailed the greatest possible inconvenience and
personal worry.

I have no inclination to go into the painful details, and I
shall merely mention that the pecuniary crisis, which Mr. Hazlitt had hoped to avert, was accelerated by a knavish account-
ant, introduced to him (in ignorance of his real character,
doubtless) by Mr. Hone. Mr. Hazlitt's strength and spirits
were completely shattered by this deplorable and shameful
affair. He removed in the beginning of 1830 to 6 Frith
Street, Soho, and there he was now threatened with a return
of his old enemies, dyspepsia and gastric inflammation.

His early friends, the Reynells, took leave of him to go over
to Havre, where they had arranged to settle ; and he was
then poorly, and under the care of a M. Sannier. This was
in June. There is a letter from Lamb to the first Mrs. Hazlitt, dated June 3, 1830, respecting a suggestion she wished
made to my grandfather through Lamb, on a point in which
the unhappy circumstances inspired her with the deepest
motherly interest and anxiety — her son's establishment in
life.

It has never been printed, and I may therefore insert it : —

[*June* 3, 1830.]

" DEAR SARAH, — I named your thought about William to
his father, who expressed such horror and aversion to the

idea of his singing in public, that I cannot meddle in it directly or indirectly. Ayrton is a kind fellow, and if you choose to consult him, by letter or otherwise, he will give you the best advice, I am sure, very readily. *I have no doubt that Mr. Burney's objection to interfering was the same with mine.* With thanks for your pleasant long letter, which is not that of an invalid, and sympathy for your sad sufferings,[1] I re-main,   In haste,

"Yours truly,

"Mary's kindest love.   [CHARLES LAMB.]

"MRS. HAZLITT,

"At Mr. Broomhead's,

"St. Anne's Square, Buxton."

The "thought" was that William should go with Mr. Braham the singer, and that he should adopt the profession. But his father's insuperable repugnance to the choice of any line of life lingered with him till the last ; he wanted to see him a gentleman, and to be able to leave him independent of the world.

In the course of the summer, my grandfather grew weaker and worse, and the services of Dr. Darling and Mr. Lawrence were volunteered. Still he was able to think and write a little. He composed a paper on " Personal Politics," in view of the then recent deposition of Charles X. and the overthrow of the Bourbon dynasty in France. It was something, he thought, to have been spared to witness *that.* The possibility of their recall occurred to him.

" Even then," he wrote, " I should not despair. The Rev-olution of the Three Days was like a resurrection from the dead, and showed plainly that liberty too has a spirit of life in it ; and that the hatred of oppression is 'the unquenchable flame, the worm that dies not.' "

The end was near. He had struggled with death through August and a part of September, and seemed to live on by a pure act of volition. But he was sinking. He asked those who were with him to fetch his mother to him, that he might

---

[1] Mrs. H. was beginning to labor under frequent and severe attacks of rheu-matism.

see her once more. He knew that he was going fast. But his mother could not come to him ; she was in Devonshire, and heavily stricken in years.

As he lay there, on his dying bed, he mentioned to Lamb, who was by, that William was engaged to Kitty,[1] and said that the idea gave him pleasure.

One Saturday afternoon in September, when Charles Lamb was in the room, the scene closed. He died so quietly that his son, who was sitting by his bedside, did not know that he was gone till the vital breath had been extinct a moment or two.

His last words were : " Well, I 've had a happy life."

" In my grandmother's handwriting I find this contemporary memorandum : —

"Saturday, 18th September, 1830, at about half-past four in the afternoon, died at his lodgings, No. 6 Frith Street, Soho, William Hazlitt, aged fifty-two years, five months, and eight days.

" Mr. Lamb, Mr. White, Mr. Hessey, and his own son were with him at the time."

In a letter written by a friend to his sister in Havre, on the following Tuesday, there is a reference to the loss which his acquaintance, his son, and literature had sustained on that 18th of September, 1830.

" Of the events which have occurred here since your departure," Mr. W. H. Reynell writes, "none will astonish you more, or at least affect you more, than the death of poor Hazlitt ; though the uncertain state in which he has been for the last two months ought to have prepared his friends for the worst. It appears, however, from all accounts, that his son has entertained a very different opinion, or at least caused a very different opinion to be entertained. His father died on Saturday, and on Friday William told me that he was much better ; and even on the following day (the day he died) gave out that he was in no danger, but that he had *something in his mind*, which would kill him if he did not dispel it. I hear that

---

[1] Miss Catherine Reynell. They were married June 8, 1833.

16   .

Mr. Lawrence and another medical man were present, besides Dr. Darling, who had been attending him throughout, and who, they think, had not treated him judiciously. Mr. Hone called in Broad Street on Saturday afternoon to inform me of the melancholy event. My father will be very much shocked to hear of the departure of his old friend so suddenly."

Talfourd observes : —

" Hazlitt's death did not so much shock Lamb at the time, as it weighed down his spirits afterwards, when he felt the want of those essays which he had used periodically to look for with eagerness in the magazines and reviews, which they alone made tolerable to him ; and when he realized the dismal certainty that he should never again enjoy that rich discourse of old poets and painters with which so many a long winter's night had been gladdened, or taste life with an additional relish in the keen sense of enjoyment which endeared it to his companion."

HAZLITTIANA.

Like Dr. Johnson, Mr. Hazlitt addressed everybody as *Sir.* The youngest and most intimate of his friends was not exempt from this rule, unless Mr. Hazlitt happened to be in an unusually happy and cordial humor. Mr. C. H. Reynell's sons, whom he knew as well as his own child, were almost invariably saluted in what would now appear a ludicrously formal manner ; but indeed this mode of allocution had not gone out then so entirely as it has in our day.

He was accustomed to speak low, like Coleridge, with his chin bent in and his eyes widely expanded ; and his voice and manner, as a rule, were apt to communicate an impression of querulousness. His was the tone of a person who related to you a succession of grievances.

But when he entered on a theme which pleased or animated him, or when he was in the presence of those whom he knew well, and *trusted*, he cast off a good deal of this air, and his demeanor was easy, yet impassioned.

" In person," writes the late Mr. Justice Talfourd, " Mr.

Hazlitt was of the middle size, with a handsome and eager countenance, worn by sickness and thought ; and dark hair, which had curled stiffly over the temples, and was only of late years sprinkled with gray. His gait was slouching and awkward, and his dress neglected ; but when he began to talk he could not be mistaken for a common man. In the company of persons with whom he was not familiar his bashfulness was painful ; but when he became entirely at ease, and entered on a favorite topic, no one's conversation was ever more delightful. He did not talk for effect, to dazzle, or surprise, or annoy ; but with the most simple and honest desire to make his view of the subject entirely apprehended by his hearer. There was sometimes an obvious struggle to do this to his own satisfaction : he seemed laboring to drag his thought to light from its deep lurking place ; and, with modest distrust of that power of expression which he had found so late in life, he often betrayed a fear that he had failed to make himself understood, and recurred to the subject again and again, that he might be assured he had succeeded."

Where Talfourd speaks of his "intense sense of his individual being," he intends, however, I should think, an euphuism for what somebody else more candidly terms "ingrained selfishness." In some people egotism is simply delightful. In children it is not unpleasant very often. We rather like it in diarists. But in the main it is an unamiable quality, there is no doubt ; and where a great man is discovered to be an egotist, and to love himself best, society takes all the worse offense. It is a surprising frailty.

Some admirer of his was astonished to find that his conversation was so ordinary. Could this be the author of " Table Talk ? " It was a gentleman who evidently expected Hazlitt to speak essays. Enough for him to have to write them ! He considered himself off duty when he was not at work on something he had thought of.

Haydon the painter was scandalized at surprising him once looking at himself in the glass. Did Mr. Haydon never look at himself in the glass ?

Southey, in the " Doctor," takes occasion to observe, as something which had come to him upon report, " that Mr. Hazlitt saw his likeness in one of Michael Angelo's devils." The writer evidently meant mischief or wit ; but was not very successful, if so, in attaining either.

My grandfather, it is well known to all who understood him often said things half in jest (did the author of the " Doctor " never do so ?) ; and this, if said by him at all, was in one of these semi-serious moods. But it was Mr. Southey's cue to interpret him literally. The injustice done to a person on the other side of the question was of course scarcely worth considering : a fling at a Jacobin and a friend of Mr. Leigh Hunt was no harm, even if the joke was not very good or very true.

Mr. Patmore has fallen rather wide of the mark here. What he chooses to characterize as *demoniacal* in my grandfather's expression, was, in the main, assuredly nothing more than grimace and willfulness. I do not pretend to dispute that bitter, gloomy recollections did not haunt his brain upon occasion, and darken his brow, producing a lowering passionate expression ; but I am convinced, from all that I have learned and understood from those who were as good judges as Mr. Patmore, that the latter has seriously, nay grossly, misconceived the truth here ; and that these physiognomical phenomena were, oftener than not, mere tricks to mislead people, as they must have misled Mr. Patmore, into the persuasion that some satanic train of thought was going on within.

Leigh Hunt used to describe my grandfather's shake of the hand as something like a fish tendering you his fin. The same gentleman, on meeting him abroad, was surprised at the change in his appearance. He used to wear his hair long and curly, and then he had had it cropped, finding that it was beginning to turn gray.

When Leigh Hunt was in Italy, my grandfather, then newly married to his second wife, paid him a visit and dined with him. It seems that Mr. Hunt had been piqued by the manner in which my grandfather on one or two occasions, in those fits of spleen which sometimes came over him, retorted on him ;

and L. H. became anxious to prove to Mr. Hazlitt that he could do the same if he chose. He selected the present opportunity to do so, and before dinner was served, L. H. said to Mrs. Hazlitt, " I have something to show Hazlitt, but I will not let him see it till after dinner, as it might spoil his appetite." " Oh ! " said Mrs. H., " it will do him good." Thereupon Hunt gave Hazlitt a paper in which he had spoken his mind pretty freely on the sore subject, and Hazlitt sat down in a chair and read it through. When he had done, he observed, " By God, sir, there 's a good deal of truth in it."

He used to visit Leigh Hunt, when the latter resided at Hampstead, in the Vale of Health. The country thereabout was much more lonely than now, and he used to be so nervous of meeting with some dangerous adventure, that Mr. Hunt was generally obliged to send some one to see him as far as the London road.

He was untidy in his dress as a rule, and with this untidiness went, as is mostly the case, a prodigality. He never enjoyed the credit of having new clothes. He appeared to best advantage when he was attired for some special occasion. A gentleman (since dead) who knew him well during the last thirteen years of his life, said that he was never more astonished than when he saw Mr. Hazlitt accoutred in readiness to go to dinner at Mr. Curran's. He wore a blue coat and gilt buttons, black smalls, silk stockings, and a white cravat, and he looked the gentleman. But he did not often do himself this justice ; the processes of the toilet proved irksome. His second wife coaxed him for a time into conforming to the gentilities, but it was not for long, I fear. She abandoned the attempt in despair. An indifference to conventionalities had set in ever since his one great disappointment in life.

Montaigne the essayist had a cloak which he prized as having belonged to his father. He used to say that when he put it on he felt as if he was wrapping himself up in his father. There is still to this day preserved in our family just such a cloak as that of Montaigne ; it is the one in which Mr. Hazlitt went habitually to the play. His son values it, though he may

not go so far as Montaigne went in his fine and fanciful enthusiasm.

I have understood that this cloak (of blue cloth with a red
lining and a cape) was made on the supposed model of one
worn by Mr. Patmore. Mr. Hazlitt found, however, to his surprise and chagrin, that although Patmore's garment passed unquestioned at the doors of the opera, his own, on some techni-
cal ground, was refused admittance.

His diet was usually spare and plain. I have before me one
of the bills of Mr. Carter, his landlord at Winterslow Hut. It
is for the month of August, 1821 ; and among the items *tea*
and *rice* are conspicuous. His breakfast seems to have cost
him eighteen pence, his supper the same, and his dinner from
eighteen pence to four shillings. There is one entry of wine,
" twelve shillings : " he must have had company on the 25th
of the month, for he did not take wine.

He met my mother one day in Piccadilly, and as he looked
more out of spirits than usual, she asked him if anything was
the matter. He said, " Well, you know, I 've been having
some hot boiled beef for my dinner, Kitty — a most *uncomfortable* dish."

He had had a pheasant for dinner one day when my mother
saw him, and it turned out that he had been at a total loss to
know what to order, and so had ordered this — pheasants that
day being ten shillings a-piece in the market. " Don't you
think it was a good deal to give ? " she asked. " Well, I
don't know but what it was, Kitty," he replied, opening his
eyes in his way, and tucking his chin into his shirt-collar.

He would eat nobody's apple-pies but my mother's, and no
puddings but Mrs. Armstead's, of Winterslow. Mrs. A. contrived to persuade him that she had the art of making egg
puddings *without eggs*.

His natural gastric weakness, which is hereditary in the
family, was a constant torment to him ; and his love of all
good things in the eatable way, and abstinence (during a long
term of years) from every description of liquid, except tea and
water, tended to aggravate the constitutional tendency to this
class of disorder.

But it was a way of his to complain of indisposition sometimes, when he called anywhere, and the people of the house
were not as pleasant as usual, or something was said which
put him out of temper with them and himself. It did not sig-
nify very much which side was in fault, so long as matters
went amiss, and he did not happen to be in the best cue.

A great deal depended on the humor he was in. He saw
things with a different eye, he judged people from a different
light. He was two different men in his own person — the Mr.
Hazlitt of Mr. Southey's " Doctor " and the " Liber Amoris,"
and the Mr. Hazlitt, metaphysician, philosopher, philanthro-
pist, who desired to see some prospect of good to mankind —
according to the condition of his mental equilbrium and his
immediate *frame* of liver.

On such occasions as I have alluded to, he would get up,
say he was very ill, with his chin in and his eyes wide open,
and make the move to go, with a " Well, good-morning."

Mr. Hazlitt was to be seen to best advantage where he was
least seen — at Winterslow. There, in the maturity of his
genius and fame, he spent many a happy month, living his
youth over again in spirit and memory.

A visit to the theatre in Mr. Hazlitt's company was not always the most comfortable thing in the world. He had a slow
way of moving on such occasions, which, to less habitual play-
goers, was highly trying. He took my mother to the play one
evening, when he was in Half-Moon Street — it must have
been in 1828 : there was a great crowd, but he was totally un-
moved by that circumstance. At the head of the staircase he
had to sign the Free Admission Book, and perfectly unconscious that he was creating a blockade, he looked up at the
attendant in the middle of the operation — a rather lengthy
one with him — and said, " What sort of a house is there to-
night, sir ? " It was a vast relief to his two companions, my
mother and her elder sister, when they had run the gauntlet
of all this, and were safe in their places.

THOMAS CAMPBELL.

Yours truly
T. Campbell

(*From Maclise Gallery.*)

THOMAS CAMPBELL.

———◆———

THE "NEW MONTHLY MAGAZINE."

Y first personal introduction to Campbell took place
in 1830, at the house of a person with whom, by one
of those temporary caprices to which, in his latter
years, he so habitually yielded, Campbell had con-
tracted an intimacy as little suitable, it might have been supposed, to his refined literary tastes and fastidious personal
habits, as it certainly was to the general tone of his intellectual character; for the person to whom I refer, though
possessing considerable talents and extensive influence in
connection with the newspaper press, was a man of coarse
mind, and of almost ostentatiously profligate personal habits.

Not but there were features in Campbell's mind and character capable of accounting for this temporary intimacy. In the
first place, it must be admitted that, notwithstanding the excessive fastidiousness of his taste and habits in all matters
connected with his position and reputation as the first of living
poets (for such at that time he was considered), Campbell partook of that propensity to which another kind of kings are
said to be addicted — that of a lurking fondness for "low company;" not "low" in this case, in the ordinary sense of the
term, as implying persons of low condition and mean mental
endowments, but as indicating that freedom from conventional
restraints which always springs from a low tone of moral sentiment, when accompanied by an open and bold-faced repudiation of those principles of personal conduct which form the

basis of all cultivated society. And Campbell's mind had a strong tendency to throw off the restraints in question, without the strength of will to do so, even if his high tone of moral feeling had not stood in the way of the step — which it certainly would have done.

The person at whose house I met Campbell, was also a furious republican ; and it is probable that the apparent and I believe real sincerity of his political views and opinions, and the daring and uncompromising way in which he advocated them, both with his pen and tongue, went far to gain for him the political sympathy of Campbell — the only sympathy to which he ever frankly yielded ; if, indeed, it was not the only one that he ever strongly felt. Campbell was, in fact, a thorough republican at heart ; and not the less so for many of his other qualities, both personal and intellectual, being more or less moulded and colored by the aristocratic principle, and some of them being the very quintessence of that principle.

There was another attraction in this quarter, which, as it points at a characteristic feature in Campbell's idiosyncrasy, I may venture to refer to, as having exercised no little influence in making the house in question the scene of his frequent visits, when (as during his later years) attractions of a more intellectual character had somewhat loosened their hold upon him. The worthy host was the father of "*two* fair daughters ; " one a piquant and sparkling brunette, with black eyes and raven hair, a commanding figure, and endowed with the full complement of flirtation power proper to her complexion ; the other, a tender, delicate, and shrinking blonde, whose winning softness of look, and pensive repose of manner, aided by melting blue eyes and golden hair, contrasted (almost to a pitch of strangeness) with the wild and vivacious character of her brilliant and bewitching sister.

This united presence gave a zest to the early part of Campbell's evenings at the house of his friend ——, which heightened by its contrast, the frank and cordial, but coarse joviality and good-fellowship of their close : for there was a redeeming *bonhomie* about the host, and a

    "Total, glorious want of vile hypocrisy,"

that in some degree glossed over the open and even ostentatious profligacy of his opinions, and the habits of life which grew out of them.

There was still another reason which took Campbell to the house of this gentleman at the time I am speaking of, which (as it breaks no "confidences") must not be excluded from Recollections, one object of which is to furnish materials for the private and personal history of the literature of our time, and for correcting some of the errors and supplying the oversights of that history. There is a work in two volumes octavo, entitled "Life of Mrs. Siddons, by T. Campbell, Esq.," and another in the like form entitled "Life of Sir Thomas Lawrence, by T. Campbell, Esq.," both of which productions, if I am not greatly misinformed (and my authority was the party better than any one else but Campbell himself acquainted with the facts), were entirely prepared and composed by the gentleman above alluded to — who was an extremely rapid and off-hand writer, and was much employed by "popular" publishers when called upon at a pinch to supply the cravings of the literary market, on any particular topic of the moment, before its more legitimate resources could be brought to bear. If the party in question was to be believed, the only share the alleged author of the above-named works had in their production was that of "overlooking" the MS., "looking over" the proof sheets, and permitting his name to stand rubric in the title-page.

The uninitiated reader must not suppose that I am disclosing any private secrets in this case. One of the modes in which Campbell himself reconciled (both to himself and others) this necessity of his literary and social position, was by making no mystery of the case, or caring that others should do so. "So far as the reading public is concerned," he argued, " all that my name does to these works is, to stand sponsor for ▸heir facts, dates, and so forth ; and for those I think I can safely depend on ——. For the rest, I am too poor to stand upon the critical niceties of literary casuistry. Besides, those who are fools enough to suppose that I *could* write such loose, disjointed, shambling stuff, as those books are for the most part composed of, are not worth caring about.   And the rest of the world will learn the truth, somehow or other, soon enough for the safety of my *poetical* reputation, which is the only one I ever aimed at."

It is with a loving eye to that reputation, and a sincere belief that Campbell himself would have thanked anybody who had made the disclosure thus publicly, even during his lifetime, that I allow it to form part of these personal records of the literary history of the nineteenth century.

This seems the proper place for me to notice the exactly similar case of his (nominal) editorship of the " New Monthly Magazine."   When a proposition was made to him through a friend, some years before, to undertake that office, he must have felt, and, indeed, I believe, he openly declared, that he was the last person in the world to be the conductor of what aimed at being a " popular " literary miscellany.   In temperament indolent, capricious, and uncertain, yet hasty, sensitive, willful, and obstinate in giving his will its way ; his habits of composition slow to a degree of painfulness ; his literary taste refined, even to fastidiousness ; and, above all, his personal position as the friend and associate of nearly all the distinguished *littérateurs* of the day, and his almost morbid sensitiveness on the point of giving pain, or even displeasure, to any of them, — Campbell was, and knew himself to be, the ideal of what the proffered office required its occupant *not* to be.

On the other hand, he knew the money value of his name in the literary market, and was too shrewd to overlook the fact that *that* was the secret of the proprietor's application to him. Moreover, he could not fail to know that his literary position would enable him to do great good to the magazine, in the way of attracting or procuring contributors whom no mere pecuniary considerations could attach to such a work.

Finally, what was he to do ?   In this land of gold-worshipers, where money is "the be-all and the end-all," not only of a man's social position, but of his personal estimation, Campbell found himself with an extremely small fixed income, and

wholly incapable of materially adding to it by any legitimate
literary employment to which his habits would permit him to
apply himself. He made no scruple, therefore, of accepting
the liberal offer that was made to him by the proprietor (of, I
believe, 600*l.* a year) for editorship and his own contributions,
leaving entirely to Campbell himself the number and amount
of the latter.

Whether or not Campbell, at the moment of his accepting
the editorship of the " New Monthly Magazine," had formed
any specific views or notions as to the duties that were expected or required of him, or that he was capable of render-
ing, is difficult to conjecture. Equally problematical is it
whether the proprietor, in making the proposition, had looked
at Campbell in any other light than as the possessor of at once
the most extensive and the most unquestioned reputation of
any literary man of the day. Certain it is, however, that the
first two months of the experiment demonstrated to both parties the entire unfitness of the poet for the anything but poetical office he had undertaken. Luckily, the same brief period
had also satisfied both parties, by the unequaled success of
the experiment in a business point of view, that the bargain
was, in that respect, a fair one ; and as the proprietor had
taken the precaution of providing, in case of accidents, an
active and industrious *working* editor (in the person of Mr.
Cyrus Redding), the arrangement continued for ten years, to
the mutual satisfaction and discontent of both parties ; the
public, in the mean time, caring nothing about the matter,
beyond the obtaining (as they unquestionably did) a better
magazine for their money than had ever before been produced.

I will here give two or three illustrative anecdotes of the
Campbell Editorship of the New Monthly, arising out of
my own anonymous connection with the magazine before I
became personally acquainted with Campbell. Among my
first proffered contributions were the two first numbers of a
series of papers, having for their object to illustrate the birth,
growth, and gradual development of the passion of Love, by

means of brief passages in the (supposed) life of the (supposed) writer; and, in order to go to the root of the matter,
and to show that, at one period of our lives at all events, the
passion is a purely intellectual one, uninfluenced by feelings
of sex, the first story related to two school-boys of nine or ten
years of age, one of whom " wasted the sweetness " of his
nascent affection on " the desert air " of the other's utter indifference and disdain. Quite anticipating the possibility of
.this reminiscence of my school-days being thought too " innocent," not to say too puerile, for a grave magazine — but little
thinking of the objection that *would* be made to it — I accompanied it by the second number of the series, which was a
love story quite *selon les règles*, so far as regarded the relations
of sex, however unorthodox in other respects.

Here is the reply I received to my communication. The
style is quite *regal* in point of form, and, like all the others
that I received on similar occasions, it is in the hand-writing
of Campbell himself : —

" To the writer of the articles entitled ' ——,' the Editor of
the ' New Monthly Magazine's ' compliments. The Editor
admires the writer's talents, and attaches not the slightest mis-
conception to the nature of the feelings described in the first
number ; but he thinks that many persons, from ignorance, or
prejudice, or ill-nature, may object to the description of the attachment in the first number, and he declines accepting it.
He will, nevertheless, not only be happy but grateful for the
writer's permission to publish the second number, and requests
to be favored with his further communications."

Now it is impossible to believe, in the face of this decision,
that the writer, who was excessively clear-sighted when he
did take the trouble to look into anything, could have read the
paper in question — which was simply what I have described
it above. The probabilities are, that he never even saw it —
that, being glanced at by the worthy proprietor of the magazine (through whose hands all communications for the editor
passed), and found to relate throughout to two school-boys, it
was thought too simple food for the intellectual appetites of

grown-up readers, and was therefore, to prevent accidents, intercepted on its way: a species of sifting which I believe everything underwent before it reached the ordeal from which there was no appeal. If I am right in this conjecture, the note I have given was probably the result of a suggestion from the same quarter, born of some vague feeling, generated by that rapid bird's-eye glance which gathers its impressions of a book from a single chapter, and a magazine article from a single page, and is seldom very far wrong — though now and then, of course, ridiculously so.

About the same time with the above, I commenced another series of papers in the magazine, entitled " Letters from England." They related to " everything in the world " connected with English life, literature, art, etc., and in order to give a little adventitious novelty and lightness to topics so hackneyed, the letters were written ostensibly under the character of a Frenchman. But the disguise was so transparent, and so loosely worn, that it was difficult to conceive — nor was it desired by the wearer — that any one should be otherwise than willfully deceived by it. Yet here is the editorial Introduction by which the series was ushered to the attention of the readers of the New Monthly.

" These letters are, we understand, the production of a distinguished Frenchman, whose original MS. journal has been obligingly submitted to us by a friend for publication. The editor admits them on account of the ability which they seem to possess.[1] For this special consideration he makes, in this one instance, a departure from his general rule, of not inserting any communications bearing the stamp of national prejudice. But he protests against being responsible for a single sentiment they contain."

Now this, like the note preceding it, may safely, I think, be attributed to a suggestion emanating from the *imperium in imperio* which the proprietor of the magazine himself was wise enough to maintain in his own literary domain. As these let-

---

[1] Here the secret of non-perusal peeps out. "*Seem* to possess!" So that they may or they may not possess it, for anything he knows about them.

ters were intended, after their appearance in the magazine, to be reprinted as a substantive work,[1] and it was their publisher's policy that they should (in the first instance, at least), be considered by the public as the *bonâ fide* productions of a foreigner, he probably took the preliminary precaution of "insinuating the plot into the boxes," through the plastic medium of the responsible editor of the New Monthly, who was the most tractable person in the world, when his own personal feelings did not interfere to make him exactly the reverse. Be this as it may, I must deny having had anything to do with this note, beyond the fact of the letters being, as I have said, ostensibly written under the character of a foreigner.

The third anecdote I shall cite illustrative of Campbell's editorship of the New Monthly relates to a series of papers entitled " The Months," [2] which had for their object to note, for present recognition and future recollection, the various facts and incidents of country and of town life which mark the passage of each month respectively. I had accordingly noted, in connection with the country life of April, the return of the shy and solitary cuckoo — so at least I had called it, and had particularly referred to its extreme rarity as an object of actual sight — a characteristic which Wordsworth has so beautifully marked when calling it "a wandering *voice*." But *this* Natural History did not accord with the supposed rural experience of the editor, who appended to the passage a note signifying that his contributor was a little at fault on this point, as he (the editor) had frequently " seen whole fields *blue* with cuckoos " — the cuckoo being of a dusky brown color, and being never by any chance seen two together, except when callow in the nest !

I need scarcely add that these little blunders and oversights are noted merely as among the minor " Curiosities " of our periodical literature, and are by no means intended to call in

[1] They were afterwards published by Mr. Colburn, in two volumes, under the title of *Letters on England.*
[2] Afterwards republished as a volume by Messrs. Whittaker, under the title of *Mirror of the Months.*

question or disparage the general merits of a joint management
that, taken altogether, raised the " New Monthly Magazine "
to a pitch, not merely of popularity, but of actual desert, which
had never before been attained by any work of a similar nature.
In fact, the accession of Campbell's name to the New Monthly
may be fairly cited as marking an era in our magazine literature.

Since the foregoing Recollections were written, I have
looked over Mr. Cyrus Redding's Reminiscences, in the " New
Monthly Magazine," with the view of either confirming or correcting my own impressions derived from an unbroken connection with the magazine during the whole of Mr. Campbell's
(nominal) editorship. The unscrupulous disclosures of Mr.
Redding on this subject in his entertaining papers, more than
confirm all that I have said on it. In one place he speaks of
the editorship as "consisting in a negative, not a positive,
realization of the duty ; " and he adds as follows : " I do
not believe the poet ever read through a single number of the
magazine during the whole ten years of his editorship."

HAZLITT AND NORTHCOTE.

Though Campbell's nominal editorship of the " New Monthly
Magazine " was pretty nearly a sinecure in respect of the actual
work it exacted from him, it was on that very account the
source of frequent and serious annoyance to him, from the
scrapes it thus got him into with his personal friends and acquaintances, arising out of that want of due watchfulness and
care as to the personal bearing of the articles admitted into it,
which it was impossible for anybody but Campbell himself to
exercise, because none else could know the precise points to
which the necessary attention in this respect was required to
be directed. One of these scrapes, the particulars of which I
was made acquainted with at the time by the two persons
chiefly interested in it, was so characteristic, in all its features,
of all the parties concerned, that I will relate it here. It refers
to a series of papers which the late William Hazlitt was writ-

ing at the time in the New Monthly, entitled "Boswell Redivivus," and which professed to report his (Hazlitt's) conversations with Northcote the painter.

As I was more than once present at the conversations so professed to be reported, and as Hazlitt has himself disclosed the fact that these reports are by no means to be taken *au pied de la lettre* as regards the precise portions to be attributed to the speakers respectively, there can be no impropriety in stating my belief that, generally speaking, very little dependence is to be placed on them in this particular, when they relate to opinions and sentiments, and especially when they relate to personal feelings about *living* individuals with whom Hazlitt was acquainted ; and that Hazlitt often puts his own feelings and opinions into the mouth of Northcote, and *vice versâ.* Sometimes this was done consciously and purposely, sometimes not ; often merely to give spirit and verisimilitude to the dialogue ; not seldom to vent a little malice prepense under a guise that would give it double pungency and force. I do not believe this was ever done with a view to escape the odium and reprisals which a system of literary personality is sure to engender ; for Hazlitt never put the slightest curb upon his inclinations in this respect. But in regard to the facts and anecdotes related in these conversations, I believe Hazlitt to have been scrupulously exact in his reports.

Northcote, on his part, had an irrepressible propensity to speak unpalatable truths of his acquaintances and friends, whether dead or alive. In fact, it was his forte to say bitter and cutting things of every one — friend, foe, or stranger — who came under his notice in the course of conversation ; and he knew perfectly well that Hazlitt listened to his talk with the view of giving portions of it to the public. He knew also that Hazlitt was wholly without scruple as to what he might put forth, provided it was either characteristic of the speaker, or true of the person spoken of, and that the parts most personally offensive would be those most acceptable to the reading public.

All this Northcote knew ; and yet he gave Hazlitt full per-

mission to make any use he pleased of what might have passed
between them in these desultory conversations — of course,
with this ostensible restriction, that he (Hazlitt) must take
care to omit anything that might get the speaker into disgrace
with his personal friends ; though Northcote must have also
known that this was virtually no effectual restriction at all —
or, if it would have been so to most men, it was none to Hazlitt in a case of this nature. The truth is, that Northcote
chuckled over the wounds he thus inflicted by the hand of
another ; and when the ill consequences (as in the instance
I am about to relate) threatened to come home to himself,
he never scrupled to offer up his instrument as a sacrifice, if
that would serve, and then, if necessary, reconcile the matter
to *him* in the best manner he could, as he had done to the
other suffering parties.

It has seemed necessary to premise thus much in explanation of what follows.

In one of the chapters of "Boswell Redivivus" there occur some passages relating to the celebrated dissenting clergy-
man, Dr. Mudge, one of the great ornaments of Sir Joshua
Reynolds's *coterie*, which show him in a light anything but
favorable. They give him ample credit for his great talents
and learning, but place his sincerity and consistency as a
teacher of religion in a very questionable point of view, and
relate personal anecdotes of him that are anything but creditable. Now that Hazlitt, in setting down these passages, did
anything but repeat what Northcote had told him, no one will
doubt who was acquainted with his excellent memory and his
mental habits. As little can it be disputed that the facts, if
such they be (of which I am wholly uninformed), related of
Dr. Mudge's private life and habits, were highly worthy of
being placed on record, as matters of literary history in one
of its most interesting features — that of the private and personal character of celebrated literary men. But the crime of
Hazlitt, in Northcote's eyes, was not to have known, as if by
instinct, what Hazlitt, so far from being bound to know, could
not possibly have been acquainted with, except through the

direct information of Northcote himself — namely, that he (Northcote) had particular and personal reasons for desiring not to be suspected of being the expositor of these obnoxious truths, which, but for him, might have remained unknown or forgotten.

The effect of this exposure, painful as it was, partook of the ludicrous, to those who could not put much faith in the sincerity of the feelings exhibited by Northcote on the occasion. I remember calling on him a few days after the appearance of the paper in question — No. VI. of the series. He knew that I was in the habit of seeing Hazlitt almost daily ; and the moment I entered the room (he was not in his usual painting room, but had retreated into the little inner room adjoining it, as if in dread of the personal consequences of what had happened) I perceived that something serious was the matter.

" I am very ill, indeed," said he, in reply to my inquiry as to his health. " I did not think I should have lived. That monster has nearly killed me."

I inquired what he meant.

" Why, that diabolical Hazlitt. Have you seen what lies he has been telling about me in his cursed Boswell Redivivus ? I have been nearly dead ever since the paper appeared. Why, the man is a demon. Nothing human was ever so wicked. Do you see the dreadful hobble he has got me into with the Mudges ? Not that I said what he has put down about Mudge. *But even if I had* — who could have supposed that any one in a human form would have come here to worm himself into my confidence, and get me to talk as if I had been thinking aloud, and then go and publish it all to the world ! Why, they will think we go snacks in the paltry profits of his treachery. It will kill me. What am I to do about it ? I would give a hundred pounds to have the paper canceled. But that would do no good now. It has gone all over the world. I have never had a moment's rest since it appeared. I sent to Mr. Colburn to come over to me about it ; but he took no notice of my message, so I went over to

him. But they would n't let me see him ; and all I could get
out of his people was, that they would tell him what I said.
I told them to tell him that it would be the death of me. But
Campbell has been a little more civil about it. I wrote him a
letter — *such* a letter ! I 'll show it you. And he has replied
very handsomely, and seems to be touched by my situation.
At any rate," added he, bitterly, " I have put a spoke into the
wheel of that diabolical wretch Hazlitt."

And then he showed me the letter he had written to Campbell, and Campbell's reply. I think I never read anything
more striking in its way than his letter to Campbell. Though
brief, it was a consummate composition — pathetic even to the
excitement of tears — painting the dreadful state of his mind
under the blow which the (alleged) *treachery* of Hazlitt had
given to it, and treating the thing as a deliberate attempt to
"bring his gray hairs in sorrow to the grave." I particularly
seem to remember that these very words were used in it. The
whole tendency of the letter was to create an inference in
Campbell's mind that the thing had come upon the writer like
a thunder-clap, and that even in regard to those parts of the
Conversations which were truly reported (which he denied to
be the case in the matter in question), he was the most betrayed and ill-used person in the world. And all this in the
face of the fact that the paper of which he complained was
the *sixth* of a series that had appeared in the (then) most
popular literary periodical of the day — that they had all appeared there with his full knowledge and consent — that he
had, ever since the commencement of them, been almost daily
complimented on the conspicuous figure he was cutting in his
new character of the best converser of the day — and that a
considerable portion of what had appeared of the " Boswell
Redivivus " up to that time had consisted (on Northcote's
part, at least) of depreciating estimates of many of the most
conspicuous *living* writers, artists, etc.

It is, of course, with reference to these facts that I have
spoken of Northcote's feelings as "ludicrous," on this unlooked-for exposure of truths of which he did not wish to be

known as the author : for the astonishing force and pungency of *unpalatable* truths that he put forth about every *living* individual of whom he spoke (sometimes in their presence, and even to themselves),[1] and the double edge and effect that were given to his words by the exquisitely simple and naïve manner in which he uttered them — as if an inspired *infant* were speaking — was the characteristic of his talk. And he knew all this better than anybody could tell him, and evidently prided himself upon it.

Campbell's reply to Northcote was, I remember, in a tone precisely correspondent with the letter which called for it. He declared his unmitigated horror at the outrage that had been committed on Northcote's feelings ; absolved himself from all participation in it by naïvely stating that he had not seen a line of the paper till its publication, having been absent from town on other business ; and declared that "the diabolical Hazlitt should never write another line in the magazine during *his* management of it." These, I think, were his very words.

"And so," said Northcote, when I had read Campbell's reply — " and so I am to be assassinated, a worthy family is to be outraged in their dearest feelings, and a whole neighborhood thrown into consternation, because he (Campbell) chooses to neglect his duties, or depute somebody else to do them who is incompetent to the task ! "

Nothing could be more characteristic than this effusion, *apropos* to a letter which had every appearance of being written under feelings of sincere and poignant regret at the occasion to which it referred. But all Northcote chose to see in it was the fact that somebody else was in fault as well as the original culprit : for as to he himself having had any hand in the mischief — (at least in an objectionable point of view) — this seemed never to enter his thoughts. He sowed the seeds

---

[1] In talking to Hazlitt once about the attacks on *The Cockney School*, in *Blackwood's* (which, by the bye, he greatly approved), he said to him, " I think, Mister Hazlitt, you yourself are the most perfect specimen of the Cockney School that I ever met with : " and then he went on to give him " satisfying reasons " for this opinion!

of the most bitter personal truths in the most fertile soil for their growth and propagation — namely, the current "table-talk" of the hour — and then was lost in wonder and dismay at finding some of them bear the unexpected fruit of a personal inconvenience to himself.

The sequel of the history of these Conversations includes the most characteristic point of all. Not very long after the incident I have referred to above, the Conversations were re-published in a separate form, with large and valuable additions from the same source, and obtained through the same means and agent ; and this with the knowledge and tacit consent of Northcote himself, and with all their obnoxious truths unex-punged, excepting those in which Northcote's own personal connections were concerned ; and the "diabolical Hazlitt" continued to write as usual in the New Monthly, under Camp-bell's (ostensible) editorship !

INCAPACITY FOR FRIENDSHIP.

At the time of my first personal acquaintance with Camp-bell, he resided in Middle Scotland Yard, and my introduction to him, as before referred to, speedily led to an invitation to one of those pleasantly assorted little dinner-parties — half literary, half social — followed by a more miscellaneous as-semblage in the evening, in which, at one time, he liked to in-dulge. But under his own roof, Campbell altogether repudi-ated that unrestrained "good fellow"-ship which he did not scruple to encourage and to act elsewhere.

Here is the first note I received from him in his private capacity, and almost the only one, except those of a similar kind ; for our acquaintance (as I have said) never extended to anything like that intimacy which begets an epistolary corre-spondence.

"1 MIDDLE SCOTLAND YARD, WHITEHALL
"26 *May*, 1830.

"MY DEAR SIR, — If you and Mrs. Patmore will favor me with your company to dinner, on Tuesday next, the first of June, you will meet, I trust, the Bard of Memory, and the

present editor of the ' Edinburgh Review,' together with our
friend ——. An American professor and his lady will complete the proposed symposium

"Of yours, very truly,
" T. CAMPBELL."

Campbell was an excellent host for a small and well-assorted
literary dinner-party. He combined all the qualities proper
to that difficult office, without a single counteracting one ; the
highest intellectual position and pretensions, without the
smallest disposition to make them apparent — much less to
placard them ; a ready wit and a fine turn for social humor,
without the slightest touch of that vulgar *waggery* which so
often accompanies and neutralizes these, and is the bane of all
the intellectual society into which it is allowed to intrude ; a
graceful, easy, and well-bred manner and bearing, without any
vestige of stiffness on the one hand, or boisterousness on the
other ; finally, a perpetual consciousness of his position and
duties as master of the house, yet an entire apparent forgetfulness of these in the pleasure he took in the presence of his
friends.

There was but one little drawback from Campbell's perfection as a host, and that did not show itself till that period of
the evening when such drawbacks are tolerated, or, at least,
used to be twenty years ago, when such toleration was sometimes needed. On returning from the after dinner table to the
drawing-room, Campbell was apt to take his place beside the
prettiest woman in the room, and thenceforth to be *non est in-
ventus* for the rest of the evening and the company.

My personal intercourse with Campbell did not (as I have
said) extend beyond that of a pleasant acquaintanceship ; nor
do I believe that the social intercourse enjoyed with him by
any one of his (so-called) friends did or could amount to much
more ; for, with all his amiable and attractive qualities, he was
evidently a man so entirely self-centred, so totally free from
personal and individual sympathies, that a friendship with him,
in anything more than the conversational sense of the term,
was out of the question.

Campbell was, in this respect, the ideal of a poet — sympathizing with, and, as it were, capable of reproducing by and to his imagination effigies and incarnations of, all our human nature in all its phases of good or evil, of beauty and deformity : and (like a god) " seeing that all was good." But, as a set-off against this godlike gift, he was utterly unable to transfer or transfuse his affections, even for a single moment, to any of the actual types of our actual humanity that he found about him in the real world of flesh and blood.

It will, I think, be found to hold universally, that they who have sympathized with mankind intensely and profoundly before they could possibly have had valid human grounds for doing so, either from self-knowledge or from experience — in other words, that they who have proved themselves to be *poets* before they were *men* in anything but intuition and instinct — can never be men at all, in the human sense of the phrase ; that, in proportion as the poetical temperament is present and becomes developed, the possessor of it must submit to the sad distinction of standing apart and aloof from the rest of mankind, unloving and unloved ; and that when the temperament in question is great in amount, and greatly developed at a very early age (as in the cases of Campbell, Keats, Chatterton, etc.), the owner of it must be content to accept his rich dower as a substitute for all things else that appertain to man as a member of human society. In proportion as the poet approaches the ideal of that condition, he typifies man in the abstract ; and he who possesses all things in common with all men, cannot feel anything in common with any individual man. Judging from what he did, or *created*, while among us, as compared with the " appliances and means " afforded him by what is called fact and experience, Chatterton was perhaps the greatest *born* poet that ever lived ; and Chatterton had nothing in common with mankind, but his marvelous intellect and his misery.

Of the only other truly *great* poets that the world has seen — Dante, Shakespeare, Milton, and Goethe — nothing is on record that would seem distinctly to impugn the opinion I

have ventured to advance ; and if applied to the personal characters of the few real poets of our own day, whether living or
dead, it will meet, I think, with anything but contradiction.
At all events, in the case of Campbell, it is not to be gainsaid.
And Campbell was greatly more of a poet in faculty than he
was in fact and performance.   Few men have approached
nearer to a poet in the former respect than he did ; and it was
only his almost morbid delicacy of taste, of tact, and of ear,
and his extreme fastidiousness, which prevented him from
turning his powers to much greater practical results than he
did.   No man ever enjoyed so high and wide a poetical reputation upon so slender an amount of actual performance.   And
yet no man ever deserved his reputation more truly than
Campbell did.   Had it not been so, he would have done more ;
and, perhaps, have done better.   But he had none of that vulgar hungering and hankering after fame which, write what
they will to the contrary, no real poet ever felt as anything
more than a momentary aspiration.   Campbell knew and felt
that he was a poet ; and as the world in some sort assented to
his own faith on this point, he was content "to know no
more."

Let it be observed, too, that Campbell never for an instant
prostituted his high and holy calling to the necessities of his
worldly condition.   The literary drudgery to which he submitted during the whole of his life included no line of verse.
It is probably true that, from the time when his poetical taste
and judgment became matured, nine tenths even of the little
poetry he did write consisted of

"Lines that dying he would wish to blot."

In fact, from the period when he regarded his critical taste as
having reached maturity, he scarcely wrote a line of poetry at
all.   Though this probably arose partly from that constitutional indolence, and Epicurean love of ease, which were leading features of his temperament.   But I do not believe that
any personal or worldly considerations would have induced
Campbell to tamper with the gift which stood him in stead of

all mundane ones, and made them all look poor and mean by comparison.

Returning to the personal results of the poetical tempera-ment in Campbell, and their effects as seen in his intercourse with the world, I may remark, that if they prevented him from becoming the *friend* of any man, they made him the acquaint-ance and boon companion for the time being of all, — from the poet on his prophetic tripos and the prince on his throne, to the beggar in his rags and the infant in its native simplicity. Destitute himself of actual living sympathy with either, he nevertheless, or perhaps on that very account, attracted the sympathies of each and all, by reflecting the true image of themselves in the clear cold mirror of his impassible spirit.

The result of this was, that when Campbell was in good health and spirits, or was made so for the nonce by those arti-ficial means which during the latter part of his life were neces-sary to his personal comfort, he was the most popular person in the world, whatever class of society he frequented ; and though I cannot believe that anybody ever loved him to the amount even of ordinary friendship, everybody *liked* him, no-body feared him, and half those with whom he came into ac-cidental contact fancied him to be an ordinary person like themselves, and

         " Wondered with a foolish face of praise "

at the vast reputation of one so little different from the Thom-sons and Johnsons of their ordinary acquaintance.

CAMPBELL AND LORD AND LADY BYRON.

On one of the occasions when I met Campbell at the house of the gentleman before alluded to, we had a long and most earnest conversation on a topic which at that time occupied universal attention, no less in general than in literary society — the quarrel between Lord Byron and his wife ; and I was not a little surprised that Campbell had taken up the cause of Lady Byron in the spirit, not of an impartial judge, or even of one who fancied or pretended that he was such, but of a paid and unscrupulous advocate; the fee, in this case, being the personal compliment on the part of the lady, of having sent for him, and confided to him her version of the true nature of her grievances. This was of course done under the seal of inviolable secrecy; so that, while it was absolutely impossible, from what Campbell said, to judge for oneself as to the validity of the alleged enormities of his "friend" Byron, his tone and words in referring to them, and the solemn earnestness with which he pronounced his own opinion as to the justice of Lady Byron's treatment of her husband, and at the same time the alleged *impossibility* of his giving any reasons for the faith that was in him on the matter in question — were calculated to produce, and in my case did produce, an impression which nothing but *facts*, testified in plain words by unbiased witnesses, ought to produce; and (I cannot help thinking) the production of such an impression ought not to have been attempted, even by a prosecutor, much less by an advocate, in the absence of the power or the will to confirm it by unquestionable facts.

It was impossible to escape the frightful inference which Campbell's words on this occasion were calculated to produce; while, at the same time, it was impossible to feel safe in admitting that inference, or even to feel absolutely certain that it was the one he intended.

I can compare the effect which Campbell produced upon me on this occasion only to that which was sought to be produced on the jury in a celebrated criminal trial a few years ago, when (as it has since been universally admitted) the advocate overstepped even the extremest limits of his professional duty, by attempting to screen his client at the risk of an innocent person's life; and which attempt, while it did but heighten public indignation against the guilty party, it would scarcely be too much to say, actually destroyed the innocent life against which it was so heedlessly and unjustifiably directed.

Whether the dark and fearful insinuations so studiously propagated by Campbell on the occasion I have alluded to above, and doubtless, therefore, on every other which offered itself, and supported by similar ones from other quarters, were not the "apple-pips" that killed poor Byron before his time, may be fairly made the subject of question when (if ever) the point becomes one capable of being freely and fearlessly discussed.

PERSONAL CHARACTER.

The personal character of Campbell exhibited that true test and constant accompaniment of a high degree of the poetical temperament when it stops short of the highest, — the power to dispense with the world and society, without the power or the desire to shun or abandon them. His mind was self-centred and self-dependent, yet social, and fond of the excitement of external thoughts and things. The objective and the subjective contended too strongly and too constantly within him to admit of his being a poet of the first order, in whom, instead of contending, they balance and strengthen each other. But that very contention it was which placed him in the highest rank of the second order; it would even have given him the capacity of attaining the first place in that rank if he had also possessed the power of sustaining his volition at the required pitch. But in this point of his personal character and temperament lay Campbell's great deficiency as a poet. He had never sufficient control over himself, never sufficient command of his intellectual condition and movements, to be sure he might not be tempted, at a moment's warning, to abandon the wide and populous solitude of his little study at Sydenham, or the sweet society of his own "Gertrude of Wyoming," while she was growing there in all her ineffable beauty,[1] for the boisterous good-fellowship and · and noisy revelry of his friend Tom Hill's after dinner table, with its anomalous *olla-podrida* of "larking" stockbrokers, laughing punsters, roaming farce-writers, and riotous practical jokers. These were occasionally embellished and kept in check, it is true, by the refined wit and elegant scholarship of a Moore and a Rogers, the rich and racy humor of a Dubois, the easy and gentlemanly pleasantry of a Horace

[1] His *Gertrude of Wyoming* was entirely written at Sydenham.

Smith, the mild and bland good-nature and good-fellowship of a Perry, etc. Still, even when any of these, or such as these, were present, there must have been an unwholesome jumble of contradictions, which, like the mixing of wines, defeated the appropriate effect of each, even when it did not turn all to mischief.[1]

There is no doubt that Campbell liked these anomalous orgies, though he could not but hate or despise many of their component parts. It is true, also, that the alternative of solitude was indispensable to his love of society ; while the converse of the proposition would be anything but true. On the contrary, the more he had courted and cultivated solitude, the more warmly she would have responded to his love till at length he might have fairly wedded her, and the world would have had cause to bless the union, for the offspring it would have yielded. Whereas in weakly alternating between solitude and society, he failed to serve either truly ; though, during the period of his health and vigor, he may be truly said to have loved both, and it would have been very difficult for himself to have determined which he loved best. The rest of the world, however — those of them, at least, who took sufficient interest in him to " look into his deeds with thinking eyes " — could have had no difficulty on this point. To them it must have been obvious that there was about Campbell, when in any society but that of a quiet and not ill-assorted *tête-à-tête*, or a pleasant little dinner-party at his own house, an uneasy and ill-disguised restlessness and want of repose, and an occasional absence, which plainly told that the home of his spirit was elsewhere.

To sum up this speculation in a word — (for I am afraid the reader will not accept it as anything more decisive, especially as coming from a mere acquaintance) — *Tom* Campbell was a very good fellow, and a very pleasant one withal : but he

---

[1] I am speaking here from conjecture merely, as regards everything but the names of the guests; for though I afterwards became intimately acquainted with Campbell's worthy neighbor and host of Sydenham, these famous meetings were at an end long before my time.

prevented Thomas Campbell from being a great poet, though not from doing great things in poetry.

There were, however, other small features in Campbell's intellectual character, each of which would alone have prevented him from attaining poetical greatness. His intense self-consciousness (which the world ridiculously translated into personal vanity) would alone have been sufficient for this ; for it rendered him incapable of wholly escaping from himself, while it prevented him from fairly appreciating other states and stages of being.

Another of these qualities was his extreme, and even finical, fastidiousness. For though this quality of mind did not prevent him from originating high thoughts, and great and noble imaginations, it wholly incapacitated him from reflecting them in their height and greatness, by causing him to detect, with a morbid keenness and microscopic power of vision, those inevitable defects of execution which a perfectly natural and healthy intellectual vision would not have discovered. For what, after all, can the best written poetry be but a sort of *cast* from the sculptured images of the poet's mind ? And what are the best casts of the finest sculpture when placed beside the originals themselves ? Nevertheless, for those who have never seen, and never can see, the originals (and in that condition are all ordinary mortals, as regards the original types of the poet's creations) good casts are of little less value and virtue than the original marbles themselves. But Campbell, in fastidiously scraping away from *his* casts all the little inequalities and defects left or made by the necessary manipulation of the working, the joinings in the mould, and the air-bubbles and impurities in the material of which the cast was formed, destroyed at the same time much of the pure and natural contour and texture of the original, and with it that truth, both of detail and of general effect, the presence of which forms so large an element in our admiration of works of high art.

As a corollary from that want of repose which marked Campbell's intellectual character, there was a total absence in

18

him of that passion for the beauties of external nature, and
that consequent love of a country life, which have marked almost all great poets. His mind was of the true metropolitan
order, and his "retreat" at Sydenham was a retreat in the
military sense of the phrase — a movement called for by the
exigences of his position in the battle of life. The solitude
that was necessary to the health and growth of his poetical
temperament he could have created for himself in great cities,
as well as he could have found it in a desert; and he did so
create it there till he "found himself famous ; " but when that
happened, the defects of his idiosyncrasy came out. He then
ceased to feel any excitement apart from populous assemblies
of men and women — acknowledged no movement but in the
march of human events from day to day — saw no beauty but
in the living human face — heard no music but in the speaking
human voice — in short, knew no salvation out of the pale of
great cities. In fact, when once Campbell was fairly recognized as the greatest of living English poets, he was never
so happy as when he was occupied in matters which a great
poet would have regarded as toys or troubles — organizing a
club, or founding a university, or standing forth as the say-
iour of an effete people that could not save itself.

It is true (as I have said) that Campbell sought his poetical
inspiration in the solitude of his own thoughts and contemplations, and found it there. But he sought it as a duty and a
task, though at the same time as a relief ; and he found it in
infinitely less abundance and purity than he would have done
had his habitual course of life been more consonate with the
requirements of that poetical temperament which he un-
doubtedly possessed in a very high degree and a very pure
form, and not a few of the results of which attain a pitch of
perfection that has never been surpassed.

While thus glancing at that feature of Campbell's intellectual character which was ill-naturedly translated into " personal
vanity," I must not omit to state that it was confined exclusively to his intercourse with women, and also, I believe, to
the latter years of his life, after the death of his wife.   But it

grew upon him as he grew in years, and at length became, or was deemed so by those who were his friends for their own sakes, the besetting weakness of his life, and occasionally led him into positions somewhat undignified, it is true, for his real friends and admirers to witness, or for his enemies (if he had any) to point at and placard. Still, absolutely alone as Campbell was, as regards family relationship, during the latter years of his life, it was but a spurious philosophy, and a questionable friendship, that would have debarred him from exercising and thus keeping alive, those semblances of sympathy which alone bound him to society, and stood him in stead of that poetical world in which he had heretofore dwelt, but which had latterly slipt from under his feet, — leaving nothing in its place but that childlike love of the beautiful, the bright, and the unattainable, which, as it always precedes and heralds the growth of the poetical temperament, not seldom, under one form or other, follows its decay, and strews flowers upon its grave. During the whole period of the youth, the manhood, and the mature vigor of his intellect, Campbell was essentially and emphatically a poet ; never attempting to blend that holy character and calling even with that of the sage or the philosopher, still less with that of the mere worldling or the mere trifler. He never was an ordinary man, pursuing the common aims and ends of men by the ordinary means. He stood apart from the world and its ways, but without openly impugning or repudiating them ; never shunning society, yet never embracing it ; never out of the world, yet never truly in it ; seeking and receiving nothing at its hands (in his intellectual character I mean), yet ever ready to help, or advance, or do it good.

In all these things Campbell exhibited the true and sure tests and characteristics of a born poet. How little reasonable then, how little humane, to exact or expect from such a man, at the close of such a career, — when he felt all these possessions slipping away from him, and leaving no mere worldly equivalents in their place, — that he should relapse, or rather be transformed, into a mere ordinary man, with the commonplace habits and associations of his time and circumstances! The natural and therefore the fitting change was that which really happened to him. Ceasing to be the POET, he relapsed once more into the little child from which the poet had emerged ; "pleased with the rattle" of hollow flattery; "tickled with the straw" of real or pretended admiration ; crying now and then for the moon, till hushed to sleep by the fondlings of mock affection or mercenary kindness; and then dreaming, childlike (as not even the poet can till he again becomes a child), of the wonders and glories and virtues

"Of that imperial palace whence he came."

APPEARANCE OF CAMPBELL AND ROGERS.

The following description of Campbell's personal appearance was written during his life-time, and formed part of what was intended as a series of Sketches from Real Life, taken at one of the chief resorts of the literary and other celebrities of the day : —

"The person of this exquisite writer and delightful man is small, delicately formed, and neatly put together, without being little or insignificant. His face has all the harmonious arrangement of features which marks his gentle and elegant mind ; it is oval, perfectly regular in its details, and lighted up not merely by 'eyes of youth,' but by a bland smile of intellectual serenity that seems to pervade and penetrate all the features, and impart to them all a corresponding expression, such as the moonlight lends to a summer landscape : the moonlight, not the sunshine ; for there is a mild and tender pathos blended with that expression, which bespeaks a soul that has been steeped in the depths of human woe, but has turned their waters (as only poets can) into fountains of beauty and of bliss.

"There are persons whom we cannot help associating together in our imagination, without feeling or being able to fancy any sufficient reason for doing so. When we see one, we think of the other, as naturally and necessarily as if they stood to each other in the relation of mutual cause and effect.

The poets Campbell and Rogers hold this imaginary relationship in many more minds, we suspect, than ours, or we should not have felt it to be worth a passing word of mention, much less have made it the reason, as we shall now do, of placing them as companion portraits in our literary gallery. But there is, in fact, a curious and beautiful assimilation between the minds and persons of the bards of Hope and of Memory, a similitude in dissimilitude, and one of a nature which corresponds as curiously with the subject of their best known works, HOPE and MEMORY; the one looking eagerly onward, as if life were in the future only; the other looking anxiously back, as if all but the past were a shadow or a dream. In the mind of the bard of Memory we see the same natural grace and elegance, the same cultivation and refinement, the same delicacy of taste, and the same gentle and genial cast of sympathy with his fellow beings and with external things, that we find in the bard of Hope. And when twenty years more of mingled joy and sorrow shall have passed through the heart and over the head of the latter, we may look to see as little difference in the personal attributes of the two, or rather, the bard of Hope will have gently subsided into the bard of Memory — the living type of the latter having, in the common course of nature, cast off the 'mortal coil' which holds him reluctantly to a state of being 'where nothing is but what is not.'

"It must not be supposed from the above, that we see or fancy any actual physical resemblance between the person and features of Mr. Campbell and those of Mr. Rogers. If we did, our visual organs would be essentially unfitted for the task we have imposed upon them. All we mean to intimate is, that a similar conformation of mind and temperament, modified by similar trains of thought, feeling, and study, have imparted to these two accomplished men, not a similarity, but a correspondence, in the general expression of the symbols by which their intellectual characters respectively interpret themselves to our bodily senses. Nobody will see any 'family likeness' between them; but every one duly qualified to catch 'the mind's observance in the face,' will perceive in each the evidences of equally high intellectual cultivation, expended upon a soil similarly composed in its chief attributes, and calculated to produce flowers and fruits of a similar generic character, however differing in species or individual instances. Finally, the main difference and dissimilarity they may observe will be, that in the one case (of the bard of Memory) the passions have yielded themselves willing servitors to that mild philosophy of the heart and senses which can alone subdue without subverting them; whereas in the bard of Hope they still burn with a bright intensity that would consume the altar on which they are kindled, were it a shrine less pure and holy than a poet's heart.

" Begging indulgence for yielding to the temptation of straying so far from the mechanical limits of our task, we return to them by pointing to the head and face of Mr. Rogers, as an object of peculiar interest and curiosity to those who are students in such living lore. There is something preternatural in the cold, clear, marbly paleness that pervades, and, as it were, penetrates his features to a depth that seems to preclude all change, even that of death itself. Yet there is nothing in the least degree painful or repulsive in the sight, nothing that is suggestive of death, or even of decay — but, on the contrary, something that seems to speak beforehand of that immortality at which this poet has so earnestly aimed, and of which he is entitled to entertain so fair a hope. It is scarcely fanciful to say that the *living* bust of the author of ' Human Life,' ' The Pleasures of Memory,' etc., can scarcely be looked upon without calling to mind the bust of marble, sculptured by some immortal hand, which he so well deserves to have consecrated to him in the Temple of Fame."

The following characteristic letters have never appeared in print, except in the ephemeral pages of a newspaper. The first was sent to me in MS., by Campbell, to be used as I might think fit, and I inserted it in a popular weekly journal of the day.

"TO THOMAS MOORE, ESQ.

" MY DEAR MOORE, — A thousand thanks to you for the kind things which you have said of me in your ' Life of Lord Byron,' — but forgive me for animadverting to what his lordship says, at page 463 of your first volume. It is not every day that one is mentioned in such joint pages as those of Moore and Byron.

"Lord Byron there states that, one evening at Lord Holland's, I was *nettled* at something, and the whole passage, if believed, leaves it to be inferred that I was angry, envious, and ill-mannered. Now I never envied Lord Byron, but, on the contrary, rejoiced in his fame ; in the first place from a sense of justice, and in the next place, because, as a poetical critic, he was my beneficent friend. I never was nettled in Lord Holland's house, as both Lord and Lady Holland can witness ; and on the evening to which Lord Byron alludes, I said, ' Carry all your incense to Lord Byron,' in the most perfect spirit of good-humor. I remember the evening most distinctly — one of the happiest evenings of my life, and if Lord Byron imagined me for a moment displeased, it only shows me that, with all his transcendant powers, he was one of the most fanciful of human beings. I by no means impeach his veracity, but I see from this case that he was subject to strange illusions.

"What feeling but that of kindness could I have towards Lord Byron ? He was always affectionate towards me, both in his writings and in his personal interviews. How strange that he should misunderstand my manner on the occasion alluded to — and what temptation could I have to show myself pettish and envious before my inestimable friend Lord Holland. The whole scene, as described by Lord Byron, is a phantom of his own imagination. Ah, my dear Moore, if we had him but back again, how easily could we settle these matters. But I have detained you too long, and, begging pardon for all my egotism, I remain, my dear Moore,

" Your obliged and faithful servant,
" T. CAMPBELL.

" MIDDLE SCOTLAND YARD, WHITEHALL,
" *Feb.* 18, 1830."

" Sir, — I am obliged to you for discrediting a silly paragraph from the ' Sligo Observer,' which is quoted in your paper to-day.

" It charges me with having abstracted the MS. of the ' Exile of Erin ' from the papers of the late Duke (you call him marquis) of Buckingham. If my character did not repel this calumny, I could refute it by the fact that I never in my life had access to any papers of either a Duke or Marquis of Buckingham. I wrote the song of the ' Exile of Erin ' at Altona, and sent it off immediately from thence to London, where it was published by my friend, Mr. Perry, in the ' Morning Chronicle.' With the evidence of my being the author of this little piece I shall not trouble the world at present. Only if my Irish accuser has any proof that George Nugent Reynolds, Esq., ever affected to have written the song, he will consult the credit of his memory by not blazoning the anecdote, for if he asserted that the piece was his own, he assuredly told an untruth. I am inclined to believe, however, that the ' Sligo Observer's' proffered witnesses are not eminently blessed with good memories, for they offer to testify that they heard Mr. Reynolds for years before his death, and prior to my publication of the song, repeat and sing it as his own. If the matter comes to a proof, I shall be happy to prove that this is an utter impossibility, for I had scarcely composed the song, when it was everywhere printed with my name ; and it is inconceivable that Mr. Reynolds could have had credit for years among his friends for a piece which those friends must have seen publicly claimed by myself.

" But the whole charge is so absurd, that I scarcely think the ' Sligo Observer ' will renew it. If they do, they will only expose their folly. I am, sir,

" Your obedient servant,

" THOMAS CAMPBELL.

· " MIDDLE SCOTLAND YARD, WHITEHALL,
    " *June* 16, 1830."

THE COUNTESS OF BLESSINGTON.

.

.

(From Maclise Gallery.)

COUNTESS OF BLESSINGTON.

AT THE ROYAL ACADEMY.

FIRST saw Lady Blessington under circumstances sufficiently characteristic of her extraordinary personal beauty at the period in question — about five or six and twenty years ago — to excuse my referring to them somewhat in detail, though they do not fall within the immediate scope of these Recollections ; for it was not till several years afterwards that I became personally acquainted with the subject of them. It was on the opening day of that Royal Academy Exhibition which contained Lawrence's celebrated portrait of Lady Blessington — one of the very finest he ever painted, and universally known by the numerous engravings that have since been made from it. In glancing hastily round the room on first entering, I had duly admired this exquisite portrait, as approaching very near to the perfection of the art, though (as I conceived) by no means reaching it, for there were points in the picture which struck me as inconsistent with others that were also present. Yet I could not, except as a vague theory, lay the apparent discrepancies at the door of the artist. They might belong to the original ; though I more than doubted this explanation of them ; for there are certain qualities and attributes which necessarily imply the absence of certain others, and consequently of their corresponding expressions.

Presently, on returning to this portrait, I saw standing before it, as if on purpose to confirm my theory, the lovely original. She was leaning on the arm of her husband, Lord Blessington, while *he* was gazing in fond admiration on the portrait. And then I saw how impossible it is for an artist to " flatter " a really beautiful woman, and that, in attempting to do so, he is certain, however skillful, to fall into the error of blending incompatible expressions in the same face ; as in fact even Lawrence's portraits of celebrated " beauties " invariably do. He was either not content to represent them as they really were, or incapable of doing so. They one and all (and the one now in question more than most others) include an artificial and meretricious character, which is wholly incompatible with the presence of perfect female beauty, either of form or expression.

I have seen no other instance so striking, of the inferiority of art to nature when the latter reaches the ideal standard, as in this celebrated portrait of Lady Blessington. As the original stood before it on the occasion I have alluded to, she fairly " killed " the copy, and this no less in the individual details than in the general effect. Moreover, what I had believed to be errors and shortcomings in the picture were wholly absent in the original. There is about the former a consciousness, a " pretension," a leaning forward, and a looking forth, as if to claim or court notice and admiration, of which there was no touch in the latter.

So strong was the impression made upon my mind by this first sight of one of the loveliest women of her day, that, although it is five or six and twenty years ago, I could at this moment place my foot on the spot where she stood, and before which her portrait hung — a little to the left of the door as you entered the great room of the old Royal Academy.

I have never since beheld so pure and perfect a vision of female loveliness, in what I conceive to be its most perfect phase, that, namely, in which intellect does not predominate over form, feature, complexion, and the other physical attributes of female beauty, but only serves to heighten, purify, and irradiate them ; and it is this class of beauty which cannot be equaled on canvas.

There is another class of beauty which may be, and which, indeed, often is, surpassed by the painter's art. This is the class formerly adopted by Westall as the *ideal* of female beauty, but now grown obsolete by the progress of a more pure, because a more natural, taste in art. This class or face, though not uncommon in nature, and more prevalent among ourselves than in any other modern people, may readily be surpassed by art, and often is so, because its beauty is that of *form* merely. It is not only distinct from expression, but incompatible with it, or nearly so — with what is understood by expression in a *general* sense ; incompatible, because if expression of any complicated kind be given to it, the perfection of form is changed, and its beauty for the time being dissipated.

This class of beauty was not the ideal of the ancients ; still less of the great Italian masters. There is no touch of it in any of those antique remains that are recognized as typical of the goddess of beauty — least of all in the most famous of all — the Venus dei Medici.

Some of Correggio's heads are the highest examples in existence of the true ideal of female beauty — the beauty of expression ; but there is not one of them that is not surpassed by actual nature at any given time. This was the ideal of Lawrence. It was this which he tried to surpass whenever it came before him, instead of merely to represent it ; and the result was that the more signal the instance which presented itself to him, the more signally he failed, — by giving that peculiar expression (not to be safely described) which is incompatible with *any* ideal of female beauty, because incompatible with the simultaneous existence of those intellectual and moral qualities on which this highest phase of female beauty depends. And he never failed more signally than in the celebrated portrait which has called forth these remarks, — a portrait which owes its celebrity to the fiat of those who had *not* seen the original at the time it was painted.

At this time Lady Blessington was about six-and-twenty years of age ; but there was about her face, together with that beaming intelligence which rarely shows itself upon the countenance till that period of life, a bloom and freshness which as rarely survive early youth, and a total absence of those undefinable marks which thought and feeling still more rarely fail to leave behind them.   Unlike all other beautiful faces that I have seen, hers was, at the time of which I speak, neither a history nor a prophecy ; not a book to read and study, a problem to solve, or a mystery to speculate upon, but a star to kneel before and worship — a picture to gaze upon and admire — a flower the fragrance of which seemed to reach and penetrate you from a distance, by the mere looking upon it ; in short, an end and consummation in itself, not a promise of anything else.

Lady Blessington had not, at the period I have just spoken of, done anything to distinguish herself in the literary world ; though the fine taste in art and the splendid hospitalities of her husband, and her own personal attractions and intellectual fascinations, had already made their residence in St. James's Square the resort of all that was most conspicuous in art, literature, and social and political distinction.   It would be difficult to name any one among the many remarkable men of that day (namely, from 1818, when her marriage with Lord Blessington took place, to 1822, when they went abroad to reside for several years — indeed, until Lord Blessington's death in 1829) who then enjoyed, or have since acquired, a European reputation, with whom Lady Blessington was not on terms of social intimacy, which amounted in almost every case to a certain mild and subdued phase of personal friendship — that only friendship which the progress of modern civilization has left among us — that, namely, which may subsist between man and woman.

A tithe only of the names of those who ranked among Lady Blessington's friends at this period, and who remained such during their respective lives, would serve to show that her attractions were not those of mere beauty, or of mere wealth and station.   Quite as little were they those of intellectual supremacy or literary distinction ; for at this period she had acquired none of the latter, and at no time did she possess the former. In fact, it was the *mediocrity* of her talents which secured and maintained for Lady Blessington that unique position which she held in the literary and social world of London during the twenty years following her husband's death. Not that she could ever have compassed, much less have maintained that position, unassisted by the rank and wealth which her marriage with Lord Blessington gave her, or even in the absence of that personal beauty which lent the crowning prestige and the completing charm to her other attractions. But none of these, nor all of them united, would have enabled her to gain and keep the unparalleled position she held for the twenty years preceding her death, as the centre of all that was brilliant in the intellect, and distinguished in the literary, political, and social life of London, had she not possessed that indefinable charm of manner and personal bearing which was but the outward expression of a spirit good and beautiful in itself, and therefore intensely sympathizing with all that is good and beautiful in all things. The talisman possessed by Lady Blessington, and which drew around her all that was bright and rich in intellect and in heart, was that "blest condition" of temperament and of spirit which, for the time being, engendered its like in all who came within the scope of its influence. Her rank and wealth, her beauty and celebrity, did but attract votaries to the outer precincts of the temple, many of whom only came to admire and wonder, or to smile and depreciate. as the case might be. But once within the influence of the spell, all were changed into worshipers, because all felt the presence of the deity — all were penetrated by that atmosphere of mingled goodness and sweetness which beamed forth in her bright smiles, became musical in the modulations of her happy voice, or melted into the heart at her cordial words.

If there never was a woman more truly "fascinating" than Lady Blessington, it was because there never was one who made less effort to be so. Not that she did not *desire* to please : no woman desired it more. But she never *tried* to do so — never felt that she was doing so — never (so to speak) cared whether she did so or not. There was an *abandon* about her, — partly attributable to temperament, partly to her birth and country, and partly, no doubt, to her consciousness of great personal beauty, — which, in any woman less happily constituted, would have degenerated into something bordering on vulgarity. But in her it was so tempered by sweetness of disposition, and so kept in check by an exquisite social tact, as well as by natural good breeding as contradistinguished from artificial — in other words, a real sympathy, not an affected one, with the feelings of others — that it formed the chief charm and attraction of her character and bearing.

IN ITALY.

My personal acquaintance with Lady Blessington did not commence till her return from abroad, after her husband's death. But as her social career from the period of her marriage with Lord Blessington in 1818, up to his death in 1829, was marked by features of great public interest, particularly that almost daily intercourse with Lord Byron for the last nine months of his strange life, which gave ·rise to her published " Conversations " with him, and her residence in Paris during the Revolution of July, 1830, the reader may like to have before him a brief summary of the events of that period, as noted in her own " Diary," which I have reason to believe she continued up to her death.

From her marriage in 1818, till the autumn of 1822, Lord and Lady Blessington resided in St. James's Square, where, as I have said, she formed an acquaintance, and in most cases an intimacy, with a very large proportion of the literary and political celebrities of that day. Here are a few of those of her early friends who have already passed from the scene, or still embellish it: Luttrell, William Spencer, Dr. Parr, Mathias, Rogers, Moore, John Kemble, Sir William Drummond, Sir William Gell, Conway, Sir Thomas Lawrence, the Locks of Norbury Park, Sir George Beaumont, Lord Alvanley, Lord Dudley and Ward, Lord Guildford, Sir John Herschell, etc. ;

Prince Polignac, Prince Lieven, the Duc de Cazes, Count
Montalembert, Mignet, etc. ; and among our English political
celebrities, Lords Grey and Castlereagh, Lord John Russell,
Lord Lansdowne, Lord Palmerston, Lord Hertford, Sir Francis
Burdett, etc.

In the autumn of 1822 the Blessingtons left England with a
view to a lengthened residence abroad. They stayed at Paris
for a week, and then proceeded rapidly to Switzerland — as
rapidly, at least, as the princely style of their travelling arrangements permitted ; for nothing could exceed the lavish
luxury with which Lord Blessington insisted on surrounding
his young and beautiful wife, whose simple tastes, and still
more her genial sympathies with all classes of her fellow-
beings, by no means coveted such splendor, though her excita-
ble temperament enabled her richly to enjoy its results.

They reached the Jura in five days ; travelled in Switzerland for about a month, and then returned, through Geneva
and Lyons, into Dauphiny, where, by one of those unaccounta-
ble fancies in which only those who are satiated with luxury
and splendor ever indulge, they took up their abode at a vile
inn (the only one the town — Vienne — afforded), and submitted for three weeks to all sorts of privations and inconveniences, in order, ostensibly, to explore the picturesque and an-
tiquarian beauties of the most ancient city of the Gauls and its
vicinity, but in reality to find in a little bracing and wholesome contrast, a relief from that *ennui* and lassitude which, at
that time of day, used to induce Sybarite lords to drive
Brighton stages, and sensitive ladies to brave alone the
dangers of Arabian deserts.

From Vienne they proceeded to Avignon, at which city they
made a stay of several weeks, and were *fêted* by the notabilities of the place in an incessant round of dinners, balls,
soirées, etc., which, marked as they were by all the deficiencies
and *désagrémens* of French provincial hospitality, were nevertheless enjoyed by Lady Blessington with a relish strongly
characteristic of that cordial and happy temperament which

19

rendered her the most popular person of whatever circle she formed a part.

Loitering for about six weeks more between Avignon and Genoa, they arrived at the latter city at the end of March, 1823, and the next day Lady Blessington was introduced (at his own particular request) to Lord Byron, who was residing in the Casa Saluzzo, at the village of Albaro, a short distance from the city.

Lady Blessington's intercourse with Lord Byron, so pleasantly and characteristically described by herself in the well-known published "Conversations," and as she was accustomed to describe it *viva voce*, and still more pleasantly and characteristically in her own conversations at Seamore Place and Gore House, formed an era in her life, and probably contributed not a little to the unique position which she afterwards held in London society for so many years : for Byron's death occurred so soon after his quitting Genoa for Greece, and the last few months of his residence in Italy had been so almost exclusively devoted to that friendly intercourse with·the Blessingtons, in which he evidently took unusual pleasure, that Lady Blessington may be considered as having been the depositary of his last thoughts and feelings ; and she may certainly be regarded as having exercised a very beneficial influence on the tone and color of the last and best days of that most strange and wayward of men.

Lady Blessington's first interview with Byron took place at the gate of the courtyard of his own villa at Albaro. Lord Blessington, who had long been acquainted with Byron, had called on him immediately on their arrival at Genoa, leaving Lady Blessington in the carriage. In the course of conversation Lord Byron, without knowing that she was there, requested to be presented to Lady Blessington — a request so unusual on his part in regard to English travellers, of whatever rank or celebrity, that Lord Blessington at once told him that Lady B. was in the carriage with her sister, Miss Power. On learning this, Lord Byron immediately hurried out to the gate, without his hat, and acted the amiable to the two ladies, in a way that was very unusual with him — so much so that, as Lady Blessington used to describe the interview, he evidently felt called upon to *apologize* for not being, in her case at least, quite the savage that the world reported him.

At Byron's earnest request they entered the villa, and passed two hours there, during which it is clear that the peculiar charm of Lady Blessington's manner exercised its usual spell — that the cold, scorning, and world-wearied spirit of Byron was, for the time being, "subdued to the quality" of the genial and happy one with which it held converse — and that both the poet and the man became once more what nature intended them to be.

On the Blessingtons' departure, Byron asked leave to visit them the next day at their hotel, and from that moment there commenced an interchange of genial and friendly intimacy between Byron and Lady Blessington which, untouched as it was by the least taint of flirtation on either side, might, had it endured a little longer, have redeemed the personal character of Byron, and saved him for those high and holy things for which his noble and beautiful genius seems to have been created, but which the fatal Nemesis of his early life interdicted him from accomplishing.

Lady Blessington seems, in fact, to have been the only woman holding his own rank and station with whom Byron was ever at his ease, and with whom, therefore, he was himself. With all others he seemed to feel a constraint which irritated and vexed him into the assumption of vices, both of manner and moral feeling, which did not belong to him. It is evident, from Lady Blessington's details of conversations which must be (in substance, at least) correctly reported, that Byron had a heart as soft as a woman's or a child's. He used to confess to her that any affecting incident or description in a book moved him to tears, and in recalling some of the events of his early life, he was frequently so moved in her presence. His treatment, also, of Lord Blessington, who received the news of the death of his only son, Lord Mountjoy, just after their arrival at Genoa, was marked by an almost feminine softness and gentleness.

Byron's personal regard for Lord Blessington had its origin
in the same gentleness and goodness of heart. " I must say,"
exclaimed he to Lady Blessington, at an early period of their
acquaintance, "that I never saw 'the milk of human kindness' overflow in any nature to so great a degree as in Lord
Blessington's. I used, before I knew him well, to think that
Shelley was the most amiable person I ever knew ; but now I
think that Lord B. bears off the palm ; for *he* has been as-
sailed by all the temptations that so few can resist — those of
unvarying prosperity — and has passed the ordeal victoriously ;
while poor Shelley had been tried in the school of adversity
only, which is not such a corrupter as that of prosperity. I
do assure you that I have thought better of mankind since I
have known Blessington intimately."

It is equally certain that he thought better of womankind
after his ten weeks of almost daily intimacy with Lady Blessington at this period; and if his previous engagement with the
Greek Committee had not in some sort compelled him to go to
Greece, where his life was sacrificed to the excitements and an-
noyances of the new situation in which he thus placed himself,
it is more than probable that his whole character and course
of life would have been changed. For what Byron all his life
needed in women, and never once found, except in his favorite sister, Mrs. Leigh, was a woman not to love or be beloved by
(he always found, or fancied he had found, more than enough
of both these), but one whom he could thoroughly esteem and
regard for the frankness, sweetness, and goodness of her disposition and temper, while he could entirely admire in her
those perfect graces and elegances of manner, and those exquisite charms of person, in the absence of which his fastidious taste and exacting imagination could not realize that ideal
of a woman which was necessary to render his intellectual intercourse with the sex agreeable, or even tolerable. Merely
clever or even brilliant women — such as Madame de Staël —
he hated ; and even those who, like his early acquaintance,
Lady J——, were both clever and beautiful, he was more than
indifferent to, because, being, from their station and personal

pretensions, the leaders of fashion, they were compelled to adopt a system of life wholly incompatible with that *natural* one in which alone his own habits of social intercourse enabled him to sympathize. Those women again who, with a daring recklessness as his own, openly professed a passion for *him* (like the unhappy Lady C—— L——, or the scarcely less unfortunate Countess G——), he either despised and shrank from (as in the first of these instances), or merely pitied and tolerated (as in the second). But in Lady Blessington, Byron found realized all his notions of what a woman in his own station of life might and ought to be, in the present state and stage of society ; beautiful as a muse, without the smallest touch of personal vanity ; intellectual enough not merely to admire and appreciate *his* pretensions, but to hold intellectual intercourse with him on a footing of perfect relative equality ; full of enthusiasm for everything good and beautiful, yet with a strong good sense which preserved her from any taint of that "sentimentality" which Byron above all things else detested in women ; surrounded by the homage of all that was high in intellect and station, yet natural and simple as a child ; lapped in an almost fabulous luxury, with every wish anticipated and every caprice a law, yet sympathizing with the wants of the poorest ; an unusually varied knowledge of the world and of society, yet fresh in spirit and earnest in impulse as a newly emancipated school-girl : such was Lady Blessington when first Lord Byron became acquainted with her, and the intercourse which ensued seemed to soften, humanize, and make a new creature of him.

That I do not say this at random is proved by the fact that within a very few days of the commencement of their acquaintance Byron wrote a most touching letter to his wife (though any reconciliation had at this time become impossible), having for its object to put her mind at ease relative to any supposed intention on his part to remove their daughter from her mother's care — such a fear on Lady Byron's part having been communicated to him. This letter (which appears in Moore's "Life of Byron") he prevailed on Lady

Blessington to cause to be delivered personally to Lady Byron by a mutual friend, who was returning to England from
Genoa.

The humanizing influence of which I have spoken lasted
less than three months, and shortly after its close Byron went
to Greece, where he died.

On quitting Genoa, in the early part of June, 1823, the
Blessingtons proceeded to Florence, where they remained
sight-seeing for three weeks, and then proceeded to Rome.
Here they stayed for another week, and then took up their
residence for a lengthened period at Naples. Having hired
the beautiful (furnished) *palazzo* of the Prince and Princess
di Belvedere, at Vomero, overlooking the beautiful bay, they
not a little astonished its princely owners at the requirements
of English luxury, and the extent of English wealth, by almost entirely refurnishing it, and engaging a large suite of
Italian servants in addition to their English ones.

In this, one of the most splendid residences of Italy, Lady
Blessington again became, for nearly three years, the centre
of all that was brilliant among her own travelling compatriots,
and of much that was distinguished among the Italian nobility and *litterati.*

In February, 1826, they left Naples, and the next year was
passed between Rome, Florence, Genoa, and Pisa. The remainder of their residence in Italy was completed by another
few months at Rome, and about a year more between the
other principal cities of Italy that the travellers had not previously visited.

AT PARIS.

In June of the next year (1828) we again find Lady Blessington at Paris, after an absence of more than six years ; and here
it was her destiny to witness the events of the last days of the
old Bourbon dynasty, and this in the almost daily presence of
and intercourse with those personal friends and near family
connections who were the most devoted and chivalrous of its
supporters, the Duc and Duchesse de Guiche, the Duc de

Grammont (father of the Duc de Guiche), the venerable
Madame Crauford, the Duc de Cazes, Prince Polignac, etc.

The splendor and luxury with which Lady Blessington was
at this, as at all other periods of her marriage, surrounded
by the somewhat too gorgeous taste of her doting husband,
may be judged of by a brief description of her own *chambre à
coucher* and dressing-room, in the superb hotel (formerly that
of Marshal Ney) which they occupied in the Rue de Bourbon,
its principal rooms looking on the Quay d'Orsay and the Tuil-
eries gardens. The bed, which stood as usual in a recess,
rested upon the backs of two exquisitely carved silver swans,
every feather being carved in high relief. The recess was lined
throughout with white fluted silk bordered with blue embossed
lace, the frieze of the recess being hung with curtains of pale
blue silk lined with white satin. The remainder of the furniture, namely, a richly carved sofa, occupying one entire side
of the room, an *écritoire*, a *bergère*, a book-stand, a Psyche-
glass, and two *coffres* for jewels, lace, etc., were all of similar
fancy and workmanship, and all silvered, to match the bed.
The carpet was of rich uncut pile, of a pale blue. The hang-
ings of the dressing-room were of blue silk, covered with lace,
and richly trimmed with frills of the same ; so also were the
toilette-table, the *chaiselongue*, the dressing-stools, etc. There
was a *salle-de-bain*, attached, draped throughout with white
muslin, trimmed with lace, and containing a sofa and *bergère*
covered with the same. The bath of white marble was inserted in the floor, and on the ceiling was painted a Flora
scattering flowers with one hand, and suspending in the other
an alabaster lamp, in the shape of a lotus.

The whole of the vast hotel occupied by the Blessingtons
during the first year of this their second lengthened residence
in Paris, was fitted up with a luxury and at a cost no less lavish than those bestowed on the rooms I have just described.
But it is proper to state here that Lady Blessington herself,
though possessing exquisite taste in such matters, by no
means coveted or encouraged the lavish expense which her
husband bestowed upon her ; and in the case of the particular

rooms just described, he so managed as not to let her see them till they were completed and ready for her reception. Indeed, Lady Blessington had, in all pecuniary matters, much more of worldly prudence than her lord. The enormous cost of entirely furnishing a hotel like that in which they now resided, may be judged of by what was said to be the original cost of the ornamental decorations of the walls alone, including mirrors, — namely, a million of francs.

With this year the more than queen-like splendors and luxuries of Lady Blessington's life ceased. In 1829 her husband died, leaving her a jointure of 2,500*l.* a year, and a large amount of personal property in the shape of furniture, plate, pictures, objects of *vertû,* etc. After witnessing all the excitements of the " Three Days " of July, 1830, and partaking personally in some of the dangers connected with them, Lady Blessington, at the close of the autumn of that year, returned to England, there to reside uninterruptedly till within a few weeks of her death.

HYDE PARK.

The following sketch was taken from the " Ring " in Hyde Park, at the period of Lady Blessington's London life now referred to : —

" Observe that green chariot just making the turn of the unbroken line of equipages. Though it is now advancing towards us with at least a dozen carriages between, it is to be distinguished from the throng by the elevation of its driver and footman above the ordinary level of the line. As it comes nearer, we can observe the particular points that give it that perfectly *distingué* appearance which it bears above all others in the throng. They consist of the *white* wheels lightly picked out with green and crimson ; the high-stepping action, blood-like shape, and brilliant *manège* of its dark bay horses ; the perfect *style* of its driver ; the height (six feet two) of its slim, spider-limbed, powdered footman, perked up at least three feet above the roof of the carriage, and occupying his eminence with that peculiar air of accidental superiority, half *petit-mai-*

tre, half plow-boy, which we take to be the ideal of footman-perfection ; and, finally, the exceedingly light, airy, and (if we may so speak) intellectual character of the whole set-out. The arms and supporters blazoned on the centre panels, and the small coronet beneath the window, indicate the nobility of station ; and if ever the nobility of nature was blazoned on the 'complement extern ' of humanity, it is on the lovely face within — lovely as ever, though it has been loveliest among the lovely for a longer time than we shall dare call to our own recollection, much less to that of the fair being before us. If the Countess of Blessington (for it is she whom we are asking the reader to admire — howbeit at second-hand, and through the doubly refracting medium of plate-glass and a blonde veil) is not now so radiant with the bloom of mere youth, as when she first put to shame Sir Thomas Lawrence's *chef-d'œuvre* in the form of her own portrait, what she has lost in the graces of mere complexion she has more than gained in those of intellectual expression. Nor can the observer have a better opportunity than the present of admiring that expression ; unless, indeed, he is fortunate enough to be admitted to that intellectual converse in which its owner shines beyond any other female of the day, and with an earnestness, a simplicity, and an *abandon*, as rare in such cases as they are delightful.

" The lady, her companion, is the Countess de St. Marsault, her sister, whose finely-cut features and perfectly oval face bear a striking general resemblance to those of Lady B., without being at all *like* them."

It is perhaps worth while to remark here, in passing, that Lady Blessington's peculiar taste· in dress and in equipage was not only in advance of her time, but essentially correct ; in proof of which it may be stated, that though their early results stood alone for years after they were first introduced, they at last became the universal fashions of the day. Lady Blessington was the first to introduce the beautifully simple fashion of wearing the hair in bands, but was not imitated in it till she had persevered for at least seven years ; and it was the same with the white wheels, and peculiar style of *picking out* of her equipages ; both features being universally adopted some ten or a dozen years after Lady Blessington had introduced and persevered in them.

LETTERS TO PATMORE.

It was shortly after her return to England that I was personally introduced to Lady Blessington by a mutual friend, and my acquaintance with her continued from that time till her departure from England a few weeks before her death.

At the period of my first introduction to Lady Blessington, she had just contributed to the " New Monthly Magazine " (then under the direction of her friend Sir Edward Bulwer) the " Conversations with Lord Byron," and they had obtained her a reputation for literary talent, of which her previous efforts, two slight works entitled " The Magic Lantern," and " A Tour in the Netherlands," had given little or no promise. But these printed " Conversations " *with* Byron, characteristic as they are both of him and of herself, are flat and spiritless — or rather, marrowless — compared with Lady Blessington's own *vivâ voce* conversations *of* him, one half hour of which contained more pith and substance — more that was worth remembering and recording — than the whole octavo volume in which the printed " Conversations " were afterwards collected. In fact, talking, not writing, was Lady Blessington's forte ; and the " Conversations " in question, though the slightest and least studied of all her numerous productions, was incomparably the best, because the most consonant, in subject and material, with her intellectual temperament, — which was fluent and impulsive, rather than meditative or sentimental. After reading any one of her books (excepting the " Conversations ") you could not help wondering at the reputation Lady Blessington enjoyed as the companion, on terms of perfect intellectual equality, of the most accomplished and brilliant writers, statesmen, and other celebrities of the day. But the first half hour of her talk solved the mystery at once. Her genius lay (so to speak) in her tongue. The pen paralyzed it, changing what would otherwise have been originality into a mere echo or recollection — what would have awakened and excited the hearer by its freshness and brilliance, into what wearied and put to sleep the reader by its platitude and commonplace. As a novel writer Lady Blessington was but a better sort of Lady Stepney or Lady C—— B——. But as a talker she was a better sort of De Staël — as acute, as copious, as off-hand, as original, and almost as sparkling, but without a touch of her arrogance, exigence, or pedantry; and with a faculty for listening that is the happiest and most indispensable of all the talents that go to constitute a good talker; for any talk that is not the actual and immediate result of listening, is at once a bore and an impertinence.

I soon found, on becoming personally acquainted with her, that another of the attractions which contributed to give Lady Blessington that unique position in London society which she held for so many years, and even more exclusively and conspicuously after her husband's death than before it, was that strong personal interest which she felt, and did not scruple to evince, on every topic on which she was called upon to busy herself, — whether it was the fashion of a cap, or the fate of nations. In this her habit of mind was French rather than English — or rather it was Irish — which is no less demonstrative than the French, and infinitely more impressible. Of French demonstrations of sudden interest and good-will you doubt the sincerity, even while you accept and acknowledge them. They are the shining small change of society, which you accept for their pleasing aspect, but do not take the trouble of carrying them away with you, because you know that before you can get them home they will have melted into thin air. But there was no doubting the cordiality and sincerity of Lady Blessington while their outward demonstrations lasted; which is perhaps all one has any right to require in such matters.

In giving a few extracts from my occasional correspondence with Lady Blessington, I cannot do better than commence them by one of the notes that I received from her at a very early stage of our acquaintance ; because it will (in my own estimation, at least) exonerate me from the charge of any un-warrantable intrusion on private life in these public notices of one whose *social* celebrity at least had acquired a European reputation.

I am not able to call to mind the occasion of the following graceful note, except that it related to something which had appeared in a newspaper I conducted at that time : —

THE COUNTESS OF BLESSINGTON TO P. G. PATMORE.

"SEAMORE PLACE, *Friday Evening*.

" DEAR SIR, — I do not think —— —— will feel any ob-jection to the mention you have made of him. Of one thing I am quite sure, — which is, that neither he nor I could mistake the motive of any use made of our names *by you*.

" I am, indeed, sorry to hear that your connection with the —— is coming to a crisis, if that crisis leads to a separation ; because I wish well to the journal, and so wishing, must desire your continuance in it.

" I have been wishing to see you for some time, and shall be glad when you can make it convenient to call. I have reason to think that Mr. —— has been misrepresented to me. But more of this when we meet.   Believe me,   ·
                    " Very sincerely yours,
                         " M. BLESSINGTON."

The two following letters relate to the subject glanced at in the preceding one. Circumstances make it proper that I should not dissipate the little mystery that involves them, fur-ther than to say that they refer to one of those literary in-trigues which are met with even in the " best regulated " re-public of letters : —

THE COUNTESS OF BLESSINGTON TO P. G. PATMORE.

" *Monday, Dec.* 10, 1832.

" DEAR SIR, — Since I last saw you, I have heard nothing on the subject we then talked of. I have not seen the person who gave me the information I reported to you, and probably shall not for some weeks or months, as I do not see him often, and in the last six months have not seen him more than twice or thrice. Of the truth of the intelligence he gave me I have not the slightest doubt, as during two years that I have known him I have never had the least cause to call his veracity in question, and I believe him incapable of any underhand or un-handsome conduct. As I know nothing of *one* of the parties, and have had no reason to think favorably of the *other*, I must give the preference of belief to the person of whom I entertain a good opinion. ·

" Believing Mr. —— to be incapable of deception or mis-representation, I can see no objection to your seeking an in-terview with him, and stating your feelings. Mr. ——, in seeking a position which he was led to believe you were on the point of losing, violated no duty to you, as he was neither your friend nor acquaintance ; but I am quite sure he would *not* seek the position had he not been assured that you are to leave it ; and I am equally sure that he never addressed him-self to Mr. —— on the subject, but that it was proposed to him by *his friends*, who represented themselves as being in Mr. ——'s confidence.

" I have now told you all I know. . . . .

" I shall be glad to see you, to talk over more fully your future prospects, and remain,

" Dear sir, very sincerely yours,

" M. BLESSINGTON."

THE COUNTESS OF BLESSINGTON TO P. G. PATMORE.

"SEAMORE PLACE, *Monday Night.*

" DEAR SIR, — I agree with you in believing that the whole story was a plot got up by the contemptible family in question, and that Mr. ——, who is, as far as I have had an opportunity of judging, an honorable well-intentioned young man, was the dupe of it.

" I wish, as an act of justice, to impress on your mind that Mr. —— behaved in the whole affair in a very gentlemanly

manner ; and it will give me pleasure to say as much for Mr.
———. . . . .

" I have such a dread of even the most remote contact with
plotters and *intriguantes*, that I bless my stars I am no longer
exposed to the vulgar observations of the persons who have
already made free with my name. It will be my own fault if,
after the experience I have lately had, I commit myself again.
. . . . I shall be glad to hear that you are going on am-
icably, and, always anxious to be of use to you,

"Believe me, dear sir, sincerely yours,

" M. BLESSINGTON."

The following notes relate to the same early period of my
acquaintance with their writer. I make no apology for the
seeming egotism of not expunging the personal compliments
to myself which these and other of Lady Blessington's notes
contain, because my object in these Recollections is to mark
the intellectual character and habits of the writer : and nothing does this more than little points of this nature.

THE COUNTESS OF BLESSINGTON TO P. G. PATMORE.

"SEAMORE PLACE, *Sept.* 10.

" DEAR SIR, — I have this moment received a very beautiful
volume entitled ' The Album Wreath,' and beg you will do me
the favor of making my acknowledgment to Mr. Francis,
whose address I do not know. The present is enhanced,
from the circumstance of its coming to me through the medium of yourself, of whose health and prosperity it will always give me pleasure to hear.

"Believe me, dear sir,

"Very sincerely yours,

" MARGUERITE BLESSINGTON."

The following note marks one of Lady Blessington's favorite studies — that of genealogy : —

THE COUNTESS OF BLESSINGTON TO P. G. PATMORE.

"SEAMORE PLACE, *Wednesday.*

" DEAR SIR, — A great mistake has crept into the notice of the death of Captain Lock.[1] He is stated to have been the grandson of the Duke of Leinster. This was not the case. The mother of Captain Lock was Miss Jennings, daughter of the celebrated *Dog* Jennings — so-called from having brought to this country the famous marble known as the Dog of Alcibaides. The brother of Captain Lock's father, the late Charles Lock, Esq., married Miss Ogilvie, daughter of the Duchess Dowager of Leinster. You have no idea how much importance people attach to such trifles as these, which after all are of no consequence. I happen to have so very numerous an acquaintance that I am *au fait* of genealogies — a stupid, but sometimes useful knowledge.

" I shall be glad to see you when you have leisure, and remain,   Dear sir, very sincerely yours,

" M. BLESSINGTON."

THE COUNTESS OF BLESSINGTON TO P. G. PATMORE.

"SEAMORE PLACE, *Monday Evening.*

"DEAR SIR, — By mistake I directed my note of Monday morning to Camden Hill instead of Craven Hill. Have you got it ?

" The forthcoming dissection of my ' Conversations,' announced, is said to be from the pen of Mr. —— ; and I think it not unlikely, for he is a reckless person who has nothing to lose, and who, if common fame speaks true, is a man

' Who dares do more than may become a man,'

or a gentleman, at least. Having been at Genoa while we were there, he is probably hurt at not being named in the ' Conversations.' But the truth is, Byron fought so shy of admitting the acquaintance to us, though we knew it existed, that I could say naught but what must have been offensive to his feelings had I named him.

[1] The singularly beautiful William Lock, of Norbury Park, who was drowned in the Lake of Como, in sight of his newly-wedded bride.

" It was one of the worst traits in Byron, to receive persons in private, and then 'deny the acquaintance to those whom he considered might disapprove of it. This was in consequence of that want of self-respect which was his bane, but which was the natural consequence of the attacks he had experienced, acting on a very irritable and nervous constitution.

" I have letters from Naples up to the 2d. Lord Bentinck died there on that day, and is succeeded in his title and fortune by his brother, Mr. Hill, who has been our minister at Naples since 1825 up to the appointment of Lord Ponsonby.

" Very sincerely yours,
" M. BLESSINGTON."

I will now give a few extracts from my later epistolary intercourse with Lady Blessington ; the object I have in view in the choice of them being, like all the rest of those Recollections, to mark those features of her intellectual character which cannot be gathered from her published writings.

Though Lady Blessington's poetical talents were not above mediocrity, she had a fine perception and an enthusiastic admiration of the poetical faculties of others, and never missed an opportunity of testifying her feelings.

THE COUNTESS OF BLESSINGTON TO P. G. PATMORE.

"GORE HOUSE, *June* 14, 1844.

" MY DEAR MR. PATMORE, — I congratulate you on the charming poems of your son. They are indeed beautiful, and as fresh and original as beautiful. My friend Mr. Procter had prepared me for something charming, but these poems, I confess, surpass my expectations, although they were greatly raised. I hope you will make me personally acquainted with the young poet when you and he have leisure. Believe me,

" My dear Mr. Patmore,
.   " Very sincerely yours,
" M. BLESSINGTON."

The note below refers to an inquiry I had been led to make relative to a criticism on " Chatsworth," said to have been written by Lady Blessington, and attributing that work to my esteemed friend Mr. Plumer Ward, who had requested me to learn, if possible, whether the graceful and gratifying things said of him in the critique in question were really written by her.

THE COUNTESS OF BLESSINGTON TO P. G. PATMORE.

"GORE HOUSE, *July* 6, 1844.

"MY DEAR MR. PATMORE, — I have no interest whatever in the —— —— beyond that of wishing it may prove a successful speculation to the owner, the Baroness de Calabrella, who is an acquaintance of mine. I have never written a notice of any book in the paper ; and a few paragraphs of fashionable movements, communicated to the baroness at her earnest request, and without any remuneration, have been the extent of my aid to the paper.

"With a fervent admiration of Mr. Plumer Ward, be assured that, had an occasion offered, I should have expressed it. Believe me,   My dear Mr. Patmore,

"Very truly yours,

"M. BLESSINGTON."

Few readers will expect to find a work like "Jerrold's Magazine" lying on the gilded tables of Gore House. But the following note will show that Lady Blessington's sympathies extended to all classes : —

THE COUNTESS OF BLESSINGTON TO P. G. PATMORE.

"MY DEAR MR. PATMORE, — I have been reading with great interest and pleasure your 'Recollections' of Hazlitt. They are full of fine tact and perception, as well as a healthy philosophy. I wish all men of genius had such biographers — men who, alive to their powers of mind, could look with charity and toleration on their failings. Your 'Recollections' of him made me very sad, for they explained much that I had not previously comprehended in his troubled life. How he must have suffered !

20

"What a clever production 'Jerrold's Magazine' is, and how admirable are his own contributions! Such writings *must* effect good.   Very sincerely yours,

"M. BLESSINGTON."

The following little bit of domestic history refers to a matter (the relinquishment of her house in St. James's Square by the Wyndham Club) which reduced Lady Blessington's income by five hundred a year. It may be here proper to remark that nothing could be more erroneous than the impressions which generally prevailed as to the supposed extravagance of Lady Blessington in her equipage, domestic arrangements, etc. There were few more careful or methodical housekeepers, and probably no one ever made a given income go farther than she did, — not to mention the constant literary industry she employed in increasing it.

THE COUNTESS OF BLESSINGTON TO P. G. PATMORE.

"GORE HOUSE, *Saturday, April* 15.

"MY DEAR MR. PATMORE, — The house in St. James's Square has been resigned by me to the executors of Lord Blessington, Messrs. Norman and Worthington, North Frederick Street, Dublin. They may be written to. Another party is in treaty for the house — a Sir W. Boyd ; so that if your friend wishes to secure it, no time should be lost. There are about four years of the lease to expire. The rent paid for the house is 840*l.* a year, unfurnished and exclusive of taxes. The Wyndham Club paid 1,350*l.* for it furnished. The furniture is now in a bad state, and the executors would let it either with or without the furniture, for the whole term, for little more than the rent they pay.

"I regret exceedingly to hear that you have been unwell, and shall have great pleasure in an opportunity of judging that your health is quite reëstablished, whenever you have time to call at Gore House.

"Believe me, dear Mr. Patmore,
"Very sincerely yours,
"M. BLESSINGTON."

THE HABITUÉS OF SEAMORE PLACE AND GORE HOUSE.
In recalling to mind the remarkable persons I have met at
the house of Lady Blessington, the most celebrated is the
Countess G——, with whom Lady Blessington became intimate after the death of Byron, and maintained a continued
correspondence with her.   Madame G—— was still very
handsome at the time I met her at Seamore Place — I think in
1832-3 ; but she by no means gave me the impression of a person with whom Byron would be likely to fall in love ; and her
conversation (for I was specially introduced to her) was quite
as little of a character to strike or interest a man so little tolerant of the commonplaces of society as Byron.   To see and
converse with the Countess G—— was, in fact, to be satisfied
that all Byron's share in the passion which has become so
famous as to render no excuse necessary for this allusion to
it, was merely a passive permitting himself to be loved — a
condition of mind which, after all, is perhaps the happiest and
most salutary effect of woman's love upon men like Byron.
And it seems to have been specially so in Byron's case ; for
the period in which the G—— family lived under his roof was
the only one in the whole of his recorded career to which his
friends and admirers can look back with feelings even approaching to satisfaction and respect.
    I remember calling on Lady Blessington one day when she
had just received a long letter from Madame G——, a considerable portion of which she read to me, as being singularly
characteristic of Italian notions of the *proprieties* of social life.
The letter was written apropos to some strictures which had
appeared in an English journal, on the impropriety or immorality of the *liaison* between Madame G—— and Byron, and on
the fact of the father and brother of the lady having resided in
the same house with the lovers.   The peculiarity of Madame
G——'s letter was the earnest, and at the same time perfectly
naïve and artless way in which she contended that the main
point of the charge against her in the English journal was precisely that on which she rested her entire exculpation from

either sin or blame. And she went on to declare, in the most solemn manner, that she had never passed a night under Byron's roof *that was not sanctioned by the presence of her father and brother.* She concluded by earnestly begging Lady Blessington to defend her character from the attacks in question, on the special ground of the fact just cited !

Among the other remarkable persons whom I met at Lady Blessington's about this period were the Duc and Duchesse de Guiche (now Duc and Duchesse de Grammont) and the Baron d'Haussez; the two former the chief persons of the household of Charles X. and his family, and the latter one of his ministers at the period of the famous Ordonnance.

The Duchesse de Guiche was extremely beautiful, and of that class of beauty the rarity of which in France makes it even more esteemed than with us, where it is much less uncommon : a blonde, with blue eyes, fair hair, a majestic figure, an exquisite complexion, and in manner the model of a high-born and high-bred French woman. She is a daughter of the late General and Comtesse d'Orsay.[1]

Baron D'Haussez, the Minister of Marine of Charles X., gave one the idea of anything but a minister of state. He was a plain, good-humored, easy-going person, with little of his country's vivacity, much appearance of *bonhomie*, and altogether more English than French in manner and temperament.

.[1] The late Duke de Grammont was, during the reign of the Bourbons, a captain of one of the companies of the Gardes du Corp, and Lieutenant-general. He did not appear to have inherited any of that *gaieté de cœur* and that happy spirit of social enjoyment which one naturally associates with the name of Grammont. His air and deportment were grave almost to severity; his manners and tone of mind were evidently tinctured by the sufferings and cruelties that his family had endured during the first Revolution. Horace Walpole has drawn the character of his mother, the Duchesse de Grammont, in no very favorable colors. Yet she displayed a spirit and courage amounting to heroism when she was dragged before the bloody tribunal of the Revolution. She was the sister of the famous Duc de Choiseul, and is believed to have exercised more influence over him, during his ministry, than any of his contemporaries.

The Duc de Guiche (now Duc de Grammont) served with distinction in the English army in the Peninsula, as Captain in the 10th Hussars. He is a descendant of *la belle Corisande.*

Another of the more recent *habitués* of Gore House was Prince (now the Emperor) Louis Napoleon, who, after his elevation to power, treated Lady Blessington with marked distinction, and whose favor, together with her family connection and long intimacy with several of the heads of the oldest and noblest families of France, would, had she lived, have given to her a position in the social circles of Paris even more brilliant than that which she had so long held in London.

But by far the most remarkable person I was accustomed to meet at Lady Blessington's was the late Count d'Orsay, brother to the above-named Duchesse de Guiche (now Duchesse de Grammont) and uncle to the present Duc de Guiche.

This accomplished nobleman and gentleman, and truly distinguished man, was for so long a period of his life " the observed of all observers " in this country, that a brief Recollection of him will perhaps not be thought inappropriate to these pages, — especially as I do not believe that any detailed notice of him has been given to the world, either here or in his native country, France, since his death.

It is a singular fact that many of the most remarkable men of recent times — those men who have exercised the most extensive influence over the social, political, and literary condition and institutions of the country to which they have attached themselves — have been strangers to that country — foreigners in the strictest sense of the phrase — in birth, in education, in physical temperament, in manners, in general tone and turn of mind — in all things, — even in personal appearance. And this has been especially the case in France. The most remarkable minister France ever had (Mazarin) was an Italian ; her two most remarkable writers, male and female, Rousseau and De Staël, were Genevese ; her most remarkable actor (Talma) was (by birth at least) an Englishman ; her most remarkable soldier, statesman, and monarch — not three, but one — was a Corsican ; and the consummate man who promises to be almost as remarkable as his illustrious relative, and has already done nearly as much good to France as *he* did, without any of the counterbalancing mischief, is Corsican by his father's side and Italian by his mother's.

The remark is perhaps less true of England than of any other European nation ; but this only makes it the more worthy of record that the most remarkable man of that country, during an entire twenty years, so far as regards that important department of a nation's habits and institutions which affect the immediate well-being and personal feelings of the great body of its cultivated classes — namely, the *social* condition and manners of these classes — was a foreigner ; and not only a foreigner, but a Frenchman — born, educated, and bred up to manhood in that country between whose manners and modes of thought and feeling, and those of England, there has ever been a greater amount of difference and dissimilarity than between those of any other two civilized people under the sun. This fact is no less worthy of note by Frenchmen than it is by the denizens of that nation for whose mingled amusement and information these sketches are more especially intended ; and it is no less creditable to one people than to the other ; to the one, for having produced the all-accomplished person whose portrait I am about to sketch ; to the other, for having appreciated his remarkable qualities, and permitted them to exercise their just and natural influence, in spite of the most rooted prejudices, and in the face of other circumstances singularly adverse to the sort of influence in question.

It used to be the fashion in England to describe George the Fourth as " the first gentleman in Europe ; " and the rest of the world seemed half inclined to admit the claim ! — George the Fourth, — who is now pretty generally allowed (even in England) to have been little better, at his best, than a graceful and good-tempered voluptuary ; a shallow egotist while young, a heartless debauchee when old, and at all times, young or old, an exacting yet faithless friend, a bitter and implacable enemy, a harsh and indifferent father, a cruel and tyrannical husband, and, as an occupant of the supreme station to which he was called, only praiseworthy as having the good sense to bear in mind that he was the ruler not of Russia but of England.

Such thirty years ago was England's beau-ideal of that

highest and noblest phase of the human character, "a gentleman." She has learned better since, and it is by a Frenchman that the lesson has been taught her ; and if now asked
to point to the finest gentleman Europe has known since the
days of our own Sidneys, Herberts, Peterboroughs, etc., she
would with one accord turn to no other than the Count
d'Orsay, — though he had nothing better to show for the distinction than his perfect manner, his noble person, his varied
accomplishments, and his universal popularity, no less with
his own sex than with that which is best qualified to appreciate the character in question.

It was the singular good fortune of Count d'Orsay — or
rather let us call it his singular merit, for it has arisen solely
from the rare qualities and endowments of his mind and heart
— to be the chosen friend and companion of the finest wits
and the ripest and profoundest scholars of his day, while all
the idler portion of the world were looking to him merely as

"The glass of fashion, and the mould of form."

He was the favorite associate, on terms of perfect intellectual
equality, of a Byron, a Bulwer, and a Landor ; and, at the
same time, the oracle, in dress and every other species of
dandyism, of a Chesterfield, a Pembroke, and a Wilton.

I have heard one of the most distinguished of English *littérateurs* declare that the most profound and enlightened remarks he ever met with on the battle of Waterloo were contained in a familiar letter from the Count d'Orsay to one of his
friends ; and of this there can be no dispute — that incomparably the finest effigies which have yet been produced of the
two heroes of that mighty contest are from the hand of
Count d'Orsay. His equestrian statues of Napoleon and
Wellington, small as they are, are admitted by all true judges
to be among the finest works of art of modern times.

In the sister art of painting, Count d'Orsay's successes
were no less remarkable. His portrait of the most intellectual
Englishman of his time, Lord Lyndhurst, is the most intellectual work of its class that has appeared since the death

of the late President of the Royal Academy ; and there is
scarcely a living celebrity in the worlds of politics, of literature, of art, or of fashion, respectively, of whom Count
d'Orsay has not sketched the most characteristic likeness extant. Most of these latter were confined to the portfolio of
the late Lady Blessington, and are therefore only known to
the favored *habitués* of Gore House. But as those *habitués*
included all that was distinguished in taste and dilettantiism,
their fiat on such matters is final ; and it is such as I have
described.[1]

But this " Admirable Crichton " of the nineteenth century
was, like his prototype just named, no less remarkable for
personal gifts and accomplishments than he was for those
which are usually attributed to intellectual qualities ; though
many of them depend more on bodily conformation than the
pride of intellect will allow us to admit. Count d'Orsay was
one of the very best riders in a country whose riders are admitted to be the best in the world ; he was one of the keenest
and most accomplished sportsmen in a nation whose sporting
supremacy is the only undisputed one they possess ; he was
the best judge of a horse among a people of horse-dealers and
horse-jockeys ; he was among the best cricketers in a country
where all are cricketers, and where alone that noblest of games
exists ; he was the best swimmer, the best shot, the best
swordsman, the best boxer, the best wrestler, the best tennis-
player ; and he was admitted to be the best judge and umpire
in all these amusements.

To crown his personal gifts and accomplishments, Count
d'Orsay was incomparably the handsomest man of his time ;
and, what is still more remarkable, he retained this distinction
for five-and-twenty years — uniting to a figure scarcely inferior
in the perfection of its form to that of the Apollo, a head and
face that blended the grace and dignity of the Antinous with
the beaming intellect of the younger Bacchus, and the almost
feminine softness and beauty of the Ganymede.

The position which Count d'Orsay held in the *haute monde*

---

[1] Fac-similes of many of these portraits have been published by Mitchell, Bond
Street.

of London society, for more than twenty years, is such as was
rarely held, at any other time, by any other person in this
country ; and this in spite of such peculiar and numerous disadvantages as no other man ever attempted to overcome,
much less succeeded. In the first place he was, as we have
seen, a Frenchman born and bred ; and he never changed or
repudiated the habits and manners of his native country, or in
any way warped or adapted them to those of the people among
whom he had nevertheless become naturalized. He spoke
English with a strong French accent and idiom, and, I verily
believe, would not have got rid of these if he could ; his tone
of thinking and feeling, and all the general habits of his mind,
were French ; the style of his dress, of his equipages, of his
personal appearance and bearing, were all essentially and eminently French.

In the next place, with tastes and personal habits magnificent and generous even to a fault, Count d'Orsay was very far
from being rich ; consequently, at every step, he was obliged
to tread upon some of the shopkeeping prejudices of English
life. Unlike most of the denizens of this " nation of shopkeepers," he very wisely looked upon a tradesman as a being
born to give credit, but who never does fulfill that part of his
calling if he can help it, except where he believes that it will
conduct him, if not to payment, at least to profit. The fashionable tradesmen of London knew that to be patronized by
Count d'Orsay was a fortune to them ; and yet they had the
face to expect that he would pay their bills after they had run
for a " reasonable " period, whether it suited his convenience
to do so or not ! As if, by rights, he ought to have paid them
at all, or as if *they* ought not to have paid *him* for showering
fortune on them by his smile, if it had not been that his honor
would have forbidden such an arrangement, even with "a
nation of shopkeepers ! " Nay, I believe they sometimes
perpetrated the mingled injustice and stupidity of invoking
the law to their aid, and arresting him ! Shutting up within
four walls the man whose going forth was the signal for all
the rest of the world to think of opening their purse-strings,

to compass something or other which they beheld in that
mirror of all fashionable requirements ! It was a little fortune
to his tiger to tell the would-be dandies dwelling north of Oxford Street where d'Orsay bought his last new cab-horse, or
who built his tilbury or his coat ; and yet it is said that his
horse-dealer, his coachmaker, and his tailors, have been known
to shut up from sight this type and model by which all the
male " nobility and gentry " of London horsed, equipaged, and
attired themselves !

Another of the great disadvantages against which Count
d'Orsay had to contend, during his whole life, was the peculiarity of his social position. And these social disadvantages
and anomalies acted with tenfold force in a country where the
pretenses to moral purity are in an inverse ratio to the practice. It will scarcely be disputed that London is, at this present writing, not merely the most immoral, but the most openly
and indecently immoral capital in Europe. Things not only
happen every day in England, but are every day recorded
there for the amusement and information of the breakfast tables where sit her matrons and maidens, that not only do not
and could not happen elsewhere, but could not be put into
words if they did. And yet in England it was, that because
Count d'Orsay, while a mere boy, made the fatal mistake of
marrying one beautiful woman, while he was, without daring
to confess it even to himself, madly devoted to another still
more beautiful, whom he could not marry — because, I say,
under these circumstances, and discovering his fatal error
when too late, he separated himself from his wife almost at
the church door, he was, during the greater part of his social
career in England, cut off from the advantages of the more
fastidious portion of high female society by the indignant fiat
of its heads and leaders. And this was in England, where
people who can afford it change wives with each other by Act
of Parliament, giving and receiving the estimated difference of
the value of the article in pounds sterling ! And where such
an arrangement does not necessarily preclude even the female
parties to it from enjoying the social privileges of their class,

and does not at all affect the males ! In England ! — where no married man in high life is thought the worse of, or treated the worse, even by the female friends of his wife, for being suspected of having a mistress or two. In England ! — where every *un*married man in high life is compelled to keep a mistress whether he likes it or not, unless he would put his character in jeopardy !

If the explanation of this apparent anomaly in the case of Count d'Orsay be asked, all that can be replied is, that his supposed conduct under the difficult circumstances in which he found himself was not exactly *selon les règles* of English society. Moreover, if he really did commit a breach of these rules (which, by the bye, half the world, and they by no means the worst-informed half, did not believe), the scandal of a tacit avowal of the breach was studiously and successfully avoided ; which is a great crime in England, where you may be as immoral as you please, provided you show no signs of being ashamed of it.

I will conclude these recollections of Count d'Orsay by some characteristic remarks, from a letter given me by Lady Blessington, relative to the Count's portrait of Lord Byron, which forms the frontispiece to her " Conversations " with the noble poet, and had previously appeared in the " New Monthly Magazine," where the " Conversations " were first published. As this is, I believe, the only passage of Count d'Orsay's writing that has ever been made public, I shall give it in the original French.

" Le portrait de Lord Byron, dans le dernier numéro du ' New Monthly Magazine,' a attiré sur lui des attaques sans nombre — et pourquoi ? Parcequ'il ne coïncide pas exactement avec les idées exagerées de MM. les Romantiques, qui finiront, je pense, par faire de Thomas Moore un géant, pourvu qu'ils restent quelque temps sans le voir. Il est difficile, je pense, de satisfaire le public, surtout lorsqu'il est décidé à ne croire un portrait ressemblant qu'autant qu'il rivalise d'exagération avec l'idée qu'il se forme d'un sujet ; et si jusqu'à ce jour les portraits publiés de Lord Byron sont passés sains et saufs

d'attaque, c'est que l'artiste ne s'étoit attaché qu'à faire un
beau tableau, auquel son sujet ne ressembloit qu'un peu. Re-
dresser l'esprit du public sur la réelle apparence de Lord Byron est sans contredit plus difficile à faire, qu'à prouver que le
meilleur compliment que sa mémoire ait reçue, est la conviction intime que l'on a, qu'il devoit être d'un beau idéal, pour
marcher de front avec ses ouvrages ; ainsi rien moins qu'une
perfection n'est capable de satisfaire le public littéraire. Il
n'en est pas moins vrai que les deux seuls portraits véridiques
de Lord Byron présentés jusqu'à ce jour au public, sont celui
en tête de l'ouvrage de Leigh Hunt, et celui du ' New
Monthly.' Qu'ils satisfassent, ou non, la présente génération
d'enthousiastes, peu importe, car trop généralement elle est
influencé par des motifs secondaries. On trouve dans ce moment des parents de Lord Byron qui se gendarment à l'idée,
qu'on le decrive montant à cheval avec une veste de nankin
brodé et des guêtres ; et qui ne peuvent digérer qu'il soit rep-
résenté très maigre, lorsqu'il est plus que prouvé, que per-
sonne n'étoit aussi maigre que lui en 1823 à Gênes. Le fait
est qu'il paroit qu'au lieu de regarder les poëtes avec les yeux,
il faut pour le moins des verres grossissants, ou des prismes
si particuliers qu'on auroit de la peine à se les procurer.
C'est pour cette raison qu'il est probable que l'auteur de
l'Esquisse regrette de s'en être rapporté à ses propres yeux,
et d'avoir satisfait toutes les connoissances présentes de Lord
Byron, qui ont alors si maladroitement intercédés pour la publication de cette triste et infortunée esquisse, qui rend le
' Court Journal ' et tant d'autres inconsolables."

Lady Blessington died suddenly at Paris on June 4, 1849,
while in the (supposed) enjoyment of her usual health and
spirits. She had dined, the day before, with her friend the
Duchesse de Grammont, and a few days previously with
Prince Louis Napoleon at the Elysée Bourbon.

Feeling unwell on the morning of the day of her death, she
sent for a physician, who was a homœopathist, and as her attack was one which demanded instant and vigorous measures,

she was, like poor Malibran under similar circumstances, lost
to that world to which she had administered so much pleasure
and instruction. Only two or three days before her death, she
had completed the furnishing of her new residence (Rue du
Cercle), and had removed into it, and all the gay world of
Paris were looking with anxiety for the commencement of her
réunions.

The following list comprises, I believe, the whole of Lady
Blessington's published writings, with the exception of Mag-
azine papers, and her contributions to her own annuals, the
" Keepsake " and the " Book of Beauty."

" The Magic Lantern," " A Tour in the Netherlands,"
" Desultory Thoughts," " The Idler in Italy," " The Idler in
France," " Conversations with Lord Byron," " The Confes-
sions of an Elderly Lady," " The Confessions of an Elderly
Gentleman," " The Governess," " Grace Cassidy," " The Two
Friends," " The Victims of Society," " Meredith," " The Lot-
tery of Life," " The Belle of a Season," and " Strathern."
Several of the latter works are novels in three volumes.

INDEX.

Divorce obtained, 236. No ill-will, 236.
Alarm about MS. and pictures, 237.
Completing his Life of Napoleon, 238.
Copyright valueless to him, 239.
Threatened with sickness, 239. Wishes
his son to be a gentleman, 240. Strug-
gling with death, 240. Death, 241.
Old fashioned manners, 243. Descrip-
tion of his person by Talfourd, 242.
Remark of Southey about him, 243.
His shake of the hand, 244. "A deal
of truth in it," 245. Dress, 245. Diet,
246. At his best at Winterslow, 247.
Creating a blockade, 247.
Hazlitt, Mrs. Sarah, marriage of, 190.
Settlement of her property, 191. Reply
to her father, 192. Disposition of, 202.
Fond of finery, 202. Opinion of her
brother's manners, 202. Character of,
204. Goes to Scotland to get a divorce,
215. Extracts from her diary, 216, 226,
230. Divorce obtained, 236.
Hertford, Lord. Anecdote of, 112.
Hone, William. Hazlitt at ease with,
135.
Hunt, John. Hazlitt's opinion of, 147.
Confined for a political libel, 147. Per-
sonal appearance, 148.
Hunt, Leigh. Attracts Hazlitt, 96. Genius of, not appreciated by Hazlitt, 154.
Effect of his social qualities, 155. Description of Hazlitt's shaking hand, 244.
Speaks his mind to Hazlitt, 245.

Jeffrey, Francis. Anecdotes of, 111.

Knowles, Sheridan. Hazlitt's regard for,
178. Harshly criticised by Patmore,
179. Patmore's introduction to, 179.
Has an explanation with Patmore, 179.
Hazlitt's criticism of, 180.

Lamb, Charles. Meets Patmore at Hazlitt's, 4. Not interested in Patmore's
book, 4. Description of, 6. His Jewish
look, 9. Not an uncommon character,
10. Personal appearance, 10. Dress,
10. Lamb done brown, by Wordsworth, 11. Character of Lamb's visitors, 12. Unconventionality of, 12.
On a par with his company, 13. His
sympathy with mankind, 13. At his
best at home, 13. Uncertainty of his
conduct, 14. Among his books, 15.
His dog Dash, 16. Letter to Patmore,
17. Letter from Patmore in reply, 19.
Domestic arrangements, 22. Beckey,
22. At Enfield, 23. Swindled by an
old couple, 24. Wordsworth fond of
sugar, 24. Self-sacrifice, 25. Bored
with the country, 25. London his
world, 26. In the country, 27. Temp-

tation of his walks, 27. Mary's salutation about ale, 28. Mary too anxious
about him, 28. Gin and water at Enfield Chace, 28. What would untie his
tongue, 29. Writing a task to him, 29.
Effect of stimulants to make him talk,
30. Letter to Patmore, 30. Intellectual character, 33. His restlessness, 34.
In his book-room, 34. Restless and
fidgety, 35. Secret of his rambles, 36.
An odd correspondent, 37. Embarrassed by a portrait. 37. Delicacy for a
sheep-stealer, 37. Intimacy with Hazlitt, 38. Joke on Almack's, 39. Anecdote of Northcote, 40. What he would
have done with L. E. L., 40. L. E. L.
in pantaloons, 40. Opinion of Bernard
Barton, 40. Remark to Crabbe Rob-
inson, 40. Discussion with Leigh
Hunt, 41. Opinion of Dryden, 41.
Pun on Adelaide Procter, 42. Remark
to Coleridge, 42. In at one ear and
out at the other, 42. Contrasted with
Hazlitt, 44. Letter to Southey, 44.
Miss Kelly hears of his death, 47. Letter to Mrs. Hazlitt, 239.
Lamb, Mary. Her impression of Patmore's book, 4. Relations with her
brother, 5. "Now, Charles, you 're not
going to take any ale?" 28. Restricts
Charles too much, 28.
Landor, Walter Savage. Hazlitt's high
opinion of, 175.
"Liber Amoris," an injury to Hazlitt's
reputation, 182.

Montagu, Basil. Hazlitt a visitor at
the house of, 80.
Moore, Thomas. Disliked by Hazlitt,
165.
Mouncey, Mr. A favorite companion of
Hazlitt, 143. Character of, 144. Early
associates, 144.

Northcote, James. Anecdote of, 40.
Conversations with Hazlitt, 93. Haz-
lett's suggestions to, 94. What attracted Hazlitt, 95. Propensity to say
cutting things, 260. Chuckles over the
wounds he inflicted, 261. Makes free
with the character of Dr. Mudge, 261.
"That diabolical Hazlitt," 262. An
old humbug, 263. Note from Campbell, 264.

Patmore, P. G. A *jeu d'esprit* of, 3.
Nervous of consequences, 3. Hazlitt
not displeased, 4. Charles and Mary
Lamb, 4. Miss Lamb's opinion of, 4.
Visits Lamb at Colnbrook, 5. Description of Lamb, 6. Letter of Lamb to,
17. Reply, 20. Conversation with

22

DR. HOLLAND'S

LATEST PROSE WORK,

SEVENOAKS.

A STORY OF TO-DAY.

BY J. G. HOLLAND.

Author of " ARTHUR BONNICASTLE," "THE MISTRESS OF THE MANSE,"
" KATHRINA," " BITTER SWEET," " TITCOMB'S LETTERS," etc.

With 12 full-page illustrations, after original designs by Sol. Eytinge.
One volume, 12mo. Cloth, $1.75.

Dr. Holland in his latest novel, " The Story of Sevenoaks," has
undertaken to present some typical American characters, and especially to throw light upon a phase of New York life, the outside of
which, at least, is familiar to every reader. Jim Fenton, the rough,
droll, outspoken, big-hearted fellow, who rises from trapper to hotel-
keeper in the Northern woods ; Paul Benedict, the gentle, easily
swindled inventor ; Miss Butterworth, the brusque, busy, and benevo-
lent little dressmaker ; Mr. Snow, the conciliatory parson ; Mr.
Cavendish, the lawyer for an emergency ; Mrs. Dillingham, the
handsome semi-adventuress ; Mrs. Belcher, the fretful, but too meek
wife ; and Belcher himself, the cunning and successful swindler, the
great manufacturer, the railroad prince, the man who gets up a corner
in Wall Street, and " pines for a theological seminary," — all these,
and other characters whose names we need not rehearse, each sug-
gests some real person whom the reader has known or read about.
But it is not merely because the characters and scenes and incidents
are thoroughly modern and familiar that the story has won so much
attention during its serial publication in SCRIBNER'S MONTHLY. The
progress of events is rapid, and graphically narrated : and it is
seldom that an American Magazine story has been followed from
beginning to end by so large an audience, and with such eager and
sustained interest. The book, too, is enlivened by those bits of out-
of-door description, sympathetic touches of character, and genial
philosophies, that his readers always find in Dr. Holland's stories,
and which constitute no small part of their attraction.

Copies sent post-paid by

SCRIBNER, ARMSTRONG, & CO.

743 and 745 BROADWAY, NEW YORK.

An Important Historical Series.

EPOCHS OF HISTORY.

EDITED BY

EDWARD E. MORRIS, M.A.,

Each 1 vol. 16mo. with Outline Maps. Price per volume, in cloth, $1.00.

HISTORIES of countries are rapidly becoming so numerous that it is almost impossible for the most industrious student to keep pace with them. Such works are, of course, still less likely to be mastered by those of limited leisure. It is to meet the wants of this very numerous class of readers that the *Epochs of History* has been projected. The series will comprise a number of compact, handsomely printed manuals, prepared by thoroughly competent hands, each volume complete in itself, and sketching succinctly the most important epochs in the world's history, always making the history of a nation subordinate to this more general idea. No attempt will be made to recount all the events of any given period. The aim will be to bring out in the clearest light the salient incidents and features of each epoch. Special attention will be paid to the literature, manners, state of knowledge, and all those characteristics which exhibit the life of a people as well as the policy of their rulers during any period. To make the text more readily intelligible, outline maps will be given with each volume, and where this arrangement is desirable they will be distributed throughout the text so as to be more easy of reference. A series of works based upon this general plan can not fail to be widely useful in popularizing history as science has lately been popularized. Those who have been discouraged from attempting more ambitious works because of their magnitude, will naturally turn to these *Epochs of History* to get a general knowledge of any period; students may use them to great advantage in refreshing their memories and in keeping the true perspective of events, and in schools they will be of immense service as text books,—a point which shall be kept constantly in view in their pre-paration.

THE FOLLOWING VOLUMES ARE NOW READY:

THE ERA OF THE PROTESTANT REVOLUTION. By F. Seebohm, Author of " The Oxford Reformers—Colet, Erasmus, More," with appendix by Prof. Geo. P. Fisher, of Yale College. Author of " HISTORY OF THE REFORMATION."

The CRUSADES. By Rev. G. W. Cox, M.A., Author of the "History of Greece."

The THIRTY YEARS' WAR, 1618—1648. By Samuel Rawson Gardiner.

THE HOUSES OF LANCASTER AND YORK; with the CONQUEST and LOSS of FRANCE. By James Gairdner of the Public Record Office. *Now ready.*

THE FRENCH REVOLUTION AND FIRST EMPIRE: an Historical Sketch. By William O'Connor Morris, with an appendix by Hon. Andrew D. White, President of Cornell University.

CRITICAL NOTICES.

www.ingramcontent.com/pod-product-compliance
Lightning Source LLC
Chambersburg PA
CBHW021108270326

41929CB00009B/772